EURIPIDES

THE COMPLETE PLAYS
VOLUME III

D1509741

OTHER SMITH AND KRAUS TRANSLATIONS
BY CARL R. MUELLER

Aeschylus, *The Complete Plays, Vol. I*
Aeschylus, *The Complete Plays, Vol. II*

Johann Wolfgang von Goethe, *Faust: Part One and Part Two*

Heinrich von Kleist, *Three Major Plays*

Luigi Pirandello, *Three Major Plays*

Arthur Schnitzler, *Four Major Plays*

Sophokles, *The Complete Plays*

August Strindberg, *Five Major Plays, Vol. I*
August Strindberg, *Five Major Plays, Vol. II*

Frank Wedekind, *Four Major Plays, Vol. I*
Frank Wedekind, *Four Major Plays, Vol. II*

EURIPIDES

THE COMPLETE PLAYS
VOLUME III

TROJAN WOMEN
IPHIGENEIA IN TAURIS
ION
HELEN
CYCLOPS

Translated by Carl R. Mueller

GREAT TRANSLATIONS SERIES

A Smith and Kraus Book

A Smith and Kraus Book
Published by Smith and Kraus, Inc.
177 Lyme Road, Hanover, NH 03755
www.smithandkraus.com

First Edition: October 2005
10 9 8 7 6 5 4 3 2 1
Manufactured in the United States of America
Cover and Text Design by Julia Hill Gignoux, Freedom Hill Design
Cover Illustration: Hermes, Eurydice and Orpheus in the Underworld.
c. 500 B.C.E. Louvre, Paris.

The Library of Congress Cataloging-in-Publication Data
Euripides.
[Works. English. 2005]
The complete plays / Euripides ; translated by Carl R. Mueller. —1st ed.
v. cm. — (Great translations series)
Contents: v. 1. Alkêstis. Mêdeia. Children of Heraklês. Hippolytos —
v. 2. Andromachê. Hêkabê. Suppliant women. Êlektra. The madness of Heraklês —
v. 3. Trojan women. Iphigeneia in Tauris. Ion. Helen. Cyclops —
v. 4. Phoenician women. Orestês. Bakkhai. Iphigeneia in Aulis. Rhesos.
ISBN 1-57525-300-3 pbk (v. 1) ISBN 1-57525-433-6 cloth (v.1) —
ISBN 1-57525-321-6 pbk (v. 2) ISBN 1-57525-434-4 cloth (v.2) —
ISBN 1-57525-358-5 pbk (v. 3) ISBN 1-57525-435-2 cloth (v.3) —
ISBN 1-57525-374-7 pbk (v. 4) ISBN 1-57525-436-0 cloth (v.4)
1. Euripides—Translations into English. 2. Greek drama (Tragedy)—Translations into English. 3. Mythology, Greek—Drama. I. Mueller, Carl Richard. II. Title.
III. Great translations for actors series
PA3975.A1 2005
882'.01--dc22   2005051719

CONTENTS

Euripides and the Athenian Theater of His Time

I ❧ THE LIFE

Of the many tragedians practicing in Athens during the fifth century (note: all dates are BCE), the work of only three of them is extant. Numerous others we know by name, from records, from stone inscriptions recording their victories in dramatic competitions, and from commentary by their contemporaries. Why, then, should the work of only three of these have survived? One answer might be that they represented the cream of the crop; that their plays were popular and received numerous productions after their first appearance in competition in Athens, productions not only in the outlying demes of Athens, but as far away as Sicily and the Athenian colonies that dotted the coast of Asia Minor. These productions would have needed copies of the original manuscript, and the proliferation of such copies gave them a chance of survival that less popular plays would not have had. Additionally, their work was taken up by schools and used as teaching tools for learning the art of rhetoric. This leaves us with the Big Three of the Athenian fifth century: Aeschylus, Sophokles, and Euripides. And little as we know biographically about Aeschylus and Sophokles, we know next to nothing about Euripides.

By the time people came to be interested in the details of his life, it was too late. The documentation was gone; letters to and from him, recollections of friends and family had been swept away by the tide of time, even as early as the age of Aristotle, midway in the fourth century. The majority of references to him remaining from the fifth century are from the Old Comedy tradition of Aristophanes and others. It was part of the art of Old Comedy to be topical. Few public figures escaped lambasting by Old Comedy: politicians, military men, civic leaders, philosophers, poets, playwrights, even the gods. Everyone was a potential target, and they must have loved it; it was part of an open society. Even Sokrates must have laughed at his not-so-flattering representation on Aristophanes' stage. These contemporary references, of course, were not meant to serve posterity as biographical source material, and yet not a few have used them as such.

It is said by some that Euripides, for example, was philosophically inclined and that that inclination served to cast doubt on Greek tragedy's religious basis. He is also said in his dramatic work to have been an antitraditionalist. But, as David Kovacs has pointed out, such imputations most likely rely on the evidence of Old Comedy. And, comedy being comedy, it has as its principal bent the art of exaggeration. If Aristophanes in *Clouds* makes Sokrates appear to be, as Kovacs writes, "a quack scientist and a teacher of dishonest rhetoric," it should be understood as part of the joke that Old Comedy not only had the right but was expected to indulge in. "For a joke to be worth making in Old Comedy, there need only be a slight resemblance between the actual person and his comic representation."

How little need be the resemblance between the comic representation and the individual being referenced is seen in Aristophanes' *Frogs* in which Aeschylus and Euripides are pitted against one another in Hades. The Aeschylus caricature is seen as retrogressive in his grandiloquence, pompous, infatuated with the past, old-fashioned in the extreme, a staunch moralist and a didact, while Euripides is faulted with the infelicity of introducing speaking slaves onto his stage and with allowing for the lowly and conventional. The truth of the matter is that slaves with speaking roles appear first in Aeschylus, and, as Kovacs points out, Orestês' wet nurse even describes her one-time ward's toilet-training, a liberty to which not even Euripides would sink. Kovacs continues:

> The Aristophanic Euripides is as new-fangled as his Aeschylus is old-fashioned. The real Euripides, of course, had made innovations in the tragic art, and on many points of style he stands at the opposite pole to the practice of Aeschylus. It makes comic sense, however, that as the representative of the new manner he should also be given other traits that may not correspond to the real Euripides any more than priggish moralism or exaggerated decorum belonged to the real Aeschylus. Where Aeschylus is pious, he is an atheist. Where Aeschylus champions the heroic and believes in tragic decorum, Euripides is the spokesman for *verismo* and dwells with artistic satisfaction on the ordinary and everyday. It is quite possible that the comic poet has here given himself a great deal of latitude to portray both the tragic poets in ways that do not necessarily correspond to the way they are or are perceived.

Or to put it another way: a major attribute of comedy in all ages is to allow for distortion to activate the risible.

Equally suspect is the tendency of some critics to interpret the plays based on "facts" from unreliable biographical sources and, contrarywise, to see in his plays intellectual and behavioral tendencies of the man himself. Was Euripides an agnostic? Was he a misogynist? If Euripides' purpose in writing *Mêdeia* was to demonstrate the evil of Woman, and if Hippolytos's condemnation of Woman is really the voice of his creator, then by all means. The problem, of course, is that there is no evidence on which to base such theses. No more (indeed far less) than we have for a similar misguided exercise in regard to Shakespeare.

What, then, do we know about Euripides with reasonable certainty? The fact is not much. He is said to have been born on the island of Salamis off the western coast of Greece on the very day of the Battle of Salamis in which Athens finally defeated the Persian Empire under Xerxes. This is doubtful, and most likely an example of remembering a difficult date by shifting it to a date that is easily remembered, as the Battle of Salamis most certainly was. It is safe, however, to say that he was born in the 480s but precisely where is suggested by only one or two bits of stone-engraved evidence, namely that as a boy he participated in a festival to Apollo Delios in Phyla, one of the demes of Athens. Another indisputable fact is that he won the prize in tragedy four times, one of those being posthumous. We know, too, that he first entered the tragic competition at Athens in 455 and that his final entry in the Great Dionysia was probably in 408, after which he left for Macedonia and the court of King Archelaus. It is said he left Athens a bitter man, possibly because he felt unappreciated. The more likely explanation, as has been suggested, is that life in Athens, after a war of more than two decades, a war, moreover, that Athens would soon lose, became too difficult. He died in 406. Athens fell to Sparta in 404.

Richard Rutherford has summarized Euripides' life rather well: "The constant parodies and references to his plays in Aristophanes' comedies are not only satirical criticism but a kind of tribute to a playwright whose work he obviously knew intimately and whose significance was beyond question."

II ⟡ THE THEATER AND ITS FORM

One of the fascinating questions in regard to the Athenian theater of the fifth century—used by Aeschylus, Sophokles, and Euripides—is what was it like? Actually we know virtually nothing about it, as little as we know about the origin of Athenian tragedy. What we do know is that the first performances of Athenian tragedy in the mid-sixth century took place in the Agora, the

Athenian market place, a place of general assembly, and that spectators sat on wooden bleachers. Then, around 500, the theatrical performance site was moved to the Sacred Precinct of Dionysos on the south side of the Akropolis. At first spectators may have sat on the natural slope of the hill to watch the performance, an arrangement most likely superceded by wooden bleachers introduced for greater audience comfort. But even this is guesswork, logical as it sounds. From here (or perhaps even before we arrive here), the general public image of the Athenian Theater of Dionysos makes a great and very wrongheaded leap some one hundred and fifty years into the future to the middle of the fourth century and the most esthetically harmonious of all Greek theaters, that at Epidauros. There we have a stone *skênê* building to serve as backing for the action, a building with from one to three doors and fronted by a line of pillars, the *proskênion*; possibly there is a second story to the *skênê* building and a *logeion*, the *skênê's* roof for the appearance of gods and even mortals. We then perhaps see a raised terrace or low stage area in front of the *skênê* where some if not most of the action takes place, and then, in front of all that, the most crucial element of all, a perfectly round and very large orchestra made of pounded earth and circled in stone. And, not least, the vast reaches of a stone auditorium, in Greek the *theatron*.

Certain as that structure may still be at Epidauros, it has no precedent in Athens until the 330s when *stoa, skênê,* and *theatron* were finally finished in stone. There is evidence, however, that the oldest stone *skênê* in Athens dates from sometime between 421 and 415, some thirty-four to forty years after Euripides first ventures into playwriting. And we know that for some years prior to that, the *skênê* was made of wood, torn down at the end of each festival, and rebuilt (perhaps newly designed) the next year. Just when, however, that wooden *skênê* was first introduced is a mystery that may never find an answer, if for no other reason than the fragility of such a structure and/or the fact that it was regularly demolished at the close of each festival. The earliest call in an extant Greek tragedy for a *skênê* of whatever construction comes in 458 for Aeschylus's *Oresteia*. But that is no indication that the *skênê* did not exist earlier in the century, that it could not have been called for by a play that no longer exists. Nonetheless, we can at least say that Euripides' first extant play, *Alkêstis*, in 438, unequivocally calls for one, as do his remaining eighteen extant plays.

As for a raised acting area in front of the *skênê* for *Oresteia*, it is possible, but it is only in the late fifth and early fourth centuries that there is evidence in the form of vase paintings of a low, raised platform for the performance of tragedy, a platform raised about a meter (roughly forty inches) and mounted via a flight of steps in the center, steps suggesting that action was not confined to the platform but spilled out into the orchestra. This, of course, still tells us nothing about the positioning of theatrical action in the earlier period from the late sixth to well into the fifth century, nor is it conclusive evidence that such a raised level actually existed in Athens in the fifth century. Nothing short of archeological evidence could do that, and of that there is none. From a purely practical standpoint, it must be asked what if anything would have been served by such a raised level, especially considering that the action of the play was looked down upon by a steeply raked *theatron* of spectators and that even the first row of seats, the thrones for priests and dignitaries, was itself raised above the ground-level playing area.

It is also not known what the original shape of the early Athenian orchestra might have been, that area where the Chorus sang and danced elaborate choreographies. There are examples of smaller, outlying Attic theaters of the later fifth century, whose orchestras were other than circular. Both Thorikos and Trachones had tiny provincial deme theaters in which the audience was seated on wooden benches in a rectangular arrangement in close proximity to the acting area, which, as well, may have been loosely rectangular, or, even more likely, trapezoidal, with only two sides being parallel. It is possible that the early shape of the theater at Athens was the same, with the exception that it would have been on a much grander scale. Where does all this lead? Not much of anywhere except more speculation. Some scholars maintain, for example, that there is no evidence for a circular orchestra in Athens before the 330s, whereas others argue that the choreography performed by the Chorus required a circular area, and thus there must have been one from the start. In any event, the question for Athens can never be answered because subsequent reconfigurations of the theater have destroyed all archeological evidence.

III ✥ THE MASK

Whatever the layout of the early Athenian Theater of Dionysos, it is a fair guess that to accommodate the numbers of male citizens of that thriving metropolis and many from its outlying demes, not to mention important foreign visitors, the structure could not have been less than sizable. And size brought with it distance from the theatrical event as the eventual *theatron* at Athens in the 330s still demonstrates, rising as it does to touch the fortified walls of the Akropolis some hundreds of feet away. The capacity of the theater has been judged to be somewhere between fifteen and twenty thousand.

Whether distance served as an incentive to the use of masks (some have speculated that they served as a megaphone to project the voice to the farthest rows) is not known, nor is it the most salient reason for the use of the mask, for there are others. There is ample evidence, for example, that in Greece the use of the mask in cult ceremonies was widespread. Adolescent rites of passage, puberty rites, known from Sparta, made use of masks of considerable grotesqueness. And the cult of Dêmêtêr and Dêspoina at Lycosura is known for its use of animal masks. Then, of course, there is the mask used closer to home, in the cult of Dionysos, from which the mask in Greek tragedy most likely derives. Whether amplification had any part in the use of masks on the Athenian stage, they at least gave a greater presence to the actor wearing one, for they were large enough to cover the entire head. Made generally of linen, the fifth-century mask represented types rather than individuals. Perhaps the most compelling reason for them is the need for two and later three actors to act out all the speaking roles.

The rationale might also have been one of economy. Considering that tragedy was a masked entertainment, it was only practical to confine the number of speaking parts in any one scene to three actors, the reason most likely being, as Easterling suggests, to enable the audience to tell "where the voice is coming from," inasmuch as facial movements were obscured by masks. This practical limitation, however, permitted an actor to be double- and perhaps even triple-cast, a practice much used and most often, one must assume, to very good effect. In any case, even though the primary reason for only three actors was very likely a financial consideration, to have a single actor play, for example, the roles of Klytaimnêstra, Êlektra, and Athêna in *Oresteia*, or, in the same play, the roles of Agamemnon and Orestês; or in Euripides' *Bakkhai* Pentheus and his mother Agavê, and in Sophokles' *Women of Trachis* the roles of Dêianeira and Heraklês—each of which possibilities offers resonances that are far-reaching and highly intriguing. One must also not forget that masks were helpful in disguising the male actor who traditionally assumed female roles, women being excluded from theatrical performance. As for the numbers of nonspeaking actors on stage, there was no limit, and exciting stage effects with scores of extras would not have been unusual.

IV ❧ THE CHORUS AND DANCE

Of all the elements of theatrical practice, the importance of the Chorus cannot be overestimated. In Athens especially there was a long tradition (even before tragedy) of an emphasis on the competition of dithyramb choruses that consisted of both song and dance. Even in the days of tragedy, there were separate competitions devoted to the dithyramb in which each of the ten demes of Athens participated. In Aeschylus's day the tragic Chorus numbered twelve, then Sophokles added three more for a total of fifteen. In his *Tragedy in Athens* David Wiles gives a brilliant and convincing exposition of the degree to which the tragic Chorus participated in the theatrical event. He posits (with help from other scholars) that not only was the choreographed movement of the Chorus not in straight lines or highly formalized, as previously thought, but that it was often particularly active. When, for example, the Chorus of Young Theban Women in Aeschylus's *Seven Against Thebes* makes its first entrance, it is anything but sedate; it is disordered in the extreme (choreographed disorder, to be sure), but their terror of the encroaching war outside their city gates is such that it prompts the agitated reentry of Eteoklês who deals harshly with them for their civic disturbance. In Sophokles' *Oedipus at Kolonos* there is a similar entry by the Chorus of Old Men who dart wildly about the orchestra in search of the intruder into the Sacred Grove.

Wiles makes a most insightful deduction when he posits that the subject of each choral ode is acted out by the Chorus in choreographed dance. And even more startling, that during long narrative speeches, such as the Persian Herald's speech in *Persians*, in which he describes the defeat of the Persian forces in the naval battle at Salamis; or the narrative in *Bakkhai* describing the death of Pentheus; or in *Hippolytos*, the bull from the sea; or the sacrifice of Iphigeneia at Aulis. In each of these, the Chorus was actively acting out a choreography that visually complemented the verbal narration. The brilliance of this deduction is staggering in indicating the degree of the participation of the Chorus in Athenian tragedy: they were seldom inactive, and not only did they wear the persona of their first function as Old Men of Kolonos or Young Theban Women, but also served as an abstract or distanced body that acted out the subject of others' narration of which in no event could they have had any foreknowledge. It helps to understand why when Athenians attended the theater at festival times they spoke of going to the "choreography" rather than to the play.

V ⟟ MUSIC

Of music in Archaic and Classical Greece we know very little. Some music scores survive, but they are largely fragmentary and date from the Hellenistic period or later. Although the Greeks were knowledgeable about a great many musical instruments, especially from their eastern neighbors, they adopted only two main sorts: stringed instrument (lyre) and wind instrument or pipe (*aulos*), not a flute but sounded with a reed (single and double). In tragedy of the fifth century, the double-pipe *aulos* was the instrument of choice to accompany the musical sections of the dramatic action, though drums may very well also have been employed, as for example in *Bakkhai* where drums are frequently mentioned.

The musical element in the performance of fifth-century tragedy was of primary importance. Every one of the extant tragedies has built into it a number of choral sections (usually five) that cover generally short passages of time and in which the singing and dancing Chorus holds the center of attention in the orchestra. In addition, there are sections in which song is exchanged between characters, as well as an alternation between spoken dialogue and recitative or song, the latter often between a character or characters and the Chorus. As Easterling rightly points out, these sections exist in the same time frame as the scenes of exclusively spoken dialogue. The rationale behind this practice being "to intensify emotion or to give a scene a ritual dimension, as in a shared lament or song of celebration." To what extent music was employed in performance is not known, but it is intriguing to speculate that its role was enormous and went far beyond those sections of the plays that call unequivocally for it.

VI ⟡ THE CITY DIONYSIA

What we know about the production of tragedy in Greece is almost totally confined to Attica, though other areas were also active producers. In any event, from the close of the sixth and throughout the fifth century, tragedy was primarily performed as part of the Great or City Dionysia in Athens, though tragedy was also a part of the Rural Dionysia during the winter months when access to Athens was inhibited because of weather. But tragedy was not the sole reason for these festivals. They also scheduled processions, sacrifices in the theater, libations, the parade of war orphans, and the performance of dithyramb and comedy. And as summary, the final day was devoted to a review of the conduct of the festival and to the awarding of prizes.

Three tragedians competed with three plays each plus a satyr play, all chosen by the *archon*, a state official who also appointed the three *chorêgoi* who undertook the expense of equipping and training the choruses, the actors and playwrights being paid for by the state. One judge from each of the ten tribes or demes of Athens was chosen to determine the winners of the competition, and the winning playwright was crowned with a wreath of ivy in the theater. Till about the middle of the fifth century, the three tragedies of each day's performance comprised a trilogy of interconnected plays; eventually each of the three plays had a different subject and were independent of one another, but always there was a satyr play.

And then there was Dionysos.

VII ᛜ· NOTHING TO DO WITH DIONYSOS?

Dionysos. What had the theater to do with Dionysos, and Dionysos with the theater? How did the two become one and mutually express one another as an indigenous Athenian institution? What is it that is quintessentially associated with Dionysos that makes him the appropriate representative of the art of drama, and in particular of tragedy?

Some scholars believe that, since the subject of the dithyramb chorus was Dionysos, tragedy, developing out of the dithyramb (as Aristotle conjectured), simply took with it its subject. Now, of course, we are less than certain of that succession, especially when one considers, as Herington puts it, the "catholicity of the art form" of tragedy in the subjects it treats; for, though Dionysos plays a significant part as a subject, he has considerable competition. Or is it his otherness that makes him tragedy's apt representative, his transformative aspect (both animate and inanimate), or simply his inability to be pinned down as being either this or that? Some would say that his cult ritual, which existed long before tragedy, possessed aspects that made it prototypical of drama: the use of masks for disguise, ecstatic possession and the capacity to assume alternate personalities, mystic initiation. And then there is wine, discovered by Dionysos, and the wildness of nature, the power of his ambivalent sexuality, his association with dance in partnership with satyrs and maenads. These are only a few of the possibilities that may have led to this inexhaustible god's association with drama. Which it was, of course, we will never know; but a fair guess might be that each of these attributes, and perhaps others, contributed

One thing, however, is certain, that in the early period of tragedy, from the late sixth and well into the fifth century, tragedy was associated with the satyr play, that light send-up of a classical mythological subject. What's more, once tragedy emerged, the same playwrights who wrote the tragedies also wrote the satyr play that culminated the day's dramatic event.

Easterling finds that all three of these forms (dithyramb, satyr play, and tragedy) share one thing: song and dance, and, as she says,

. . . among them it was satyr play that was the most obviously
Dionysiac element, since the chorus of satyrs, far more than any other
choral group, was explicitly and by definition part of the god's en-
tourage, and satyrs of various types, as we have known from vase-
paintings, had been associated with Dionysus well before the dramatic
festivals were established.

The question remains: what made Dionysos the god uniquely suited to
drama? Authentic, testable proof from the time of its formation doesn't exist,
and we have only the extant plays (a small remnant of the total production of
those years) to look to for possibilities.

Perhaps one of the most salient reasons for Dionysos as god of theater is
the mask, for at its core it is the very essence of the Dionysiac, which, ultimately, is escape. But who would think of Greek tragedy as escapist fare, the
means of leaving reality behind? And yet, is it so impossible that tragedy's removal from real life gave the same satisfaction, then as now, albeit of a different kind? Greek tragedy, after all, is filled with Alienation devices. Just as the
Elizabethan playgoer didn't speak the language of Shakespeare's stage in the
street, the diction, the vocabulary, the very syntax of Attic tragedy (not to
mention the emotional manipulation possible through various skillfully applied metric systems) was even more removed from the daily patter of the
Athenian Agora, especially in Aeschylus and Sophokles, though perhaps less
so in Euripides, dramatic dialogue in whatever age never being the argot of
the marketplace.

And as for the mask and its Dionysiac potentialities, it permits an actor
to take on not just one but as many roles as needed in the course of the tragic
trilogy and its culminating satyr play. In the early days of tragedy, there was
one actor, then Aeschylus added a second, and Sophokles a third. No matter
how many actors (one or three), they were required to play as many speaking
roles as the play called for, each time changing masks to assume another character. And since only males were permitted to act, a male would as easily perform a female as a male role. Pentheus, for example, in *Bakkhai*, also plays his
mother Agave who at the end enters carrying her son's severed head. In other
cases an actor could play four or even five roles. Furthermore, each of the four
Choruses in a tetralogy would assume another, separate, identity, finally and
inevitably ending up as a band of cavorting and lascivious satyrs. And then,
of course, there is the distancing of the music as well as the elaborate choreography of the Chorus.

So fictive is this convention of masks in the Attic theater that it is as
iconoclastic in regard to everyday reality as is the Epic, anti-illusionist, theater

of Brecht. No Athenian in that Theater of Dionysos could have failed finally to be aware of the game openly and unashamedly being played on him, and he must have relished it, knowing by subtle means, by the timbre of a voice, by delivery, or some other telltale sign that Pentheus was now (in the terrible/wonderful deception that was theater) his mother carrying his own head. Which doesn't mean that theater couldn't also be the bearer of weighty messages, such as: as you sow, so also shall you reap—a lesson Pentheus learns too late. In any event, an illusion of reality was deliberately broken that said to that vast audience that this is not life as you know it, and besides, there's always the down-and-dirty ribaldry of the satyr play to send you home laughing at its unmediated escapist function, just in case you fell into the trap of taking things a bit too seriously.

One other thing regarding the mask needs saying. As we know from Greek pottery (in particular large *kraters* for the storage of wine), in the cult rituals of Dionysos, the god was frequently "present" in the form of a large suspended or supported mask, suggesting two intriguing possibilities: (1) that he served as an observer, and (2) that he observed the playing out in the ritual of many of his characteristics. It is fascinating to associate that spectatorship of the ritual Dionysos with the fact that at the beginning of every City Dionysia at Athens a large statue of Dionysos was placed dead center in the *theatron* to oversee the day's theatrical representation of himself in the form of mask, transformation, disguise, ecstatic possession, dance (to name only a few), and, in the satyr play, debauchery, drunkenness, and general ribaldry.

And then there was sex.

VIII ᴄᴏ· THE ALL-INCLUSIVE GOD

The sexual import of Dionysos and his cult is quite beyond refutation. His most formidable aspect *in absentia* is the giant phallus, a sign of generation and fertility, a ritual instrument that was prominently displayed and carried through the streets in procession on various holidays, as well as ritually sequestered (in small) in a cradlelike enclosure and treated at women's festivals as the product of its fertility, a baby. In small, it was a piece of polished wood looking like nothing so much as a dildo.

As a subject for Attic tragedy, sex cannot be denied; it appears so often as not only a motif but as a catalytic motivational force in one play after another, so significant an element that Attic tragedy could scarcely do without it.

One has only to think of Phaidra and Hippolytos; the Suppliants and their Egyptian suitors; Mêdeia and Jason; Laïos, Oedipus, and Iokastê;

Heraklês and Dêianeira; and Pentheus and Dionysos. In each of these relationships, sex is dark, disruptive, tragic, leading inevitably to the resolution of all problems: count no man happy till he is dead.

Dionysos and death? The Dionysos who gives wine, who causes milk to flow from the earth and honey to spout from his ritual *thyrsos*, who carouses with his satyrs and maenads in the mountains? The answer can only be yes, as much death as freedom, as much death as liberation, as escape, as dissolution, as sex itself—no infrequent carrier of the death motif as rapture in destruction. Death is, after all, the only total escape, the only true liberation from pain and distress and dishonor and fear, the only unalloyed pleasure that ultimately is nothing less than the paradoxical absence of that pleasure in nonbeing.

When we consider how often the death expedient is invoked in Athenian tragedy—and particularly, perhaps, in Euripides—and how often it is the only answer to the dark shadow of sex that enfolds these plays, we come to the realization that the Dionysos situated commandingly dead center in that Athenian theater that bears his name, watching himself onstage in every event that transpires on it, from the playful to the tragic, is not only watching, not merely observing from his place of honor, but, like the gods in various of his plays, directing, manipulating the action and the fate of his characters—like Aphroditê and Artemis in *Hippolytos*, like Athêna in *Aias*, like Dionysos himself in *Bakkhai*. In the end, Dionysos is the god of the theater because Dionysos is Everything, All: light-dark, hot-cold, wet-dry, sound-silence, pleasure-pain, life-death. And if he lures his Athenian audience unsuspectingly into his theater to escape "reality" by raising life to a level that exceeds, indeed transcends, reality, whether by means of language, or dimension, or poetry, or the deceptively *fictive* games he plays with masks and actors playing not only their own characters but others as well, he does so with a smile (he is, after all, known as the "smiling god," though at times demonically, eyes like spiraling pinwheels, tongue hanging lax from languid lips). He knows what they don't know—that it really is life up there on his stage, a mirror of him and of all things, of his all-encompassing fertility (which also includes death). As such there can be no question why he is the god of theater, but most specifically of tragedy, because in the end death is the only answer, and sex, life's greatest pleasure, becomes the catalyst that ultimately leads to death, which is the greatest pleasure of all and has everything to do with Dionysos.

Carl R. Mueller
Department of Theater, School of Theater, Film and Television
University of California, Los Angeles

The Plays

TROJAN WOMEN

I

The date of *Trojan Women*, 415, is one of the few secure dates of Euripides' extant plays and that only because it was listed as winning second prize at the City Dionysia in Athens. It was also the year when the Peloponnesian War, which began in 431, took a breath. Athens was, technically speaking, at peace. But peace or no peace, Euripides, by the time he wrote *Trojan Women*, had witnessed enough atrocities to decide that, particularly regarding prisoners of war, neither Athens nor its enemies were above contempt.

The litany of these horrors regarding the fate of war prisoners is recorded in Thucydides. In 431, even before the declaration of war between Sparta and Athens, a party of more than three hundred Thebans, collaborating with a group of Plataian traitors, attempted to seize their near-neighbor city Plataia, an ally of Athens. When the operation failed, the Thebans surrendered, assuming their lives would be spared. Some 180 of them were, however, summarily executed. Four years into the war, in 427, Plataia surrendered to the Spartans and Thebans only to have its defense force of more than two hundred executed along with twenty-five Athenians who had been with them in the siege. "The women were made slaves," writes Thucydides. "As for the city . . . they razed it to the ground from its very foundations." In the same year, Athens put down revolts in several cities on its ally-island Lesbos, in particular Mytilene. Athens voted to punish Mytilene by executing all its men of military age and by enslaving its women and children. A ship was dispatched to Lesbos with the decision, but as it happened, Athens changed its mind.

> Immediately another trireme was sent out in all haste, since they feared that, unless it overtook the first trireme, they would find on their arrival that the city had been destroyed. The first trireme had a start of about twenty-four hours. The ambassador from Mytilene provided wine and barley for the crew and promised great rewards if they arrived in time, and so the men made such speed on the voyage that they kept on rowing while they took their food (which was barley

mixed with oil and wine) and rowed continually, taking it in turn to sleep. Luckily they had no wind against them, and as the first ship was not hurrying on its distasteful mission, while they were pressing on with such speed, what happened was that the first ship arrived so little ahead of them that [General] Paches had just had time to read the decree and to prepare to put it into force, when the second ship put in to the harbor and prevented the massacre. So narrowly had been the escape of Mytilene. . . . The other Mytilenians whom Paches had sent to Athens as being the ones chiefly responsible for the revolt were, on the motion of Cleon, put to death by the Athenians. There were rather more than one thousand of them.

In the summer of 421, Athens recaptured and reduced Scione, an ally city in northern Greece that had revolted. "They put to death," writes Thucydides, "the men of military age, made slaves of the women and children, and gave the land to the Plataians to live on." This treatment of Scione (along with that of Melos) was held in the fourth century as a standard reproach against Athens. As for the Spartans, in the winter of 417 they marched against Argos and in the process "took the Argive town of Hysia, putting to death all the free men who fell into their hands."

And then there was Melos, the island city that joined Athens in winning the battle of Marathon in 480 by contributing ships. It had remained neutral ever since, a neutrality that rankled Athens. Grube writes eloquently of the encounter.

In 415 BC the Athenians sent out an expedition to Melos, a small island in the southern Aegean, whose only crime was to have maintained its independence from Athenian influence. They laid siege to the town and captured it; all men of military age were put to death, the rest of the population sold into slavery. *The Trojan Women,* perhaps the finest war-play of all time and certainly Euripides' masterpiece on the subject, was produced the following spring, at the very time when the great fleet that was soon to start out upon the conquest of distant Sicily was gathering in the harbor of the Piraeus. Neither Sicily nor Melos are mentioned in the play; they are not directly relevant to its appreciation, but the contemporary background undoubtedly accounts for the passionate intensity that inspires this drama, in which the poetry is uniformly great. It is that same conquest of Melos which Thucydides puts into such bold relief in his history of the Peloponnesian War. His condemnation of it as a terrible example of conquering brutality is clear in the famous Melian Dialogue, where he makes the Athenian uphold, brutally and without shame, the doctrine that might is right. We can thus still feel the horror with which the more cultured and thoughtful among the Athenians witnessed this cruel exhibition of power-politics on the part of the city which they loved so well.

Whether the Melian slaughter was in Euripides' mind as he wrote *Trojan Women* is not certain. Scholars have thought it to be so for a considerable time, and yet it is now believed that the author hadn't the time to write the play between the time of the incident at Melos and its early March production in Athens. In any case, even without Melos, there were other examples, as we have seen, of such brutality regarding captured populations. And even if Melos wasn't on Euripides' mind as he wrote his play, Melos was unquestionably on the mind of the Athenian spectator in the Theater of Dionysos in 415.

II

Trojan Women is unique in its form and content among not only Euripides' oeuvre but in extant Athenian tragedy. If many have complained about Euripides' penchant for writing episodic plays, *Trojan Women,* though broken down into four or five scenes (depending on where the breaks are made), is uniquely united by not only the character of Hêkabê, who is onstage throughout but by the narrow time frame of the action and the almost inevitable succession of scenes. "It has a less intricate plot than many [plays of Euripides]," as Barlow observes,

> [it] is more static and it differs markedly from other Euripidean episodic representations too in its representation of character. It is not only that most of its characters are women but also that those roles are on the whole interpreted as those of *normal* people caught up in abnormal circumstances. There is an ordinariness about Hêkabê and Andromachê which cannot be said about Êlektra, or Orestês, or Mêdeia, or Phaidra, or Pentheus. These women's feelings for their children and grandchildren , husbands and parents, are the feelings of millions of people for their families—not feelings out of balance, as are so often depicted elsewhere in Euripides—but feelings *naturally* felt. The tragedy occurs not from some neurosis in them, but from

cruelty imposed from outside which draws out their natural responses of love, protectiveness, and grief. The germ of naturalness must be there in all tragedies, but often in Euripides it is distorted, so that it becomes something else—an obsession, a pathological condition. Here there is none of that in the case of Hêkabê, Andromachê or indeed Talthybios. Only Kassandra's reaction is one peculiar to her special function as priestess. This normality in the midst of cruelly imposed circumstances somehow gives hope in the midst of an otherwise bleak play. For as the women work through their natural emotions, so they become for the audience more than just passive victims. They *do* respond—they *do* articulate, they *do* rationalize and they *do* grieve. And even if they face only despair, the play had brought them to vibrant life for the audience even in that expression of despair. And in that vibrant life is a tribute to the human spirit in the face of cruelties imposed upon it.

But no tribute, one might say, to the Greeks—the Athenians and Spartans alike—who have imposed precisely such cruelties on enemies and former allies in a war that is now merely in intermission: Mytilene, Scione, Hysia, and, only months earlier for those Athenian male citizens sitting on that March day in the Theater of Dionysos at Athens, Melos.

❧

IPHIGENEIA IN TAURIS

I

There is scarcely an event in the body of Greek myth that is definitive, which is to say that variations abound, and so the tragedians of the Athenian fifth century were free to choose among numerous versions, say, of the myths regarding Iphigeneia. But it goes even further: the playwright had the freedom to improvise on whatever myth he chose as long as the myth's core was left unchanged. This, it appears, is what Euripides did in his *Iphigeneia in Tauris*. But not only did he rewrite the myth of Iphigeneia, giving it, among other things, a new ending, he grafted onto the Iphigeneia myth that of her brother Orestês, in the process rewriting it as well. Orestês, then, is assigned by Euripides not merely the rescue of the cult statue of the goddess Artemis but also of his sister Iphigeneia.

According to M. J. Cropp in his edition of the play: "The mythical Iphigeneia was partly a figure of epic poetry (the princess killed by her father to allow his conquest of Troy) and partly a figure of cult, a subordinate or 'faded' goddess connected with the rituals and myths of Artemis," two elements that were intertwined as early as the archaic period. The *Cypria,* too, an archaic epic poem that treats of the first nine years of the Trojan War (up to the point where the *Iliad* begins), mentions Iphigeneia's removal to Tauris, or so it is believed inasmuch as only a summary from a much later date survives.

> When the expedition had gathered for the second time at Aulis, Agamemnon shot a deer while hunting and claimed to be excelling Artemis. The goddess took umbrage and held them back from their voyage by sending storms. Calchas explained the goddess' wrath and told them to sacrifice Iphigeneia to Artemis, so they sent for her on the pretext of marriage with Achilles and set about sacrificing her. But Artemis snatched her away, transported her to the Taurians and made her immortal, setting a deer on the altar instead of the girl.

That, of course, was the summary of the *Cypria,* whereas the first surviving text to mention the Iphigeneia-Tauris connection is in the fourth book of Herodotos's *Histories,* the source that Euripides cannot but have used:

> [The Taurians] sacrifice to the Maiden Goddess all shipwrecked sailors and such Greeks as they happen to capture upon their coasts; their method of sacrifice is, after the preliminary ceremonies, to hit the victim on the head with a club. Some say that they push the victim's body over the edge of the cliff on which their temple stands, and fix the head on a stake; others, while agreeing about the head, say the body is not pushed over the cliff, but buried. The [Taurians] themselves claim that the goddess to whom these offerings are made is Agamemnon's daughter, Iphigeneia. Any one of them who takes a prisoner in war, cuts off his head and carries it home, where he sets it up high over the house on a long pole, generally above the chimney. The heads are supposed to act as guardians of the whole house over which they hang. War and plunder are the sources of this people's livelihood.

It's fair to surmise, then, that earlier Athenian tragedy (as opposed to epic) did not deal with an Iphigeneia who was saved and immortalized by Artemis, for neither Aeschylus in *Oresteia* (the first in tragedy), nor Sophokles and Euripides in their own *Êlektra* plays did so; in each instance her death is taken for granted, as is most likely also the case with the lost *Iphigeneia* plays by Aeschylus and Sophokles.

As for Euripides' invention of the restoration to Greece of the statue of the Taurian Artemis as well as Iphigeneia by Orestês and Pyladês, it is highly possible if not absolutely certain. Conacher says of the

> particular *kind* of explanation of the "restoration" of Iphigeneia and Artemis, [that it] has that blend of mythological improbability and poetic appropriateness suggestive of Euripidean virtuosity: thus, while the pacification of the Furies (Orestês' interest in the matter . . .) seems to have little to do with the statue of Artemis for which Orestês is sent by Apollo, there is, nonetheless, a certain artificial neatness in employing the guilt-laden Orestês, the end product of the violent deeds involving Agamemnon's immediate family, for the rescue of Iphigeneia, from whose initial suffering the subsequent violence all stemmed.

There is some conjecture that Sophokles' lost play *Chryses* may indeed have involved Orestês' and Iphigeneia's escape from Tauris, "but so little is known of this play," writes Conacher, "that this possibility can do no more than cast a faint shadow over the reasonable belief, itself incapable of proof, that Euripides invented Orestês' rescue and establishment in Attica of Artemis' statue and its priestess."

II

Iphigeneia in Tauris (of about 414) is probably the earliest of Euripides' tragedies that is not truly a tragedy (the others being *Helen* and *Ion*). What exactly to call this genre has been the source of discussion for years. David Kovacs in his Loeb edition of the plays, sums up the question from a historical perspective:

> To most modern readers, a tragedy with a happy ending is a contradiction in terms: if promised a tragedy we expect to see a play like *Oedipus* or *Hamlet,* in which the characters we have come to care about are dead or in misery at the end of the play. In antiquity there was no such firm expectation, and tragic poets not rarely produced as *tragoidiai* plays where the sympathetic characters, after a harrowing escape, reach safety and the prospect of lasting happiness. In the fifth century *tragoidiai,* unlike "tragedy" in English, meant a dramatic rep-

resentation of the deeds of heroes of myth, in contrast to a *komoidia* (comedy), which is about ordinary characters in the present day.

Kovacs then, in addressing the question of Aristotle in his *Poetics,* points out that for him the aim of tragedy was to create the tragic emotions of pity and fear by means of a "deed of violence, usually between close kin." In *Oedipus Tyrannos,* it is a violent deed committed years before the play's opening, namely Oedipus's, albeit unwitting, killing of his father on the road to Thebes, the discovery of which propels him into a condition of abject misery. Aristotle, however, allows for another means of eliciting pity and fear, namely, to quote Kovacs, to "dramatize a situation in which the deed of violence between kin is on the point of happening but is in the end avoided." Kovacs elaborates:

> In a play like *Oedipus* we see the malignity of Apollo, who is determined to bring to an end the cursed race of Laius and whose management of circumstances known to him but not to the characters is breathtakingly cruel. In the other sort of play the gods operate, overtly or covertly, to bring about rescue and blessing for the principal characters. That is what happens in [*Iphigeneia in Tauris*].

What, then, *do* we call such plays? Romances, as with Shakespeare's last four works for the stage? Tragic-comedies? Romantic tragic-comedies? Perhaps Polonius has a term for it. In any case, it really doesn't matter. It is what it is. And if the play (whatever its genre) is good, we have our reward.

ION

I

Written and produced sometime around 413, *Ion* is one of Euripides' nontraditional tragedies—a tragedy that is not a tragedy—at least by our more limiting standards, though Aristotle in his *Poetics* not only termed it tragic, he rather approved of a tragic clash of forces that had a benign conclusion. Technically speaking, however, inasmuch as the work was presented at the annual tragedy competition at the Great Dionysia in Athens, it must in any case (in fifth-century terms) be considered a tragedy.

We, of course, may call it what we will. Perhaps the most realistic description is to call it a domestic comedy. Not that Euripides would have known it, for that genre was sometime, well in the future, to be known as New Comedy. Nonetheless Euripides' plays with happy endings following upon serious subject matter undoubtedly strongly influenced that genre's development. One must remember, too, that even in his tragedies Euripides regularly introduces matter and characters from everyday life (such as Phaidra's earthy Nurse in *Hippolytos*) in an attempt to make tragedy more immediate.

II

The scene is Delphi, at the temple of the Delphic oracle of Apollo. The god Hermês opens with a monologue in which he tells what will transpire in the play. We learn that years earlier Apollo raped Kreousa, the daughter of King Erechtheus of Athens, in a cave beneath the Athenian Akropolis. Secretly she bears a male child and exposes it in the same cave in which she was raped. Apollo, knowing of the exposure, orders his brother Hermês to save the child and to bring it to the temple at Delphi, where the baby is brought up by the Delphic Priestess, who knows nothing of his true identity. He grows to young manhood while serving as a temple attendant.

In the meanwhile, Kreousa marries Xouthos, an Achaian and now king of Athens. Their marriage has been childless, so together they have come to Delphi to learn from Apollo how they can have children. Hermês tells us that Apollo has a strategy: to conceal his liaison in the affair, he will tell Xouthos that Ion is his son, and, back again in Athens, the boy, now established in his rightful place and position, will later be revealed to Kreousa as her child. He will be called Ion and will be the founder of Ionia, known throughout all Greece. It is at this point that Ion enters the scene, as Hermês takes cover in the nearby laurel grove.

III

Ion enters chanting and singing. He goes about his duties of cleaning the temple with his laurel broom, singing of Apollo and his service to him, reminding us that he has no father or mother and so has grown up in the temple. The Chorus of Kreousa's Female Attendants enters. They are new to Delphi and bustle about like tourists, admiring the scene and the sculpture that decorates Apollo's temple.

Kreousa enters and immediately there is a rapprochement between her and Ion. She is brought to tears by the thought of being so near the domain of a cruel god. Ion is moved by her pain and inquires of her ancestry. She explains that Erechtheus was her father, and she is now queen of Athens. Ion questions her about her royal line having been born directly from the earth. She informs him of her and her husband's mission and their inability to have children.

Kreousa then pretends to Ion that she has also come to Delphi on behalf of a friend who was violated by Apollo, had a child by him, and longs now to know what has happened to that child. Ion, still a naïve boy, is shocked by the revelation and denies that Apollo could have done such a thing—it was some man who wronged her friend and she is too ashamed to admit it. Kreousa denies this. Similarities between Kreousa and Ion are established. She is a mother without her child; he is a child without a mother. Innocently, Ion suggests that Apollo may have rescued the child and taken him to raise him in secret. Kreousa protests: "How dare he not share that pleasure!" To which Ion replies: "The god was unjust. I pity the mother." Unfortunately, however, the oracle, he says, will not shame the god by revealing his secret. Kreousa's husband Xouthos enters and almost immediately goes into the temple.

With Kreousa's exit, Ion registers serious concern that the gods should be capable of such wrong. Gods are meant to do good, and when men do evil, the gods punish them, so how can gods punish men for what they do themselves with impunity? The Chorus sings in supplication to Athêna and Artemis to end the childlessness of Kreousa and Xouthos and bemoans the unfortunate union of Apollo and Kreousa.

IV

Just as Hermês revealed in his prologue, when Xouthos comes joyfully from the temple he has been told that the first person he meets will be his son. That first person is an unsuspecting Ion. Xouthos embraces him exuberantly, causing some consternation to the perplexed Ion, who thinks that Xouthos may have lost his mind. Xouthos explains, surmising that Ion was born of some youthful encounter. Xouthos is jubilant, whereas Ion, despite his happiness at having found his father, is depressed about his future in Athens, the bastard son of a non-Athenian, not to mention the usual miserable fate of a stepson at the hands of a stepmother, let alone one who is childless. He is also troubled by the fact that one day he will be king, and kings live unhappy lives with the crush of duty to burden them. He prefers a life of moderation, such as he has in Delphi serving Apollo. Xouthos convinces Ion to come to Athens and assures him that his identity will be kept secret from Kreousa.

The two go off to celebrate their reunion, but first Xouthos warns the Chorus on pain of death to reveal nothing of this to Kreousa. The Chorus sings of its pity for Kreousa and bitterly denounces Xouthos and Ion.

V

Kreousa and an old male Slave, her doddering former tutor, enter. Then the Chorus reveals to Kreousa that she will never have children and that Xouthos has a son. Crushed, Kreousa laments her fate. The Slave concocts a story of Xouthos siring a son on a slave woman and spiriting him off to Delphi for safekeeping, only then to reclaim him as inheritor of his throne, thus ending the ancient house of Erechtheus. He advises Kreousa to kill both husband and son and devises a plan. Kreousa berates Apollo for abandoning her and her baby and determines at the cost of her good name to reveal the god's outrage to her. Shocked by the revelation, the old Slave urges her even more importunately to kill young Ion. Ignoring the Slave's earlier plan, she gives him poison and instructions to carry out the deed.

VI

After an ode praying for Kreousa's success, there enters a Slave Attendant of Kreousa to report the failed attempt to murder Ion. While Ion was busy preparing a feast to honor his reunion with his presumed father, Kreousa's old Slave entered to offer help in preparing refreshments. He manages to put the poison in Ion's cup, is discovered, and confesses. In consequence, the Delphians have voted the death of Kreousa and are out to kill her.

The Chorus laments the circumstances, and Kreousa enters in a state of terror at being pursued. She takes a suppliant's position at the altar as Ion, and the Delphians rush in. Ion, she says, has no claim to the Athenian throne. Just as he is about to drag her from the altar, saying that the unjust have no claim to protection, the Pythia, Apollo's priestess, enters with the wicker basket in which Ion was brought to Delphi as a baby. It still contains the tokens placed there by his mother, which will help him to discover her. After she has described each article, Ion is convinced that she is indeed his mother. Kreousa then tells him with some hesitancy that Apollo is his father. Confused by how to reconcile this with Apollo's declaration that Xouthos is his father, Ion is about to enter the temple to confront Apollo, when Athêna appears on the temple roof.

She has come in Apollo's place because he feared reproach for things past. In any event, all will turn out right she assures them. Ion will go to Athens and there become king, and he will also found the race of Ionians and be known throughout all Greece. As for Xouthos, he must not be told that Ion is not his son. And finally, Kreousa and Xouthos will have children, two sons, Doros and Aiolos, ancestors of the Dorians and the Aiolians. Together, mother and son go off, but before that Kreousa withdraws her earlier severe criticism of Apollo.

VII

There are strong opinions regarding *Ion* that range from it being a play of dead seriousness to a light-hearted send-up. To one critic, it is a diehard glorification of Athens, a play of "predominantly propagandist appeal," to use Conacher's phrase, "glorifying the position of Athens as the natural leader of the Greeks," especially when one considers the "constant references, mythological and topographical, to things Athenian, and with the (on the whole) sympathetic treatment of Kreousa, championed by an Athenian chorus. . . ." The problem here is that the god Apollo, who is so central to the play's action, is in many ways a fallible deity, not to mention more of a liability to Athens than a credit. In Conacher's words, he is

> shifty, devious and bungling, the Apollo of this play lacks even the foresight (a conspicuous lack in the god of prophecy) required to plan successfully his own solution of the Ion problem. Indeed, it is only through the unforeseen human element that the divine parentage of Ion (and with it all the *kudos* which it brings to the Athenians) becomes common knowledge to all, and Apollo (who had meant to keep his paternity a secret) is forced, in order to prevent matricidal bloodshed, to let the truth appear.

Athêna, of course, in her strong propagandist conclusion to the play, in which Ion and the two Athenian sons to be born to Kreousa and Xouthos are to become founders of leading Greek dynasties, somewhat dispels this bad press of Apollo. And yet even she, his goddess sister, can't fail to suggest his not exactly honorable reason for not appearing: "The god thought it best," she explains, "not to appear himself, in the event there be blame for past occurrences." At the same time, however, one feels that she isn't terribly proud of her brother's behavior even if it is a feather in the Athenian cap to have Ion, the future Athenian king, be the son of the god, a worthy complement to Athenian pride in its autochthonous origins. This fact of divine parentage must have been important to Euripides, for it was almost certainly he who invented it and added it to the myth.

VIII

Religion, then, with Apollo at its center, has been seen as the play's focus. And yet it is not quite so easy as that. One camp sees it as the "satirical condemnation of Apollo and traditional religion," while by another camp it has been seen, in K. H. Lee's words, "as giving full approval to the god, whose providence, despite appearances to the contrary, is thoroughly vindicated." He continues:

> Are these appearances too earnest, and should we read the play as a light-hearted piece which sees everything come right in the end, and allows us to laugh quietly at human failings, some more excusable than others, but all redeemable in a world whose standards "though not perfect are sound"? Such divergent readings, with many and varied nuances, have been expounded by sensitive, well-informed critics. This leaves us with not interpretive chaos, but with the conviction that ambiguity and absence of closure are central to this drama. This is not because Euripides failed to present a clear message, it is the message itself. The play of light and shade, the amalgam of error and virtues like loyalty, piety and compassion, the benevolence of a god who yet seems to act in fits and starts produce the remarkable texture of a play which reflects mortal uncertainty. Ion grows to find a life which, though splendid, will not evoke the joy and peace of his opening song. Kreousa never loses our sympathy even when hate seems to be her only emotion. Apollo is worthy of neither blame nor unqualified approval. So the play, like Ion himself, is a hybrid in its tone and in the judgments it provokes. It leaves us at the end continuing to brood over the scales which balance the grand Athenian future against Kreousa's image of her abandoned baby, holding out its arms and appealing to its mother for warmth and nourishment.

David Kovacs tends to see the play, for all its comedic features, in much the same way. He calls it a work more tragic even than *Oedipus Tyrannos* in its bolder underscoring of the "utter difference between mortal and immortal life."

> Apollo, to be sure, is watching out for his son and the mother who bore him, but he takes too little cognizance of what it is like to live as a human being. We may well be right to hear an undertone of loss and sadness in the apparent joy at the play's end. Kreousa's long years of

sorrow are no small portion of her life, and they can never be recalled. This means nothing to a god who lives forever. Ion has greatness ahead of him, but the blessed life of Delphi, where he has been completely immersed in piety and goodness, is to be no more. Though both Ion and Kreousa praise Apollo, the impression remains that, as in the first book of the *Iliad,* the world is run by gods on Olympus who do not understand the realities of the mortal condition. That is a good image for the tragedy of human life.

IX

H. D. F. Kitto, who tends to see the play largely as a brilliant and an elegant romp, is not insensitive to the play's serious elements. One thing he rejects out of hand, however, is the imposition of a tragic theme. To him it is alien not only to the play's structure but to its genre as tragic-comedy. "Intellectual profundity is as alien to this tragic-comedy as is moral profundity; we look in vain for any serious purpose beyond the serious purpose of creating such elegant drama." He sees brief "flashes of satire and criticism such as we can take in our stride; passages of serious moralizing, common in the tragedies, are altogether absent." He continues:

> The *Ion* is full of obvious criticism of Delphi, but it is conveyed easily, never allowed to stand for long in the foreground. Ion may briefly expound the doctrine that if the gods are not just they are not gods, but the interest of the passage lies in the manner rather than in the matter, in Ion's delightful ["Oh, but I really must have it out with Apollo. What's he thinking?]; and in his conclusion that if they do not mend their ways the gods will find their temples empty. The play indeed contains more ridicule than criticism; the keynote is given by the ludicrous behavior of Hermês in the prologue—hiding in the laurels in order to see the play not proceeding according to plan.

HELEN

I

If Euripides' *Iphigeneia in Tauris* and *Ion* have exercised critics and audiences in the matter of what genre they belong to, perhaps his *Helen* of 412 (a firm date for once in the extant plays of our playwright!) takes the prize for numbers of genres that have been applied to it, both ancient and modern. I use here the list offered by Cedric Whitman:

> Although commonly classed as one of the "tragic-comedies," it has been called everything from a "parody of the *Iphigeneia in Tauris*," a "farce," "no tragedy," and "comedy from beginning to end" to "a brilliant failure," "a powerful and moving drama," "a comedy of ideas," "tragedy *manqué*," and a mixture of "theology and irony."

Whitman's solution regarding this contentious (he calls it "desperate") matter is to call it what the Greeks themselves called it, a tragedy, at the same time "admitting that it is made up of elements some of which seem ill at ease in the art created by Aeschylus and Sophokles." Not a bad solution, especially considering that even Aristotle in his *Poetics* sanctions that genre description: a tragic clash of events that finds a happy resolution.

In any case, it is not too long before Whitman, too, takes his stance with his own generic description—for him *Helen* is a "romance," and for good reason. Having pointed up the striking plot similarities between *Iphigeneia in Tauris* and *Helen,* he suggests that Euripides took great pains in *Iphigeneia in Tauris* not to "put too great a strain on the credulity of his audience," whereas in *Helen* he appears deliberately to gear his play to the implausible, so as to emphasis the "unlikelihoods" of his fable.

> The result is that, for all their similarity, there is a great difference between the two plays, the *Iphigeneia* being more properly called melodrama, while in the *Helen* the emphasis on the improbable, the magical, the unascertainable suggests rather the term romance. The terms perhaps do not matter, but the difference does, for the romantic mode admits of a far wider play of imagination and requires greater suspension of disbelief, together with more of the element of reflection and a more distanced perspective.

II

The series of tragedies that are no tragedies (*Iphigeneia in Tauris, Ion,* and *Helen*) have frequently been described as having as their foundation the discontinuity between illusion and reality, which is to say between truth and nontruth, and in none of these plays is it more pronounced than in *Helen.*

In *Iphigeneia in Tauris,* the heroine is whisked away by Artemis from the sacrificial altar at Aulis and deposited at what might as well have been the end of the earth, in Tauris. But at least she's in that barbarian land in body, in reality, and her place on the Aulian altar is taken by a doe. That doe, however, is perceived by the Greek army of onlookers not as a doe, but as the heroine herself. And so, Iphigeneia "lives" in Tauris and is "dead" in Aulis. In *Helen,* the heroine is alive, body and soul, in Egypt, whisked off there by Hermês at Hera's command, before Paris could claim her as his prize. The "prize," therefore, that Paris claims is a phantom (*eidolon* in Greek), fashioned out of clouds and air by the gods. It is this insubstantial nonbeing that the unwitting Paris takes with him to Troy. It is for this same illusion that countless numbers of Greeks and Trojans fought and died for ten long years and for which Troy was razed to the ground. This is the greatest and most devastating of the illusions at the heart of *Helen.*

III

There are numerous versions of the tale of Helen in Egypt. Book four of Homer's *Odyssey* gives us one of the earliest, and Herodotos in book two of his *Histories* gives another:

> I questioned the priests about the story of Helen, and they told me in reply that Paris was on his way home from Sparta with his stolen bride, when, somewhere in the Aegean Sea, he met foul weather, which drove his ship towards Egypt, until at last, the gale continuing as bad as ever, he found himself on the coast, and managed to get ashore at the Salt-pans, in the mouth of the Nile now called the Canopic. . . . On their arrival Proteus [king of Egypt] asked Paris who he was and where he had come from, and Paris gave him his name and all the details of his family and a true account of his voyage; but when he was further asked how he got possession of Helen, then, instead of telling the truth, he began to shilly-shally, until the runaway servants convicted him of lying and told the whole story of his crime. Finally Proteus gave his judgment: "If," he said, "I did not consider it a matter of great importance at I have never yet put to death any stranger who has been forced upon my coasts by stress of weather, I should have punished you for the sake of your Greek host. To be welcomed as a guest, and to repay that kindness by so foul a deed! You are a villain. You seduced your friend's wife, and, as if that were not enough, persuaded her to escape with you on the wings of passion you roused. Even that did not content you—but you must bring with you besides the treasure you have stolen from your host's house. But though I

cannot punish a stranger with death, I will not allow you to take away your ill-gotten gains: I will keep this woman and the treasure, until the Greek to whom they belong chooses to come and fetch them."

Paris is let go and returns, without Helen, to Troy, which the Greeks take after ten years, but find no Helen, neither real nor phantom. Finally, after a seven-year ordeal of sailing home, Menelaos is reunited with her (as in Euripides) when he is driven off course by storms and lands in Egypt.

IV

The most famous of the tales of Helen is that told by Stesichorus, the poet from Himera who flourished between 600 and 550. Stesichorus, according to Whitman,

> was said to have been blinded by the deified Helen for having condemned her elopement with Paris. In order to regain his eyesight he composed a palinode, or rather two, one each against Homer and Hesiod, reversing the traditional tale and declaring that Helen never went to Troy, but that what Paris carried off was a phantom Helen, while she herself was spirited away to Egypt. . . . Menelaus recovered her in perfect chastity, and Stesichorus recovered his eyesight. How much of all this is the poet's invention is not known; there may have been a Spartan myth to this effect. . . . Spiriting-away is a very common motif in both epic and folklore . . . and the substitution of a phantom for the object of desire finds a parallel in the story, as told by Pindar in *Pythian* II, of Ixion, who made an attempt on Hera but was fooled by Zeus into sleeping with a cloud in her shape, and was then damned to eternal torments. Whoever invented the phantom Helen, or *eidolon,* Euripides' choice of this version set the main theme of the play, and the kindred antinomies, body *versus* name, reality *versus* appearance, occur constantly throughout, pointing to the elusiveness of truth amid ironical webs of ignorance.

The play has no more than begun than Euripides introduces the first such example. Helen is introducing herself and the story in her prologue when she herself raises a doubt about the mythical (as opposed to the realistic) story of her birth.

> As for me, I come from no obscure land myself. Sparta is my home, and Tyndareos my father. There is, of course, the tale that Zeus in the form of a

swan, pursued by an eagle, took refuge at my mother Lêda's breast, and through not very gentlemanly means, helped himself to what he sought. True or not true? Who knows. In any event, my name is Helen.

And it continues, example after example (in her prologue alone) of story incident. Under normal (tragic) circumstances (in which utter reality is demanded, as Kitto so rightly insists), this ambiguity would jar the mind, but not here in this romance, where illusion is happily at home and soars.

V

Though versions of the myth that describe Helen as spending the war years in Egypt as opposed to Troy were current in Euripides' day, they were not widely known. Euripides' play, therefore, must have come as a bombshell, titivated, in addition to the alternate take on the myth, as well by the playwright's own (expected) additions.

There was Herodotos's version in his *Histories,* except it took a rationalist approach: Paris was sent on to Troy alone, and Helen remained behind in Egypt in safekeeping for Menelaos when the time came. What is missing here is the marvelous imaginative element of the ambiguous that is so central in Euripides, namely the phantom Helen that the playwright had borrowed from one of the myth's most primitive sources, the *Cypria.*

Euripides' original inventions added to his version of the myth are most likely to be the role of Theonoê, the barbarian princess capable of being persuaded by moral and ethical reasoning, and Theoklymenos, the son of Proteus, jealous and deeply in love with Helen and determined that he will have her as wife. As for Euripides' use of the phantom Helen, Conacher writes: "Even the business of Helen's wraith, though borrowed from Stesichorus, must have been developed by Euripides, for the particular kind of ironic effect in the scenes involving the real and the phantom Helen can only be imagined in dramatic terms—and in Euripidean dramatic terms at that."

But the most remarkable, bold reconsideration of the Helen myth must have been the character of Helen herself. Traditionally, she is the reviled wanton strumpet, not least in the several plays of Euripides in which she appears. She is also frequently seen as a "pawn of the gods," as Conacher says, "sometimes even a Zeus-sent *Erinys.*" At the same time, however, "these frequently shade into one another with precisely that degree of ambiguity with which the Greeks, particularly in earlier times, tended to surround all ideas of moral responsibility." So deviant from other treatments of Helen was that of Euripides in this play, that she was called by Aristophanes "the new Helen." And

Conacher concludes: "The poignant grass-widow now presented must have struck Euripides' audience as startling and even incredible, and must have contributed in no small part to that air of fantasy on which the whole feeling of this play depends."

A play ignored by producers in modern times, possibly because of the question of what genre it belongs to, the *Helen* of Euripides, if understood, is one of the most perfect of Euripides' creations. Grace, wit, charm, melancholy, splendid poetry all contrive to make it a thing of great beauty—and add to that more than a pinch of the comic to spice up the concoction.

❧

CYCLOPS

I

Cyclops is decidedly the odd man out. If the genre of certain plays by Euripides is in dispute, there is no question regarding *Cyclops*. It is a satyr play, pure and simple, and what's more, the only complete extant satyr play from Greek antiquity.

As with most of Euripides' extant plays, its date of composition is unknown, though there is speculation that it was written somewhere around 411 and perhaps first produced in 408. What we do know with certainty is that the satyr play is a form of drama based on classical myth (the stuff of Athenian tragedy), except that it treats its subject lightly, farcically, or even parodically. We also know that it was a major part of the City Dionysia at Athens in the early spring of every year, where it was performed as the final play of a tetralogy, the *envoi*, so to speak, of the tragic trilogy that preceded it, a trilogy that could be either a continuous story (as in Aeschylus's *Oresteia*), or a series of three unrelated tragedies by the same author, who wrote the satyr play as well. The satyr play could also be based on, or be independent of, the myth or myths of the tragic trilogy. And being the concluding segment, it may be assumed that in general the satyr play was relatively brief (*Cyclops*, in Greek, is 709 lines, as opposed to the average 1,700 lines of Euripidean tragedy.) In any event, it is speculated that it allowed the citizen audience to leave the theater in a good humor rather than in tears or gloom, a clever enough thought, though far too simple to be taken at face value. One ancient critic described the satyr play as "tragedy at play."

II

Inasmuch as satyr plays take their subject matter from myth, and not many myths at first entertained satyrs, one expectable theme of the satyr play (which is committed to the appearance of satyrs) is to explain how the satyrs got into a context that is not native to them. One answer might be that they are taken captive, which is indeed the situation in *Cyclops*, where they are slave laborers of Polyphêmos. And what naturally follows, then, is liberation, a major concern of the last half of *Cyclops*. To be sure, before being taken captive by the Cyclopes, the satyrs were also the slaves of Dionysos, but it was a servitude they relished in comparison with that of Polyphêmos.

Another theme is that of musical instruments. Athêna invents the *aulos*, a reed instrument used to accompany the tragic chorus in its choral odes and gives it to a satyr. We learn from a fragment of another satyr play that "the satyrs dance and sing their consternation, and then their delight, at the sound of the lyre invented by the infant Hermês."

Fire, as seen painted on numerous vases of the period, was perceived by the satyr as a grand novelty, as, of course, was wine, the gift of their favorite master, Dionysos. In *Cyclops*, it plays a large role in Odysseus's dealings with both Silênos, the fat old father of the satyrs, and Polyphêmos.

Emergence from the underworld (as in the prosatyric *Aklêstis* of Euripides) is an occasion frequently seen on fifth-century vase paintings and a delight of the satyr, as in the case of Persephonê rising from Hades. The care of divine or heroic children is no less prevalent a motif. In *Cyclops*, Silênos remarks that he once raised from infancy Maron, the "wine-god's son." But we know, too, that he raised the infant Dionysos, for Silênos was known as a protector and educator of children, and "satyrs may have been imagined in a pedagogic role," according to Seaford in his edition of the play, "even in the public celebrations of the Anthesteria."

Sex appears to be an obsession of the satyr. Not only in *Cyclops* but in numerous other of the lost plays, as well as on many vase paintings. And then, as Seaford has it, there is athletics. "It is conceivable that the surprising association of the theatrical satyrs with athletics derives from the participation in the athletic contests of the Anthesteria of men and boys dressed as satyrs."

III

But what of the satyrs/silens themselves? Who and what are these young and vivacious male creatures, the upper half of whose body is human, the lower half at first equine, then becoming more human, and only in Hellenistic times (perhaps from association with Pan) becoming more goat than horse?

They have been equated with the "wild men" of European folk tradition, and indeed they are of the wild. The *Oxford Classical Dictionary* describes them as "unrestrained in their desire for sex and wine, and generally represented naked." As for what to call them, sometime in the sixth century the silens of Attika/Ionia were amalgamated with the satyrs of the Peloponnese (causing their names to be used interchangeably) "to form, along with nymphs or maenads, the sacred band (*thiasos*) of Dionysos."

The first literary mention of silens is in the seventh-century *Homeric Hymn to Aphrodite,* where they are discovered making love to nymphs in caves: "With them the Sileni and the keen-eyed slayer of Argos mingle in love in the innermost nooks of delectable caves." And satyrs are first described in a fragment of the eighth-century poet Hesiod as "worthless and mischievous."

Satyrs were featured also in the Athenian Anthesteria, a celebration held in the month of Anthesterion (late February) and associated with the new wine. For this festival, men dressed up as satyrs and frolicked, as seen on the "Choes" vases. Another event of the Anthesteria was the arrival of Dionysos on a ship cart in the company of satyrs. As to their private side, satyrs are known also to have conducted mystic initiations, as seen on wall paintings at the Villa of the Mysteries in Pompeii. According to Seaford: "To be initiated might be to join a satyric *thiasos,* a community of this world and the next. Hence the occasion of satyrs in funerary art throughout most of antiquity." Seaford continues:

> Analogous to this contrast is the ambiguity of the satyrs as grotesque hedonists and yet the immortal companions of a god, cruder than men and yet somehow wiser, combining mischief with wisdom, lewdness with skill in music, animality with divinity. In satyric drama they are the first to sample the creation of culture out of nature in the invention of wine, of the lyre, of the pipe, and so on. Silênos is the educator of Dionysos. King Midas extracted from a silen, whom he had trapped in his garden, the wisdom that for men it is best never to have been born, second best to die as soon as possible.

And Ion of Chios, a versatile fifth-century tragedian, says of the satyrs (in Plutarch's *Periklês*) as quoted by Seaford, "that virtue, like a performance of tragedies, should not be without a satyric element." A wise reminder whether ancient or modern.

❧

A Note on the Translation

Every translator feels obligated to explain his or her aim in making a translation, and that is a salutary endeavor, for at least it tells the innocent reader what to expect as well as what not to expect. As a translator for many years, I have always (perhaps even before deciding whether or not to buy a particular volume of translations) insinuated my fingers between the covers to peek briefly at the obligatory "note on the translation" that I know cannot help but be there. What am I looking for? Usually only one word; the word that must be the bête noire of the true translator: *accuracy*. What's accuracy to the translator—or the translator to accuracy—that he or she should lust for it? A flippant query perhaps, but perhaps not, for it is a question that boggles the mind of all but the pedant. And it is in the name of *accuracy* that many a translator's hour (lifetime?) has been wasted, not to mention the hours wasted on his or her product by the unsuspecting reader who sets out to enjoy a Dante or a Homer or a Goethe, only to plow his or her way through sheer will and in the end wonder what all the fuss has been about.

There is no question that there is a place for literal translation, for translation that is bound to the word. The most convenient example that comes to mind is the long-lasting and successful Loeb Classical Library that publishes the original text and the translation on facing pages. The aim of its volumes is to aid the reader with a little Greek (or Latin), or a lot of Greek (or Latin), but not quite enough to read the original by casting a glance at the translation when knowledge fails or falters. David Kovacs is completing a new six-volume Euripides in that series that admirably fulfills its function as support in reading the original. He says about his translation: "I have translated into prose, as literally as respect for English idiom allowed." And he's correct. He's also "accurate," but that's what the series' mission is to be, and for good reason. Yet what his translations are not (and I suspect he would agree) are performable versions for the stage, and for one reason: accuracy has destroyed the poetry.

But enough of this.

What is good translation? The answer to that question is different with each good translator who has ever wrestled with the problem. Listen to St, Jerome, the great fourth-century translator of the Bible into the Latin Vulgate, in speaking of Plautus and Terence and of their translations of Greek plays into Latin: "Do they stick at the literal words? Don't they try rather to preserve the beauty and style of the original? What men like you call accuracy in translation, learned men call pedantry. . . . I have always aimed at translating sense, not words." Fourteen hundred years later the translators of the King James Bible of 1611 expressed their thoughts on literal translation: "Is the kingdom of God become words and syllables? Why should we be in bondage to them?" And in the seventeenth century, John Dryden, the translator of many a classical text, from Plutarch to Virgil and Ovid, expressed his theory of translation at length, but most succinctly when he said: "The translator that would write with any force or spirit of an original must never dwell on the words of the author."

To bring it now to our own day and to the prolific translator of many classical and modern texts, William Arrowsmith: "There are times—far more frequent than most scholars suppose—when the worst possible treachery is the simple-minded faith in 'accuracy' and literal loyalty to the original." To read an Arrowsmith translation, say, of a classical Greek play, side by side with the original, is to see a fertile and poetic mind undaunted by the mere word of the original. He realized that he was translating a fifth-century BCE Greek play for a middle- to late-twentieth-century English-speaking audience and had one obligation: to make that ancient play work on the contemporary stage for an audience that had few if any ties to the play's original context or audience. His duty was to make it work and to make it work with style and the best poetic means at his disposal.

And finally the contemporary Roger Shattuck: "The translator must leave behind dictionary meanings and formal syntax. . . . Free translation is often not an indulgence but a duty." And to that one must add that dramatic texts require perhaps even greater freedom than nonverbal texts (and poetry in whatever form is a verbal text). On the stage, rhythm is every bit as important as what is being said; at times even more important. A stinging line has to sting not merely with what it says, but with how it says it, with its rhythm. One phrase, indeed one word, too many in a sentence destroys a moment that in the end can destroy an entire scene. Effect on the stage is everything, whether one is Aeschylus or Tennessee Williams. What to do with that rebellious word or phrase? Cut it if it adds nothing of importance. And if it is important and can't be cut, then write a new sentence that gets it all in, just be certain that it has grace and style and wit, or horror if that's what's needed, and serves the moment in the best and most theatrical way possible.

What, then, is the purpose of the translations in this book and its companion volumes? And the answer to that is simple. They are aimed at the theater, at performance, at as high a level of communication to a contemporary public as is possible. That was the aim of the plays' fifth-century author, and it must remain the aim of any translator, for a dramatic text performance is all. This doesn't mean that a text meant for the theater is not communicable to a reader. At the same time, however, any theatrical text is a challenge to a reader unacquainted with the exigencies of the stage. A novel, a short story, any piece of fiction, is a thing in and of itself; it communicates totally. And if it is great writing, it also sends the imagination on all sorts of flights of possibility. A dramatic text, on the other hand, is a part of a whole; it is not totally defined. It suggests, and in suggesting it invites the spectator/auditor to bring as much to the experience as is given, and the thing that is brought is imagination.

On the stage a scene between two characters is defined by the director who arranges the action, the stage movement, in such a way as to elicit as great a sense of tension or horror (whatever is called for) as possible. A scene in which two characters whisper to each other has one effect; but play the same text with a separation between the two characters (enforced or voluntary) so that they have to speak at full volume, or even shout, and you have another effect entirely—and possibly another kind of play as the result.

This, of course, is all the work of the director whose choices determine what the bare text will convey. For the reader that visualization is lacking and the imagination is called upon to provide it. No easy task for the neophyte to the theater. Reading a play is a test even of the most experienced theater person.

Nor will a supply of translator-generated stage directions do much good. The Greeks, of course, had no stage directions in their texts, and for the translator to add them is to freeze the play's meaning, as opposed to opening it up to all kinds of possible interpretation. The stage directions in the present texts are held to a minimum.

What these translations are not is philological. One might ask why? And the best response might be that there are many such translations around, and more currently in development. The Loeb Classical Library is actively pursuing a splendid contemporary renewal of its older texts with new ones, currently Sophokles and Euripides by Hugh Lloyd-Jones and David Kovacs respectively, as well as Aristophanes by Jeffrey Henderson. Aris and Phillips (Warminster) is gradually building up a splendid library of newly edited texts and highly annotated philological translations. Penguin Classics is in the midst of renewing its Euripides collection to replace the thirty-year-old Vellacott texts with new ones by John Davie. Oxford is underway with a Euripides series translated variously by James Morwood and Robin Waterfield. Each of these publications is translated, annotated, and provided with textual notes by classical scholars. It would be fair to say, then, that the philological translation scene of Greek tragedy and comedy is well covered.

But there are also other approaches being taken. One of the most distinguished is The Oxford Greek Tragedy in New Translations series. Begun in 1973 under the inspired general editorship of the late William Arrowsmith, it is only now coming to its too-long-delayed conclusion. Arrowsmith was a demanding classicist, but he knew intuitively that Greek drama was theater first and then poetry, even if for him those two factors existed on one and the same level. He invited major American poets (W. S. Merwin, C. K. Williams, and Anthony Hecht, to name a few) to work together with classical scholars (in Anne Carson he got both in one) in producing translations of astonishing theatrical brilliance—and, one must add, translations conceived in an astonishing degree of freedom for a major university press like Oxford.

The University of Pennsylvania Press has only recently published the latest complete Greek Tragedy and Comedy series under the editorship of David R. Slavitt and Palmer Bovie. It is a series that takes enormous risks and is bound to rub some academics quite the wrong way, and yet it is never less than exciting and provocative. Literal fidelity in the Penn series is frequently dismissed as pedantic, and frequent attempts are made (not always successfully) to adapt rather than merely translate; the intent being to bring the original into a modern frame of reference.

Perhaps the most famous translation of a classical text in the last decade is the *Oresteia* by Ted Hughes for production at Britain's Royal National Theatre. Here is a distinguished English-speaking poet attacking one of the monuments of world culture in a manner that is, to say the least, unique. It is, in fact, difficult to call what Hughes has done to the *Oresteia* a translation, and yet it is that all the same. But there is also in his work on that masterpiece of world theater almost as much of himself as there is of Aeschylus. He will begin a speech as an inspired translation and then, after a dozen lines or so, segue into a lengthy speech of his own. Apt, yes, given the context, insightful, but not Aeschylus. But should one complain? I think not. We're lucky to have his thoughts. Though it might have been more direct if the product had been labeled as an adaptation/translation, as was his *Alcestis* of Euripides.

Why, then, another attempt at the Greek tragedies? Perhaps because, though much good work has been done, there is still much to do and different things to try. The reader of the present texts will have to test those new attempts for him- or herself, but one factor of these new translations must be commented on, and that is the prominence of music, song, and dance in the plays. To understand the Greek theater properly is to give full weight to these utterly essential factors. The translations in the present volumes indicate very clearly where music, chant, song, and dance were called for in the original.

Whether a modern director chooses to use music as fully as did the classical Greeks is a personal choice. In any event, the change of mood dictated by chant, song, and music in the original must ideally be created in some way in any successful modern production. It can be accomplished with voice, with mode of delivery, with style of acting, but it must be with *something,* because there is a range of tones in these plays that must be dealt with other than realistically.

Again: What is the purpose (methodology, if you will) of the translations in the present volumes of the plays of Euripides? In a word, it is to heed the warnings and advice given to translators through the millennia by practitioners of the art from St. Jerome to Roger Shattuck, to allow the original texts to breathe freely rather than to be suffocated by demands that may be proper in the classics classroom but out of place in the study of the humanities and in performance on the stage.

One final comment must be added regarding the text of these volumes. Even in classical times, the plays of Aeschylus, Sophokles, and Euripides were subject to interpolation by producers, directors, and actors. In the case of an actor, for example, his aim was to amplify his role. In all but a very few instances such interpolations have been been excised on the basis of the most recent scholarship.

✌

TROJAN WOMEN

(ΤΡΩΙΑΔΕΣ)

CHARACTERS

POSEIDON *god of the sea*
ATHÊNA *goddess protector of Athens*
HÊKABÊ *widow of Priam and once queen of Troy*
FEMALE SLAVE ATTENDANTS *of Hêkabê*
CHORUS OF CAPTIVE TROJAN WOMEN
FIRST CAPTIVE TROJAN WOMAN *leader of first half-chorus*
SECOND CAPTIVE TROJAN WOMAN *leader of second half-cho-
rus*
TALTHYBIOS *Greek officer and herald*
KASSANDRA *daughter of Priam and Hêkabê, a prophetess*
ANDROMACHÊ *widow of Hêktor*
MENELAOS *king of Sparta, husband of Helen*
HELEN *wife of Menelaos*
ASTYANAX *young son of Andromachê and Hêktor*
SOLDIERS

TROJAN WOMEN

The plains of Troy.
The camp for captive Trojan women.
Behind it the smoking ruins of Troy.
Tents for the captives dominate the scene.
HÊKABÊ lies prostrate on her back outside one of them.
Enter POSEIDON.

POSEIDON: I am here. Poseidon. Come from the depths of the salty sea on whose floor Nêrêids dance their dances in graceful rounds. Apollo and I once raised these walls of stone, stone on stone, towers, raised them straight and true along the plumb line, to embrace this city of Troy. And Troy has never been far from my heart.

But now, Troy is no more. Nothing will ever rise from this mound again. Sacked. Gutted. A smoldering ruin. Toppled by Argive spears. The work of Athêna's cunning, and the crafty hand of Epeiros, carpenter from Parnassos; Epeiros who raised a monstrous horse of wood that, pregnant with Argives spears, and burdened with its cargo of doom, rolled its way in through Troy's mighty gates.

The groves of the gods are desolate now, and their altars polluted with human blood. And Priam, great king of Troy, lies slain, cut down at the base of Zeus Protector's statue. Wagons piled high with loot, golden treasures of Troy's greatness, the spoils of war, roll noisily down to Achaian ships whose holds are heavy with war's proud plunder. All that keeps them here, these Greeks who brought war against my city, is lack of a favoring wind to belly their sails. In the seed time of this tenth year of conflict they are eager to rejoice again in the sight of their wives and children.

I, too, am leaving my city. Argive Hera and Athêna win out against me, those two who together destroyed Troy. I leave behind me fabled Ilion and my altars. When desolation cruelly embraces a city, its worship sickens and the gods are no longer honored. The Skamander's banks resound with the shouts of captives, women, waiting to learn what master will win them by lot. Some fall to the Arcadians, some to the Thessalian army, and others to the sons of Thêseus who lead the Athenians. Those not yet allotted wait in these tents, choice flesh for the likes of princes, among them Tyndareos's daughter, Helen of Sparta, by everything that's fair classed as a captive slave.

If anyone is interested, there's Hêkabê over there in front of the main entrance, weeping tears, many tears for many reasons. She doesn't know it, but her daughter Polyxenê has been piteously slaughtered at Achilleus's tomb. Priam and all their sons are dead. And Kassandra, whom Apollo abandoned a prophecy-maddened virgin, will become flesh for the pleasure of Agamemnon's bed— Agamemnon to whom piety and respect for the gods mean nothing.

Oh city, once prosperous Troy with your proud squared towers, farewell! Athêna, Zeus's daughter, did this. Had she not, you would be standing firm on your foundations.

ATHÊNA: *(Enters.)* You are a great god, my lord, and my father's brother; is it possible, do you think, to sweep my feud with you under the carpet so that we may talk?

POSEIDON: You may. Kinship, lady Athêna, is no weak charm to capture the heart.

ATHÊNA: I thank you for the thought. But I have a question that concerns us both.

POSEIDON: News from heaven perhaps? From Zeus or some other powerful deity?

ATHÊNA: No, I've come for Troy's sake, on whose ground we now stand. Is it possible, do you think, we might join powers and become allies?

POSEIDON: But you hate Troy, always have. Do you pity her now that she's a smoking ruin?

ATHÊNA: Let's return to my earlier point. Can we two take counsel together and join in whatever it is I want to do?

POSEIDON: Of course. But what do you have in mind? Are you here for the Trojans' sake or the Greeks'?

ATHÊNA: The Trojans, whom I hated so recently. I want to give the Greeks a homecoming they won't easily forget.

POSEIDON: Why are you so fickle in your allegiance? First this one, now that. Why do you hate and love with such excess?

ATHÊNA: But they outraged me and my temples!

POSEIDON: And Aias dragged off Kassandra.

ATHÊNA: And they did nothing, the Greeks! Not a word of reprimand!

POSEIDON: And yet, thanks to you, they sacked Troy.

ATHÊNA: Precisely why I intend to make them suffer—with your help.

POSEIDON: I'll do whatever you say. What's your plan?

ATHÊNA: Their homecoming will be a disaster.

POSEIDON: On land? At sea?

ATHÊNA: Their sea journey home from Troy. Zeus will send rain and hailstorm, hurricanes to blacken the sun's clear light. He has promised me the blazing bolt of his lightning to set the Greeks' ships ablaze. And you, you in your own domain, must make the Aegean churn with towering waves and whirlpools, line the coast of Euboia's bay with corpses to teach them respect for my temples and to honor the other gods.

POSEIDON: As you wish. The fewer words the better. I'll toss the Aegean's waters into mad confusion. The beaches of Mykonos and the rocky reefs of Dêlos, and Skyros and Lêmnos, and Kaphêreion's headlands will be glutted with the corpses of many a Greek.

Go back to Olympos. When you have your father's lightning bolts, wait till you see the Greek ships set out in full sail. That man who sacks fallen cities is no fool; but a fool when he then lays waste and desolates temples and tombs, places sacred to the gods. He has sown his own destruction. *(Exeunt POSEIDON and ATHÊNA.)*

(HÊKABÊ rouses herself.)

(Music. Song. Dance.)

HÊKABÊ: *(Chants.)*

Up, rise up, wretched head,
rise, rise from the dust;
neck, lift this stricken weight.
Here is Troy that is no Troy,
Troy no longer Troy
and we no longer Troy's rulers;
Troy's kings,
Troy's kings are dead.
Tides turn, turn with the tides,
endure, endure,
change is all.
Ebb and flow, helpless,
no struggle,
no breasting disaster where destiny rules.

AIIII!
AIIII!

Misery, oh misery,
what have I not suffered?
My city, my children,
my husband, gone!
Where are you now,
proud swelling sail of ancestors past?
Pride, wealth, heaped high,
where are you now?
Nothing, nothing now,
sunk in oblivion!
Shall I grieve, shall I not grieve?
Shall I keen my lament?
Look at me, wretched,
stretched out on the hard earth!

IOOOOO!
IOOOOO!

Oh head, oh temples, oh sides!
How lovely, like a ship,

endlessly shifting,
now this way, now that,
as I keen my lament!
This, too, is music to the wretched—
to chant the joyless dirge of doom.

(Sings. Dances.)

Ships prows sailing the purple sea,
skirting the fair harbors of Hellas,
you came on swift-flying oars,
you came to sacred Ilion,
oars plowing the salty sea,
speeding to the harsh high shrill of the pipes,
to the hateful song of the tuneful flute.
Here, to my pain,
here, here, you lowered hawsers
of Egyptian weave,
here in Troy's bay,
to search her out,
the hateful wife of Menelaos.
Helen, Kastor's disgrace,
Helen, blight of Sparta,
Helen, slayer of ancient Priam,
father of fifty sons,
Helen, who has run aground ancient Hêkabê,
here, on this shore, Hêkabê destroyed.

Look at me now,
behold Hêkabê,
ancient Hêkabê,
where she has ended,
where she now lies,
close by the tents of Agamemnon.

Led away, captive, slave,
from my house, head ravaged,
shorn in my grief,
pitiable, mourning Hêkabê.

Come, sad wives of bronze-speared Trojans,
come, virgin daughters, brides of disaster,
let us raise our voices for Ilion in flames.
Like a mother bird crying for her fledglings,
I will lead the dirge,
our song of lamentation;
now no longer the song I sang once
to honor, to praise the gods of Troy,
when I led the proud beat of the dancing chorus,
while Priam looked on, leaning on his scepter.

(Enter from the tents the FIRST HALF-CHORUS OF CAPTIVE TROJAN WOMEN.)

(Music continues. Song. Dance.)

FIRST CAPTIVE TROJAN WOMAN: *(Chants.)*
What are these cries, Hêkabê?
What news is there?
I heard your mournful keening through the walls.
Your words have stabbed with fear
the hearts of Troy's women,
those of us inside mourning our slavery.

HÊKABÊ: *(Chants.)*
Oh my dears, dear children,
the Argives are on the move,
on the way down to their ships,
to set sail, the oarsmen!

FIRST CAPTIVE TROJAN WOMAN: *(Chants.)*
OI 'GO!
What? What do they want?
To carry me off,
away from my native land,
my home?

HÊKABÊ: *(Chants.)*
I don't know.

But I see disaster,
ruin!

FIRST CAPTIVE TROJAN WOMAN: *(Chants.)*
IO! IO!
Unhappy women of Troy,
come, come from the tents,
come hear of the pain you must suffer!
The Greeks are heading for home!

HÊKABÊ: *(Chants.)*
É! É!
Don't, I beg you, don't bring her,
not here, not my raving Kassandra,
my Kassandra driven mad,
to be outraged by the Greeks!
I have sorrow enough to bear.
IO! IO!
Troy, oh Troy,
wretched Troy,
this is your end,
and we who leave you are wretched,
wretched both living and dead!

(Enter from the tents the SECOND HALF-CHORUS OF CAPTIVE TROJAN WOMEN.)

SECOND CAPTIVE TROJAN WOMAN: *(Chants.)*
OIMOI!
Trembling with fear, I have left the tents
of Agamemnon to hear you, my queen.
Will the Greeks end my life of misery with death,
or are the sailors now manning the ships,
ready to set to sea?

HÊKABÊ: *(Chants.)*
Dear daughter, dear child,
I have been here since dawn,
panic stricken,
my heart stabbed with terror.

SECOND CAPTIVE TROJAN WOMAN: *(Chants.)*
>Have the Greeks sent a herald?
>Have they let it be known whose wretched slave
>I am destined to be?

HÊKABÊ: *(Chants.)*
>They are near now to the drawing of lots.

SECOND CAPTIVE TROJAN WOMAN: *(Chants.)*
>IO! IO!
>What man of Argos,
>what Phthian or islander
>will lead me away,
>drag off my wretched life,
>away from Troy?

HÊKABÊ: *(Chants.)*
>FÉU! FÉU!
>Whose slave shall I be,
>wretched, unhappy,
>miserable old crone,
>where in all the world shall I serve?
>Where?
>I, a drone, a living corpse,
>feeble adornment of the dead!
>Shall I guard their doors,
>shall I nurse their children,
>I who once was proud queen in Troy?

CAPTIVE TROJAN WOMEN: *(Sing.)*
>AIIII!
>AIIIIIIII!
>How pitiful,
>how pitiful are your
>shame and your laments!
>Never again,
>never,
>will I,
>never,

move my whirling shuttle
back and forth,
back, forth,
on a Trojan loom.
Never again,
never,
will I see my parents' home.
I will know greater troubles,
greater far than these,
brought to the bed of a Greek
(I curse that night,
I curse that fate!),
or draw water
at the sacred fountain of Peirênê,
a pitiable slave.
I pray I may come to famous Athens,
land of Thêseus, blessèd land.
But never,
never let me come to Sparta,
never to the swirling Eurotas,
detested Sparta,
home of Helen,
and the sight of detested Menelaos,
sacker of Troy!

I have heard of the lovely, the hallowed ground,
the pedestal of Olympos where the Pêneüs flows,
a land of great wealth and abundant fruitfulness.
That would be next after glorious Athens.
And I have heard, too, of the land of Aitna,
Aitna and Hephaistos, fire-god,
opposite Carthage, Sicily,
mother of mountains,
praised by heralds for its crowns of excellence.
And the land washed by the Ionian Sea,
watered by the loveliest of rivers, the Krathis,
that dyes the hair red-gold with its waters,
blessing the land with its holy streams
and making it happy in its brave men.

FIRST CAPTIVE TROJAN WOMAN: *(Chants.)*
>But here comes a herald from the Greek camp.
>He has news, look at him hurry.
>What can it be?
>What will he say?
>Remember, we're slaves now of a Dorian land.

(Enter TALTHYBIOS with a detail of ARMED SOLDIERS.)

TALTHYBIOS: *(Speaks.)* Hêkabê—I may call you that, I trust, for I have often come to Troy as a herald from the Greek camp, and so I'm not unknown to you, Talthybios, here with a new message.

HÊKABÊ: *(Sings.)*
>Now it comes,
>dear daughters of Troy,
>now, now,
>what I've dreaded for so long!

TALTHYBIOS: *(Speaks.)* You have been assigned to your masters by lots, if this was your dread.

HÊKABÊ: *(Sings.)*
>Where, then?
>Tell me?
>A city in Phthia?
>Or the land of Kadmos?
>Where?

TALTHYBIOS: *(Speaks.)* You are assigned separately, each to a man.

HÊKABÊ: *(Sings.)*
>Who to which man?
>Which of Troy's women
>has a happy fate?

TALTHYBIOS: *(Speaks.)* I know the answer, just don't ask all at once.

HÊKABÊ: *(Sings.)*
>My poor Kassandra?

Poor daughter?
Who has won her?

TALTHYBIOS: *(Speaks.)* King Agamemnon chose her as his special prize.

HÊKABÊ: *(Sings.)*
As a slave to his
Spartan wife?
My poor child!

TALTHYBIOS: *(Speaks.)* No, you misjudge. As his concubine.

HÊKABÊ: *(Sings.)*
Apollo's virgin girl,
who had from the golden-haired god
the gift of a virgin life?

TALTHYBIOS: *(Speaks.)* Passion pierced his heart for your god-possessed
daughter.

HÊKABÊ: *(Sings.)*
Tear, tear away, then, the consecrated laurel,
the holy branches of the god,
the god's sacred garlands!

TALTHYBIOS: *(Speaks.)* Is there greater honor than winning a king's bed?

HÊKABÊ: *(Sings.)*
And the child you took from me,
my youngest? What of her?
Where is she?

TALTHYBIOS: *(Speaks.)* Is it Polyxenê you mean? Or who?

HÊKABÊ: *(Sings.)*
Polyxenê, yes.
What lot was chosen for her?

TALTHYBIOS: *(Speaks.)* Her assignment is to serve the tomb of Achilleus.

HÊKABÊ: *(Sings.)*
    OMOIIIII!
    My daughter,
    to serve attendance at a tomb!
    Tell me, friend, is this some quaint
    custom of the Greeks?

TALTHYBIOS: *(Speaks.)* Consider your daughter blest. She couldn't be happier.

HÊKABÊ: *(Sings.)*
    What are you saying?
    Is she alive?

TALTHYBIOS: *(Speaks.)* She has met her destiny. She's free of care.

HÊKABÊ: *(Sings.)*
    And the wife of Hêktor,
    mighty in battle,
    Andromachê,
    poor woman?

TALTHYBIOS: *(Speaks.)* The son of Achilleus took her as prize.

HÊKABÊ: *(Sings.)*
    And who am I to serve,
    I, doddering crone,
    who need a third leg to walk?

TALTHYBIOS: *(Speaks.)* Odysseus, King of Ithaka, got you as his slave.

HÊKABÊ: *(Sings.)*
    É! É!
    Beat your shorn head, ancient woman!
    Score your folded cheeks with your nails!

    IO MOI MOIIII!

    Condemned by lot to slave for a foul,
    a treacherous man, enemy to justice,

lawless, a beast, a monster!
Twists, he twists,
twists truth to falsehood,
and evil to good,
turns love to hate!

AIIII!

Weep for me, women of Troy, weep!
I am ruined! All hope dead! All gone!
The worst lot of all, fallen to me!

(Music out.)

FIRST CAPTIVE TROJAN WOMAN: Your fate is known now, lady. But
   what of mine? What Hellene or Achaian will master me?

TALTHYBIOS: Bring her out, men, Kassandra, quickly. I'll deliver her first
   to our commander, then distribute the rest of these women to the men
   who won them by lot. *(Several SOLDIERS start for the tent.)* But
   what's this? What's that flare of a pine torch gleaming inside there?
   Are they setting the tents afire, burning their bodies to escape their
   fate in Argos? Are they so eager to die? What? I understand the love
   for freedom, especially in such circumstances. A free spirit doesn't take
   misfortune lightly. Open these doors! Open! This may be to their
   advantage, but not to the Greeks'. I refuse to accept the blame!

HÊKABÊ: Burning the tent? No. But my Kassandra, my own, caught in a
   whirl of frenzy, rushing out to us here.

(Enter from the tent KASSANDRA brandishing flaming torches.)

(Music. Song. Dance.)

KASSANDRA: *(Sings.)*
   Raise it,
   raise it high,
   bring it, bring,
   bring the light,
   bring it!

I honor this place,
this holy place,
Apollo's sacred temple,
I honor,
Lord Hymenaios,
this holy place,
see it, oh see!
Blest is the bridegroom,
blest, oh blest am I,
married to the royal
bed of Argos!
Hymen, oh Hymenaios, Hymen!

Poor Mother,
you weep,
weep and moan,
tears without end,
for Father,
dead,
for country,
destroyed,
and so I, I hold high the flame,
the blaze, the radiant glow,
lighting the way,
the path to my
marriage,
for you, Hymenaios,
and you, Hekate,
custom's way when
young girls marry!

Lift high,
lift high the foot!
Lift high the foot in
dance,
in dance!

EVAN EVOË!

In dance,
as we danced in my
father's prosperity,
in happiness, joy,
the holy dance, holy!
Lead it, Apollo, lead the
dance!
I wear your crown,
your laurel crown,
I tend your temple,
Hymen, oh Hymenaios, Hymen!
Dance, Mother, dance!
Lead,
lead the way,
this way and that,
ripple the air with your
delicate foot,
join with me now,
join, join,
weave your foot with mine,
weave, weave,
in this joyful step,
and shout,
cry out,
the cry of Hymen,
cry out for the bride with
shouts of happiness,
songs to celebrate the
virgin bride!
Oh daughters of Phrygia,
daughters of Troy,
daughters dressed in
splendid gowns,
sing to me, sing,
of the Argive husband
fate has decreed
will lie beside me.

(Music out.)

FIRST CAPTIVE TROJAN WOMAN: My queen, you must stop your mad daughter before she whirls lightly into the Argive camp!

HÊKABÊ: Hephaistos, fire-god, you hold high the torch when mortals marry, but this flame is one of pain and misery, and far from the high hopes I once cherished.

Oh my child, how could I ever have imagined that your marriage would be at the point of an Argive spear. Give me the torches. In your mad frenzy you aren't in your right mind, my dear, to carry them properly. Nor has your fate brought you to your senses. I see no relief. *(She takes the torches.)* Women, take them inside and extinguish them. Let us change her wedding songs for tears.

(Two of the WOMEN take the torches into the tent.)

KASSANDRA: Crown my head, Mother, for I am victorious, the conqueror, so rejoice in my royal marriage. Escort the bride on her way, and if it seems I am less than eager, urge me on by force.

If Apollo is Apollo still, then Agamemnon, the glorious lord of the Greeks, will, in his marriage to me, win a wife more disastrous, more fatal, than Helen ever was. I will kill him, and I will lay waste his house, and so have my revenge for my dead brothers and father. But I will say no more of that, nor sing of the ax that will fall on my neck and on the necks of others, nor of the struggle that will come from a mother's murder thanks to my marriage, nor of the fall of the house of Atreus.

Possessed by the god though I am, yet I will step free of my frenzy and show how our city is infinitely more blest than the land of the Greeks. I call to mind the countless lives they lost in their rescue mission for one woman and her passion. Their oh-so-clever general destroyed what he most loved for the sake of what he most hated, offering up in his brother's honor the joy of a house of children for the sake of a woman, a woman whose abduction was no abduction but a freely willed, unforced flight.

From the time they arrived at the banks of Skamander, they began dying, day after day, though they had lost no territory nor any of the high-towered cities of their fatherland. Those caught by Arês in his fatal net, never again saw their children, nor were they wrapped for burial by the hands of their wives, but lie buried in foreign soil. And back home it was no better. Wives who had lost their husbands died widows, while others who raised children in vain, died childless in their homes, no one to tend their tombs with blood offerings. So much for the Greeks, for now I address the Trojans.

Their greatest glory was to give up their lives for their country. Those killed in battle were carried home to their houses by those who loved them and prepared for burial by hands that had every right and found quiet rest in native soil. And those Trojans who did not die in battle, lived every day surrounded with wives and children, pleasures denied to every Greek. As for Hêktor and his fate, so great a disaster in the eyes of you Greeks, let me give you the truth.

He may be dead, but he won a reputation of such glory that has no equal, and that would never have happened if the Greeks had not made it possible. Had you Greeks stayed at home, his bravery would have passed unnoticed. And so, too, for Paris. As it is, he married Zeus's daughter, but had he not, the bride of his house would have faded unknown, untalked of, unremarkable in the course of time. A man of sense should shun war. But if war comes, a noble death for a city is no disgrace, no, but a crown of glory—disgrace comes with ignoble death.

And so, Mother, shed no more tears for our country or my marriage. It is with that marriage I will destroy those we most hate.

FIRST CAPTIVE TROJAN WOMAN: How easily you smile at your disasters. Will you one day illuminate the meaning of your song?

TALTHYBIOS: It's a good thing Apollo distempered your wits; otherwise I'd see you pay dearly for your words—sending my generals from your land like that. And yet it appears that those honored and thought wise are of no more account than any other. The high commander of the Greeks, Atreus's beloved son, has stooped to engage his passion in this madwoman—and of his own choosing, her above all others. Plain man though I may be, I would never have chosen her as a slave for my bed.

As for your taunts against the Greeks and your praise of the Trojans, I ignore them and toss them to the winds because of your brain-sick idiocy. Follow me now to the ships. A choice prize for the general's bed! To you, Hêkabê, I say, when Laërtês's son Odysseus comes for you, follow him. You will be the slave of a good woman. Everyone who comes to Troy says so.

KASSANDRA: My mother, you say, will come to the palace of Odysseus. Then what of Apollo's words to me that she will die in Troy? I leave the rest unsaid; I refuse to insult her.

Poor Odysseus, poor man, knows little of the suffering he has in store. My troubles and those of Troy will seem to him golden by comparison, for he will add to the ten years he has spent at Troy another ten before he lands on his native shore. And he will do so alone and have troubles enough to hound him. And in those wandering years of endless homecoming, he will know, Odysseus will, the rock-bound strait where dread Charybdis dwells, the flesh-eating Cyclops of the mountains, the Lygurian witch Circê who makes men into swine; he will suffer shipwreck on the salty sea, longing for the lotus, and the sacred cattle of the Sun, whose flesh will speak from the spit and mean bitter times for him.

But to be brief, he will descend alive to Hades, and when he has escaped the perils of the sea, he will make his way home to find a flood of troubles in his own house. But why am I hurling out the trials that Odysseus will meet?

Hurry, Kassandra! Quickly! Waste no time! Go marry your bridegroom in the house of Death! And you will have a wretched death, wretched general of the Greeks, you whose fortune seems so grand, you whose burial will have night, not day, for witness! And I, whose corpse will be cast out, naked, will be washed down some ravine by storm waters near my bridegroom's grave and be delivered to wild beasts to rip apart and gorge on, I, Apollo's servant. Farewell garlands of the god I love best of any! Farewell mystic ribbons of inspiration! I leave behind the festivals I took such joy in. I tear you now from my flesh while my body is still pure and throw you to the winds to carry to my Lord of Prophecy!

Where is this general's ship? Take me to the place where I go onboard. Now is not too soon to be looking for a wind for your sails, for when you take me from this land, you will take in me one of the Furies, one of three.

Good-bye, Mother. You mustn't weep. Dear land of my fathers, and my brothers beneath the earth, and Priam, father of us all, you will welcome me soon. I will come triumphant to the land of the dead, leaving behind the ruins of the house of Atreus at whose hands our own house was destroyed.

(Exeunt KASSANDRA, TALTHYBIOS, and the SOLDIERS. HÊKABÊ collapses.)

FIRST CAPTIVE TROJAN WOMAN: You, attendants of the old woman, your mistress has fallen and lies there without a word! Do something! Help her! Wretches! Or will you leave her lying there?

HÊKABÊ: No. Leave me. Let me lie where I've fallen. An unwanted kindness is no kindness, my dears. What better response is there than collapse to what I have suffered, am suffering, and have still to suffer? Oh gods! What wretched, faithless allies you are—gods I once trusted! If I call on you now, it is only because one does that when disaster strikes. But I will sing first of my blessings one last time, so that when I come to my miseries I will seem the more pitiable.

Born of a royal house, I married into one, and there gave birth to sons of great eminence, destined to be lords of the Phrygians, the likes of which no mother, Greek or barbarian, could boast having given birth to. And these I saw slain by the Greek spear. And I cut my hair in mourning at their tombs. Their father Priam I didn't mourn at others' reports but saw slaughtered at the household altar, and my city taken. The daughters I raised in purity for the arms of no ordinary husbands, I brought up for the benefit of others—for they have been taken from me without hope I will see them ever again, or they me.

Finally, to crown this tale of my misfortunes, I will go to Greece an ancient slave, there to be charged with tasks unfitting to my age. Guardian of the door and keeper of keys, baker of their bread, I who once birthed Hêktor. I slept once in royal splendor and will now be forced to lay my withered back on the hard earth, and dress my broken body in tattered rags, a disgrace for one who was prosperous. How can so much suffering, so much unhappiness, have come and continue to come from a single marriage, from one woman?

Dear Kassandra, dear child, who once shared inspiration with the gods, how wretched the loss of your purity in devotion to the god! And dear, poor Polyxenê, where are you? So many, so many children, and not one now to help me in my pain. So why raise me up? In hope of what? Lead me now, lead me, who once tread so delicately in Troy, now a slave, to my pallet on the ground with its pillow of stone, and let me lie down, worn with weeping, and waste away to death. Fortune's favorite? No. Call no man happy until he is dead.

(FEMALE SLAVE ATTENDANTS lead her back to the pallet.)

(Music. Song. Dance.)

CAPTIVE TROJAN WOMEN: *(Sing.)*
Sing for me, Muse,
sing for me of Ilion,
sing me a tale,
a new-minted tale,
a song of lamentation and tears,
for I will sing now of Troy,
Troy whose destruction came from that beast,
that four-footed monster that brought me death,
brought me to slavery,
that horse,
wooden beast,
left by the Greeks,
horse spangled with golden adornments,
clattering to the skies with its belly of spears!
Troy's people shouted from the tallest battlements:

FIRST CAPTIVE TROJAN WOMAN: *(Sings.)*
"Trojans, come, the war is over!
Your troubles are past!
Bring in this gift,
this holy image,
sacred to the goddess,
Zeus's own daughter!"

CAPTIVE TROJAN WOMEN: *(Sing.)*
What girls did not go,
what old men did not rush
from their houses in song,
to lead through Troy's gates
Troy's lurking destruction?

All of Troy's masses sped to the gates,
sped to bring this polished-wood ambush
to the goddess,

the goddess,
this treacherous haven of death,
a gift to the goddess of immortal steeds,
this gift of the Greeks.
Like a ship's dark hull,
snared with nooses of flax,
they brought it to the goddess'
stone-floored temple,
goddess Athêna,
stone floors that would soon run blood-red,
death to the land,
death to Troy.
But night brought an end to their joyous labor,
and the shrill screech of the Libyan pipe sounded,
and Phrygian strains soared,
and young girls,
lifting their feet in dance,
sang joyous songs,
while inside houses
torches blazed bright to banish sleep.

At that hour, I sang and danced round the temple
in honor of Artemis,
Zeus's mountain-dwelling daughter,
when a bloody shout rang out through the city,
and with trembling hands
children grasped at mothers' skirts.
War god Arês stalked from his ambush.
This was the work of Pallas Athêna,
this was Pallas Athêna's will.
The blood of Trojans,
slaughtered,
flowed around altars,
and in our chambers,
those who had husbands still,
had them no more,
killed in their beds by headsmen's blades,
and we,
rounded up,

Troy's young women,
a prize to Greeks to breed them sons,
and pain,
pain and desolation,
grief,
grief,
grief to Troy.

(Enter ANDROMACHÊ and ASTYANAX on a mule-drawn cart led by several Greek SOLDIERS. The cart is piled high with Trojan spoils of war.)

FIRST CAPTIVE TROJAN WOMAN: *(Chants.)*
Hêkabê! Look! Andromachê!
On an enemy wagon!
And Hêktor's dear son Astyanax at her breast!

Poor woman, where are they taking you,
where, with their loot from Troy and Hêktor's bronze armor?
Spoils that Achilleus's son will hang in Phthia's shrines!

ANDROMACHÊ: *(Sings.)*
The Greeks, my masters, are carrying me off.

HÊKABÊ: *(Sings.)*
OIMOI!

ANDROMACHÊ: *(Sings.)*
Why sing a sorrow that is mine

HÊKABÊ: *(Sings.)*
AIII! AIII!

ANDROMACHÊ: *(Sings.)*
for all this grief

HÊKABÊ: *(Sings.)*
Oh Zeus!

ANDROMACHÊ: *(Sings.)*
    for all these miseries.

HÊKABÊ: *(Sings.)*
    Oh my children

ANDROMACHÊ: *(Sings.)*
    once yours,

HÊKABÊ: *(Sings.)*
    no more

ANDROMACHÊ: *(Sings.)*
    Troy lost,

HÊKABÊ: *(Sings.)*
    Troy's power

ANDROMACHÊ: *(Sings.)*
    gone

HÊKABÊ: *(Sings.)*
    unhappy

ANDROMACHÊ: *(Sings.)*
    Troy!

HÊKABÊ: *(Sings.)*
    And my noble sons!

ANDROMACHÊ: *(Sings.)*
    FÉU! FÉU!

HÊKABÊ: *(Sings.)*
    FÉU!
    Yes, for my own

ANDROMACHÊ: *(Sings.)*
    misfortunes.

HÊKABÊ: *(Sings.)*
  Oh pity the

ANDROMACHÊ: *(Sings.)*
  destiny

HÊKABÊ: *(Sings.)*
  of our city

ANDROMACHÊ: *(Sings.)*
  our Troy

HÊKABÊ: *(Sings.)*
  a smoldering ruin.

ANDROMACHÊ: *(Sings.)*
  Dear husband, come back

HÊKABÊ: *(Sings.)*
  My son you're calling
  is dead now, poor child.

ANDROMACHÊ: *(Sings.)*
  to defend your wife.
  You destroyer

HÊKABÊ: *(Sings.)*
  of the Greeks

ANDROMACHÊ: *(Sings.)*
  firstborn

HÊKABÊ: *(Sings.)*
  of my children

ANDROMACHÊ: *(Sings.)*
  to Priam

HÊKABÊ: *(Sings.)*
  once mine.

ANDROMACHÊ: *(Sings.)*
>Take me down to you in death.
>These yearnings are strong.

HÊKABÊ: *(Sings.)*
>Cruel,
>cruel

ANDROMACHÊ: *(Sings.)*
>the pains we endure

HÊKABÊ: *(Sings.)*
>for my lost city.

ANDROMACHÊ: *(Sings.)*
>Pain lies heavy

HÊKABÊ: *(Sings.)*
>pain upon pain

ANDROMACHÊ: *(Sings.)*
>because the gods hate us that Paris lived
>to destroy Troy's towers for a hateful marriage.
>The bloody bodies of our young men
>lie sprawled at the feet of Athêna's statue
>for vultures to carry off.
>The yoke of slavery was his gift to Troy.

HÊKABÊ: *(Sings.)*
>Oh unhappy land,
>unhappy Troy

ANDROMACHÊ: *(Sings.)*
>I weep as I leave you

HÊKABÊ: *(Sings.)*
>and see your pitiable final hour

ANDROMACHÊ: *(Sings.)*
>and weep for the house
>where I bore my children.

HÊKABÊ: *(Sings.)*
> Children, my sons,
> your mother leaves you now
> in a city deserted,
> a city now dead,
> with lamentation and keening
> and tears on tears,
> tears of pity,
> for our house now dead.
> The dead at least know no grief.

(Music out.)

FIRST CAPTIVE TROJAN WOMAN: How sweet are tears for the unfortunate, keening laments and the music of sorrow.

ANDROMACHÊ: Mother of Hêktor who killed so many Greeks with his spear, do you see this? Do you see what has become of us?

HÊKABÊ: I see what the gods can do. How they build tower high those that are nothing and tear down what only seems mighty.

ANDROMACHÊ: We are carted off, my boy and I, with the spoils of war; noble turned slave in a grand transformation.

HÊKABÊ: How dreadful is the power of Necessity. Kassandra has just now left me; torn from my arms by force.

ANDROMACHÊ: FÉU! FÉU! Another Aias to drag her off by the hair! But there are other troubles you must suffer.

HÊKABÊ: Yes, without measure, without number. Evil does battle with evil.

ANDROMACHÊ: Polyxenê is dead. Cut down. Her throat slit at Achilleus's tomb; a gift to warm his cold and rotting corpse.

HÊKABÊ: AIIII! Now I know the riddle Talthybios told, so cryptic then, now clear as day.

ANDROMACHÊ: I saw her, saw her myself. I leapt from the wagon to cover her body with garments and mourn her.

HÊKABÊ: AI! AI! Oh dear child, dear dead child, I weep for your slaughter! AI! AI! Once more, once more for your shameful death!

ANDROMACHÊ: She died as she died; and yet her death is a happier state than my life.

HÊKABÊ: No, my dear, you mustn't confuse them. Death is nothing; life offers hope.

ANDROMACHÊ: No. Death and not being born are the same. And death is infinitely better than living a life of pain. After life's painful struggle, the dead feel nothing, no pain, because they no longer experience evil. But to know happiness and then to fall from its grace confounds the mind in a hostile world. Polyxenê is dead; and in death she has no memory of seeing the light of day, nor know the misery she suffered.

    As for me, as Hêktor's wife, I aimed my arrows high, at a good name, a splendid reputation, and in large part I hit the mark, but fell short in finding happiness. Everything that brings credit to a woman, such as modesty, modest behavior, I strove to achieve while in Hêktor's house.

    From the first I foreswore my pleasure in the out-of-doors, for whether or not a woman is blameworthy, she attracts scandal just by venturing from her house. And so I remained indoors. Nor did I allow women into my rooms, clever women, with their clever talk, but contented myself with trusting to my own wise counsel. In my husband's company I guarded my tongue and adopted a serene gaze. I also knew when it was right to insist on my own way, and when to resign to my husband's will and award him the victory. Word of this made its way through the Greek camp, and it proved my undoing. For when I was captured, the son of Achilleus wanted me for his wife. And so I shall slave in the house of my husband's murderers.

    If I wipe clear of my mind the beloved memory of Hêktor and let into my heart my present husband, I will seem disloyal to the dead man I love. But if I prove hostile to my present husband, I will be inviting my own master's hatred. And yet it's said that a single night in a man's bed overcomes any loathing a woman may have. But I have only contempt for the woman who rejects her former husband and opens her arms of love to a newcomer. Not even a young mare, torn from its running mate, will easily bear the yoke, despite that it's a beast without reason and inferior to man in its nature.

Dear Hêktor, when I had you, I had all I could want in a husband: a man great in understanding, rank, wealth, courage. You took me, a virgin, from my father's house and were the first to come to my innocent bed. And now you're dead. And I will sail to Greece, a prisoner of war, to wear the yoke of slavery.

No, Hêkabê, don't you see? How is the death of Polyxenê that makes you grieve so worse than my own fate? I don't share with other mortals what is left to them in the end: hope. Nor do I deceive myself that I will ever know happiness again—however sweet it is to dream such dreams.

FIRST CAPTIVE TROJAN WOMAN: Our misery is a pair, my dear. And as you mourn your fate, we learn the true depth of our own sorrows.

HÊKABÊ: I may never myself have been aboard a ship, but from paintings and conversation I have learned certain things. I know that when the stormwind is not too fierce, sailors are eager to brave it and escape danger. One mate steers, another trims the sails, while a third tends to the bilge. But let a violent tempest strike, with decks awash and the vessel threatening to split, they resign themselves to the run of the waves and give everything over to Chance.

It's that way with me, my dear. So great are my misfortunes that I give myself over to them and say nothing, for the great wave of misery sent by the gods threatens to destroy me. So listen to me now. You must stop your mourning for Hêktor. Your tears can never bring him back. Accept your new master; do as he says; win the love of this husband with the charm and grace of your goodness. Do this and you will bring joy to all of your loved ones. You will raise this boy to manhood, this, my grandson, raise him to be Troy's greatest helper, so one day his descendants will resettle Troy and make it a grand city again.

But here comes another subject to take us from the old. Who is this servant of the Greeks come to announce what news?

TALTHYBIOS: *(Enters with a detail of ARMED SOLDIERS.)* Wife of Hêktor, Troy's greatest warrior, I ask you not to hate me for what I'm to say, but I have no choice. This is my message from the Greeks and the sons of Pelops.

ANDROMACHÊ: What is it, this ominous hint of sorrows to come?

TALTHYBIOS: The council has decreed that your son—
How can I say this?

ANDROMACHÊ: Will serve a different master than I?

TALTHYBIOS: No Greek will ever be his master.

ANDROMACHÊ: You surely won't leave him here, Troy's pitiable sole survivor?

TALTHYBIOS: I don't know how to say this easily.

ANDROMACHÊ: Thank you for your courtesy—unless your news is good.

TALTHYBIOS: The hard fact is—your son is to be killed.

ANDROMACHÊ: OIMOI! Worse, far worse than all my miseries together!

TALTHYBIOS: Odysseus spoke in the assembly and won the day.

ANDROMACHÊ: AIIII! AIIII! More, more grief than anyone can bear!

TALTHYBIOS: His argument: a hero's son must not be allowed to live—

ANDROMACHÊ: I hope someday his own sons find such mercy.

TALTHYBIOS: —but be thrown from the highest of Troy's battlements. Take my advice, Andromachê, give in to it, don't fight it, it will do you no good. First of all, don't cling to your son, give him up freely, that's the wise way. Bear your pain nobly, as befits your birth, and realize that you are weak. You mustn't suppose you have any power to help, and there's no one will defend you. Your city is destroyed, your husband is dead, and you are at the mercy of those who, I assure you, are in no way incapable of doing battle with a single and defeated woman.

So renounce your passionate nature for now. There's no disgrace. You won't be laughed at or scorned. Above all, do nothing undignified or vengeful, or hurl curses at the Greeks. Say anything at all to provoke the army, and your son will be denied the mercy of a burial. But if you're brave, and endure this in silence, your boy's corpse will not be left behind unburied, and you will find the Greeks more kindly disposed to you.

ANDROMACHÊ: Oh my dear, my dearest child, too much loved for your own good, you will die at enemy hands and leave your mother desolate to mourn alone. Your father's nobility, which was salvation for others, will for you be your undoing. Nor will memory of his bravery be to your benefit. The bed was doomed, that marriage bed we shared, and doomed the bridal ceremony when I came to Hêktor's house, not to give birth to a sacrificial victim for Greeks to slaughter, but a ruler, a king over the fruitful fields of all Asia.

Oh my dear, why are you crying? Do you know what is to happen to you? Clutching me, holding me fast, like a fledgling seeking the protection of my wings. Hêktor will not burst from the earth wielding his fabled spear to protect you, nor will any of his kinsmen, nor the united strength of Troy. Yours will be a terrible leap, head first, from Troy's battlements, your skull smashed on the stones below, and no one to have pity. Oh my loved dear that my arms held as a baby, how sweet the smell of your body. It was for nothing I nursed you, my labor in vain, the pain that all but killed me. Kiss me now, this once, the last, your mother, let me hold you, hold you, your arms around me, your lips against mine.

Greeks! You call yourselves Greeks but contrive atrocities worthy of barbarians! Why are you killing this child? What has he done to you? And you, Helen, you, daughter of Tyndareos, never a daughter of Zeus! It was many fathers fathered you! Vindictiveness, Hate, Slaughter, Death, and all the wickedness the earth breeds! Zeus was never your father, that much I know, for you were born a plague to Greeks and barbarians alike! I curse you! You whose ravishing eyes brought ugly death to the glorious plains of Troy!

So, come, then, Greeks, come take him, take him and toss him, hurl him to his death, if that satisfies your will! Feast on his flesh!

We're pawns in the gods' game, and they're destroying me who cannot save my child from death. Cover me, my wretched body, and fling me onto your ship! What a splendid marriage I go to across the death of my child.

FIRST CAPTIVE TROJAN WOMAN: Unhappy Troy! The countless sons you have lost for one woman's lust!

(TALTHYBIOS lifts ASTYANAX gently from ANDROMACHÊ's arms.)

(Music. Song. Dance.)

TALTHYBIOS: *(Chants.)*
　　Come, boy, it's time.
　　Leave your loving mother's arms
　　and let her mourn.
　　Climb to the towering
　　peak of your father's walls
　　where your life will end.
　　The order is given.
　　Take him.

(He hands ASTYANAX to a SOLDIER.)

　　A herald should be without pity
　　to deliver such messages.
　　I am not that man.

(Exeunt TALTHYBIOS and the SOLDIERS with ASTYANAX; then ANDROMACHÊ in the cart led by SOLDIERS.)

HÊKABÊ: *(Sings.)*
　　Oh child,
　　son of my
　　sorrowful
　　son,
　　how can they
　　do this?
　　How can they

rob you,
from me,
from your mother,
without reason,
no
reason?
What can I
do?
What, what can I
do for you?
Tear my face?
Beat my breast?
This is all.
All I can do.
Over this
I have
power.
I cry,
I cry for
my city!
I cry,
I cry for you, child!
What is left to
suffer?
What is left but
destruction,
total ruin?

CAPTIVE TROJAN WOMEN: *(Sing.)*
Oh Telamon, king of wave-washed Salamis,
bee-haunted Salamis,
there where you founded your city,
where you made your home,
in sight of the shore and the holy hill,
the sacred hill,
where Athêna revealed the first shoot of the gray-green olive,
heavenly crown and glory of bright shining Athens.
You came, you came,
from there you came,

Telamon,
on your great venture with bow-wielding Heraklês,
son of Alkmênê, Heraklês, partner, to sack proud Ilion,
Ilion, our city, our Troy,
so long, so long ago,
came from Hellas so long ago.
From Hellas he brought the land's finest flower,
Heraklês, cheated of the promised mares,
and there at the fair flow of the Simoïs
he shipped his sea-plowing oars,
secured with cables the ships' proud sterns,
and took from his ship the well-aimed bow that was death,
death to Laomedon.
With fire, with fire's crimson blast,
he split the stones straight-hewn by Apollo's hands,
and lay waste, sacked, the land of Troy.
Twice now, twice, in two battering attacks,
murderous spear and fire,
fire, have razed,
have tumbled the god-built towers of Troy.

It is for nothing, son of Laomedon,
for nothing, Ganymede, lovely Ganymede,
that you step in delicate pride among golden wine jugs,
in noble service on high Olympos,
filling Zeus's cups,
for your city, the land that birthed you,
Troy your mother,
is ablaze, burning, flame-devoured,
while her beaches groan like a bird calling her young,
here wives mourning husbands,
here children, crying, lost,
and here ancient mothers keening,
keening for dead sons, dead.
The gleaming pools you bathed in once, gone now.
Gone, too, the courses where once you ran,
destroyed now, no more.
And still you sit, Ganymede, by Zeus's throne,
ravishing youth of the serene smile,

while Priam's kingdom falls to the dust
at the point of the Greek spear.

Love, oh Love,
you who came once to the halls of Dardanos,
Eros, love god,
you who incited,
you who ignited
passion in their hearts,
the hearts of gods,
binding knots of marriage between us,
Dardanos's offspring and high Olympos,
how greatly you exalted Troy!
And yet, for Ganymede's sake, Zeus—
but enough; no more reproach for Zeus.
But Dawn, the light that all men love,
white-winged Dawn,
looked calmly on as Troy was destroyed,
as Pergamon lay ruined,
Dawn,
in whose bed lay a Trojan husband
to give her children, Tithonus,
snatched up in the golden chariot,
planting, raising strong hope for our land.
But the god's love for Troy is no more.

(Music out.)

MENELAOS: *(Enters with a detail of ARMED SOLDIERS.)* Bright splendor
of sun breaking on this glorious day, this day when I will again lay
hands on my wife! I came to Troy with my armies, I, Menelaos, not
so much, as everyone supposes, for my wife, as to find the man who
entered my house a guest, and left it a treacherous thief, a wife stealer.
But the gods, thanks to them and the spears of the Greeks, have seen
fit to punish him; he's paid with his life; and so has his city that lies in
ruins behind us.

That done, I'm here now to retrieve *her*, the Spartan woman, as I
call her, for I take in speaking her name no particular pleasure. She's

there, in this tent set aside for the captive women, numbered as one among the lot of them, a slave, and rightly, too.

Those men whose spears brought down this city to win her, have given her to me to do with as I will: kill her on the spot or, if I choose, not to kill her, but return her to the land of Argos. And so it is. I've decided not to trouble with her death in Troy but to take her back by ship to Greece and slit her throat there, just penalty for the deaths of friends killed in Troy.

All right, men, get on in there and drag her out by her murderous hair! When the winds blow fair we'll cart her off to Greece.

(Exeunt several ARMED SOLDIERS into the tent.)

HÊKABÊ: Oh Zeus, the earth's support, whose seat is on it, Zeus, so hard to know, whoever you are, Law of Necessity in nature or Law of Reason in man, I call upon you! For on your noiseless path you direct the affairs of men toward justice.

MENELAOS: What's this? What strange new prayers to the gods!

HÊKABÊ: Kill her, Menelaos, kill your wife, and bless you for it. But never look at her. She captures with desire. She enchants men's eyes, makes them her slaves, destroys cities, sets houses blazing. She knows the black arts; she has power. We both know her, as do all who have been her victims.

(Enter HELEN, richly dressed, brought on roughly from the tent by the ARMED SOLDIERS.)

HELEN: Menelaos! This rude treatment by your men doesn't promise a happy future! Forced out of my chambers! Put on display in front of the tents like any common piece! Really! Oh, I know you hate me; at least I have a fair idea. But I want to ask you a question, if it's not too much trouble. My life. What have the Greeks decided to do with it? What have *you* decided? Do I live or die?

MENELAOS: Your answer is there's been no decision. The army entrusted me with the right to kill you. I am, after all, the man you wronged.

HELEN: Am I allowed to argue against that, to prove that my death—if I *am* put to death—will be unjust?

MENELAOS: I didn't come to argue. I came to kill you.

HÊKABÊ: No, Menelaos, hear her out; let her present her argument. She shouldn't die without being heard. But give me the chance to offer a counter argument. There's no way you can know the miseries we suffered at Troy. Once the full fabric is stitched together, her death will be inevitable.

MENELAOS: This will take time, but if she wants to speak, let her. She has my permission. But I want to make it clear, I do this not for her sake, but for yours, at your request.

HELEN: Well, Menelaos, since to you I am an enemy, it makes no difference whether I speak well or not, because you'll refuse to answer me in any case. For my part, I can only assume what accusations you will make in arguing against me, and so answer them with just accusations of my own. But I will begin. First! This woman is the beginning of it all. She gave birth to Paris, giving rein to this evil. Paris was her child. Second! Doddering old Priam refused to kill the infant Alexandros, as Paris was so heroically called at birth—that woeful dream image of a firebrand—and so destroyed both Troy and me. But that's not all. I have more. Listen.

Paris passed judgment over that trinity of goddesses in a beauty contest. Pallas Athêna offered him conquest and total desolation of Greece at the head of the Trojan army. Hera, if he gave her the victory, promised rule over all of Asia and the farthest reaches of Europe. And Aphroditê, long admirer of my loveliness, bribed him with thepresent of me, my beauty, if her own beauty outstripped the others in the contest. Very well, then, so much for that, but here's what followed.

Aphroditê won, and winning, gave me to Paris in marriage. And that marriage has benefited Greece in this regard: Greece is neither destroyed nor tyrannized by barbarians. Yet Greece's good fortune was my own downfall. I, once sold for my physical loveliness, now stand accused and reviled by those who should have crowned my head with garlands. Oh, yes, you'll be saying anytime now that I'm not addressing the issue in question. So I'll answer it.

I *did* slip from your house. And I did it in secret. I *did* run away. But when he came—when Alexandros, or Paris, or whatever it is you choose to call him—when he came, he came with a goddess on his side, and no minor one, at that—he came, Paris, this woman's evil genius, bringing destruction and annihilation. And it was this man, *he,* you despicable creature, that you left with me, alone, in the house, and set sail from Sparta to Krete!

Well, then, here's my next question that I put to myself, not you. What could I possibly have been thinking, was I, in fact, in my right mind, when I slipped from the house with a stranger, deserting my country and my home? No, blame the goddess, not me, blame her, Aphroditê, and be more powerful even than Zeus! Zeus who holds power over the other gods, but is himself the slave of Aphroditê. If my fault is pardonable in Zeus, it's pardonable in me.

Now: there's another point against which you might raise a specious argument. You will object that when Paris died and descended into the dismal gorges of death beneath the earth, and my marriage arranged by the gods was annulled, I should have left my house in Troy and sped on down to the Greek ships. The fact is I attempted that very solution, and I have witnesses to attest it. The warders and watchmen of the towers and battlements. They often discovered me trying stealthily to lower myself by ropes to the ground.

So, then, husband, how am I to be justly put to death, rather than justly pitied by you, when I was the bride of force, and the victim of my own natural endowment which brought me slavery rather than a crown of victory? Is it to be stronger than the gods you hanker for? If so, what a foolish thing.

FIRST CAPTIVE TROJAN WOMAN: Come, defend us, Hêkabê, your children, your country. She's persuasive and she speaks eloquently, guilty though she is, and a terrible thing that is.

HÊKABÊ: First, I will set out to defend the goddesses against this woman's lies. How is it possible that Hera or the virginal Athêna could be so foolish as to sell Argos to the barbarians or Athens to the Trojans to enslave? And why would they have gone to Ida for the childish nonsense of a beauty contest? Why should the goddess Hera want to be more beautiful? Was she out to win a husband the superior of Zeus? And Athêna? Was she out to find a husband in the first place?

Athêna who begged her father Zeus to make her virginity a permanent state and who shunned marriage? Don't make the gods look foolish just to hide your own evil nature. You'll never persuade the wise. You say that Aphroditê went with my son to Menelaos's house. What a ludicrous idea! Wouldn't it have been easier for her to have stayed comfortably in heaven and transported you—indeed the whole town of Amyklai with you—to Troy?

My son was beautiful beyond all measure, and when you saw him your heart *became* Aphroditê, for what else are acts of foolish human intemperance but Aphroditê? Her name, after all, begins with the word for folly.

You saw him, my son, a starburst in his barbaric robes of gold from the East, and you lost your senses to luxuriance. Argos being modest of means, you strained at the bit to be rid of Sparta for Troy, whose streets flowed with gold, where you could lavish your extravagance without check.

Well, then. You maintain that my son dragged you off by force. But who of the Spartans heard you? Your cry for help? Kastor, after all, was still there, your brother, a young man, with his twin. They hadn't yet been translated to the stars. Then, once you'd arrived in Troy, with the Greeks hot on your trail, and the murderous battle had begun, every time Menelaos won the day you lauded him to the skies to make my son miserable with the knowledge that he had a great lover as rival. But when the Trojans were on top you denigrated Menelaos as being a cipher, a nobody. You kept a steady eye on Fortune, making certain she never escaped you, and cared little for virtue. And then you claim to have tried escaping, letting yourself down with ropes from the walls as though you were being kept against your will. But when, on what occasion, were you found with a noose in hand, or sharpening a sword—actions any woman of nobility would do if she longed for her husband's return?

And yet, how many times did I advise you: "Escape, my dear! Leave here! My sons will arrange other marriages. I'll see to your getting safely and secretly to the Greek ships. Save us, save us both from this war." But, no, you had other ideas. You wanted to continue luxuriating in Paris's palace and have barbarians bow to the ground before you. That was always the most important to you. And now you have the gall, you despicable creature, to come out here in the full light of day and in front of your husband, tricked out in all your finery! You had best come a beggar, dressed in rags, trembling, head shaved bare, modestly rather than brazenly, shamed by the life you've lived.

And here, Menelaos, I conclude my argument. Do Greece the honor, crown her with the glory of killing this woman and honor yourself as well with an act of such noble worth! No! Establish it as a custom: Death to women who turn whore in their husbands' house!

FIRST CAPTIVE TROJAN WOMAN: Take up the reins, Menelaos, punish her, prove your ancestors' worth and that of your house! Greece calls you a woman! Prove them wrong!

MENELAOS: We've arrived at the same conclusion, Hêkabê—that this woman left my house of her own free will to tumble into a stranger's bed. As for Aphroditê, she was only window dressing, gilding the lily. Let her now go out to face the soldiers who will stone her to death and in an instant atone for the years of hardship she has caused the Greeks and learn not to dishonor the name of Menelaos.

HELEN: No, Menelaos, don't, don't blame me for the sickness sent by the goddess! I beg you! Don't kill me! Have pity!

HÊKABÊ: Don't be a traitor to the men she sent to their death! I beg you in their name and the name of my sons!

MENELAOS: Enough, Hêkabê. She means nothing to me now. I'm ordering my men to take her down to the ships and cart her off to Greece.

HÊKABÊ: Just don't put her on the same ship as you.

MENELAOS: Why's that? Is there more of her than there used to be?

HÊKABÊ: Once a lover, always a lover.

MENELAOS: That depends on the lovers' viewpoint. But I'll do as you say. We'll sail on different ships. Good idea. But once we arrive in Argos she'll die a death as evil as the life she lived, an example to all women to live lives of restraint. Which won't be easy. Still, her death will put

the fear of god in the dissolute hearts of women who are even more
dissolute than she!

(Exeunt MENELAOS and HELEN with the ARMED SOLDIERS.)

(Music. Song. Dance.)

CAPTIVE TROJAN WOMEN: *(Sing.)*
So, then, Zeus, you betrayed us,
betrayed us lightly to the Greeks,
betrayed your temple in Ilion
and its incense-misted altar,
the flame of offerings and the
scent of smoking myrrh
rising to the heavens,
betrayed Pergamon,
holy Pergamon,
and the glens of Ida,
Ida's glens heavy with ivy,
washed by torrents of melting snows,
Ida whose peaks are first touched by the sun,
holy, radiant, sacred place!

Gone are your sacrifices,
gone the singing,
the lovely singing of sacred choruses,
and nightlong festivals of the gods,
and your statues,
gold on wood,
molded figures,
and moon-shaped cakes,
fed to the flames,
twelve in number,
sacred number.
It matters, Zeus,
it matters much if you care about this,
or have you forgotten from your throne in high heaven,
your airy seat, have you forgotten
that Troy is undone, Troy perished,

laid waste by the cruel fire storm that broke it?

Dear husband, dear friend, you wander in death,
unwashed, unburied, while I speed through waves
with flashing oars, to Argos, Argos,
horse-loving land,
where men live surrounded by walls of stone,
heaven-high walls, walls built by giants.
Children in multitudes stand at the gates,
clinging to gates, tears streaming,
crying cries scarcely heard:
"Mother, Mother, they're taking me,
taking me away, away from you, Mother,
to the ships, the Greeks,
to their dark-hulled ships,
and across the sea to holy Salamis,
or to the peak of the Isthmus between the two seas,
where Pelops's palace stands with its gates!"

Oh how I pray,
how I pray that at sea Menelaos's ship
is struck by the bolt,
the fire-streaming bolt of Zeus's lightning,
struck midship between the oars,
for he takes me from home,
takes me in tears from Ilion,
a slave to Greek shores,
while Helen,
that hated daughter of Zeus,
primps and preens with her mirrors of gold,
mirrors that pretty girls so love!
I pray he never reaches Sparta,
never again crosses his ancestral hearth,
nevermore walks the streets of Pitana,
or does honor to Athêna of the bronze gates,
for he has forgiven his wife's evil marriage,
forgotten the shame of the Greeks at Troy,
the shame they won by the banks of the Simoïs,
that brought us such grievous sorrow.

(Enter TALTHYBIOS and SOLDIERS with the body of ASTYANAX on Hêktor's shield.)

FIRST CAPTIVE TROJAN WOMAN: *(Chants.)*
IOOOOOOOOOOO!
IOOOOOOOOOOO!
New evils come upon us!
Sorrow on sorrow in exchange for the old!
Behold him, Astyanax, his torn body,
behold him, unhappy wives of the Trojans!
Dead, hurled without pity from the walls,
a cruel missile, by the hateful Greeks!

(Music out.)

TALTHYBIOS: Hêkabê, there's one ship left, oars at the ready, to carry the remaining spoils of Achilleus's son back to the shores of Phthia. Neoptolemos has already sailed. News came that his grandfather Pêleus had been driven out of the country by Pêlias's son Akastos. Being denied a leisurely departure, he set off in haste, taking Andromachê with him. I must confess, her leaving brought many tears to my eyes, her farewell to her land and Hêktor's tomb, and begging that you be allowed to bury this child, your Hêktor's son, hurled to his death from Troy's battlements.

She also begged that this bronze-backed shield, Hêktor's shield, the terror of every Greek, the shield he used to protect his side, not be among the war spoils brought onboard. It must not be taken to the home of Pêleus, nor to the room where this dead child's mother would become the bride of her new husband and she might see it and be reminded. The boy is to be buried in it instead of in a cedar coffin and a stone tomb. She asked the body be placed in your arms to be wrapped in winding sheets and strewn with flowers as best you are able under the circumstances. She does this because now she's gone, hurried off by her master's haste, and unable to bury the boy herself.

When you've finished preparing the body, we'll bury it under a mound of earth and set sail. Do what you must as quickly as possible. And yet, there's one labor I've spared you. As we forded the waters of the Skamander, I washed the body and cleaned the blood from its wounds. I'm going now to dig the grave so that together our tasks are swiftly done and we can set sail.

HÊKABÊ: Lay it on the ground, Hêktor's circled shield, no easy sight for me to see. *(The SOLDIERS lay down the shield with ASTYANAX's body and exeunt with TALTHYBIOS.)* Greeks! You whose spears show more wisdom than your brains! What so frightened you in this child that you had to kill him so savagely? Terror that fallen Troy might one day be raised up again by him? If so, then your strength was worthless. Even when Hêktor and the multitudes of strong men fighting with him were successful on the field of battle, there was still blood shed on our side. Yet when Troy is fallen, and every Trojan man destroyed, you are still afraid of a child? I despise the fear that has no basis in reason.

Dear darling child, what a miserable death yours was. If you had grown to manhood, had married, become king with power like a god's, and then died defending your city, you would have died happy, assuming happiness lies in such things. As it is, you have only witnessed and learned of such matters without ever having experienced or enjoyed them.

How cruelly, poor boy, your father's walls, walls built by Apollo, have mangled you, shorn those curls I so often smoothed with my hand and smothered with kisses. Crushed, now, your head, blood smiles through the torn, broken bones—too horrible, too horrible not to speak it out. Dear hands, how sweetly they look like your father's, slack now, limp at the joints, tiny wrists broken in the plunge. Where are your promises now, loved mouth, once so brave, so sure, when you would run and dive into my bed, screeching: "Grandmother, when you die I'll cut a great lock from my head and bring it to your tomb, my friends and I, and say such loving good-byes!"

How cheated of that I am now, for now you are no more, for now it is not you burying me, but I who bury you, so young, and I an old woman, homeless, childless, and you a wretched corpse. How sad to think of those many kisses, the care I gave you, the times I held you in my arms in sleep, all, all gone now, those lovely nights. What words will a poet write on your tomb? "Here lies a child killed by the Argives—in terror"? An epitaph of shame for the Greeks. Though you will never have your father's patrimony, at least you will have his bronze-backed shield as a coffin to bury you in.

Oh shield that protected Hêktor's fine strong arm, you have lost the great hero who best guarded you, for he is dead. How sweet is the mark of his body on your sling, and his sweat on the circle of your rim, when in battle he pressed you against his chin and you caught the drip from his brow.

Everyone, come, come bring adornment for this pitiable body, the best we have to offer in our misery, small though it is. And yet you will have all I can give. The man who imagines prosperity is his forever and rejoices in it is a fool. For like a madman Fortune leaps this way and that, and no one is happy forever.

(Enter from the tent FEMALE SLAVE ATTENDANTS bringing robes and flowers of the field.)

FIRST CAPTIVE TROJAN WOMAN: Here are your women, Hêkabê, with garments from Troy's spoils to deck the body.

HÊKABÊ: Child, it is not to celebrate your victory over friends in riding or archery that your grandmother dresses you in rich robes once your own—for Helen, hated by the gods, has stolen it from you, and with it your life and the life of your entire house.

(Music. Song. Dance.)

CAPTIVE TROJAN WOMEN: *(Sing.)*
É! É!
You have touched my heart, dear child,
who were once, once in my eyes
the lord of the city!

HÊKABÊ: *(Speaks.)* These robes, these robes so rich and fine, the glory of Troy, you would have worn on the day of your marriage to the noblest princess of all Asia—these robes that I now lay on your body. And you, oh, you, beloved shield of Hêktor, victorious so often in battle, mother of a thousand conquests, receive this garland, for you will die with this dead child, and yet you shall not die. Better far to honor you than the arms of the clever but wicked Odysseus.

CAPTIVE TROJAN WOMEN: *(Sing.)*
AIAIIIIII!
The earth,
the earth will take you, child,
take you,
take you,
bitter object of our sorrow,
sorrow!
Cry, Mother,
cry aloud—

HÊKABÊ: *(Sings.)*
AIII!
AIAIIIIII!

CAPTIVE TROJAN WOMEN: *(Sing.)*
—the dirge for the dead!

HÊKABÊ: *(Sings.)*
OIMOIII!

CAPTIVE TROJAN WOMEN: *(Sing.)*
OIMOIII!
Evils,
not to be forgotten!

HÊKABÊ: *(Speaks.)* I will tend you, I will bind your wounds, a sorry
physician, in name only, no use, no use. Your father will see to the
rest down there among the dead.

CAPTIVE TROJAN WOMEN: *(Sing.)*
Strike,
strike your head,
strike,
strike again,
again,
in rhythm,
like oars!
OI MOI MOIIIIII!

HÊKABÊ: *(Speaks.)* Women, oh women, dearest women—!

CAPTIVE TROJAN WOMEN: *(Chant.)*
>Speak to us, Hêkabê!
>We're here,
>we're with you!
>Why did you cry?
>Why did you cry aloud?
>Tell us!
>Tell us!

HÊKABÊ: *(Speaks as if in a trance.)* Now, now it is revealed, now—the gods don't care, the gods don't hear, the gods are nothing and all that matters is pain, my pain and Troy's, Troy of all cities most hated by the gods. It was for nothing, the sacrificing, the hecatombs, the oxen, all in vain, their smoke never reached the heavens. And yet had the god not crushed our city, not turned our world on its head, deep, deep in the dark earth, we had been nothing, we had faded into oblivion, unknown in obscurity, never the subject of song sung by the Muses in time to come.

>Go bury the boy now in his wretched grave. He has all the adornments that are due the underworld. What difference can it make to the dead how lavish the funeral. This is an empty pretension of the living.

(Exeunt several FEMALE SLAVE ATTENDANTS with the body of ASTYANAX.)

CAPTIVE TROJAN WOMEN: *(Sing.)*
>IOOOO!
>IOOOO!
>I weep for your mother, child,
>your wretched mother,
>whose hopes for your life were so large,
>hopes now dashed,
>nothing,
>nothing!
>Blest in your birth,
>blest in your noble birth,

you died a grim death, child,
a horrible death.

FIRST CAPTIVE TROJAN WOMAN: *(Chants.)*
>Look there, there,
>on Troy's heights!
>Those men!
>Who are they?
>Hands ablaze with torches!
>What new agony
>must Troy suffer!

(Enter TALTHYBIOS and SOLDIERS.)

(Music out.)

TALTHYBIOS: *(Shouts to men on the city walls.)* You captains, you with orders to set blazing the citadel of Troy, I order you now to make useful the torches you carry and make Troy burn! When the city is no more, we set sail for home with happy hearts!

As for you, daughters of Troy, not to waste words, when the generals sound the shrill trumpet, hurry down to the Greek ships that will take you from this land. And you, ancient Hêkabê, unhappiest of women, follow me. These men have come to fetch you for Odysseus, for by lots you are assigned to be his slave.

HÊKABÊ: OI 'GO TALAINA! Now I reach the end of my agony's road. I leave my land, my city in flame. Come, doddering feet, one last proud effort, so I may hail my afflicted city in its death. Oh Troy, Troy, once so proud in your greatness among Asia's barbarian cities, you will soon be stripped of your name, no more glory! They are burning you, you are fed to the flames, and we, we are dragged away, dragged to the ships to sail into slavery. Gods, hear me! But why should they hear? They did not hear before when we implored them!

Come, women, come, hurry, into the pyre! How much nobler to die in the flames as our land burns to its end!

TALTHYBIOS: Poor woman, your suffering has driven you mad. Take her, men. Don't hesitate. To Odysseus. She's his. Deliver to him his prize.

(Music. Song. Dance.)

HÊKABÊ: *(Sings.)*
OTOTOTOTOI!
Son of Kronos,
lord of Phrygia,
father of our race,
do you see the
dishonor
we must suffer?

CAPTIVE TROJAN WOMEN: *(Sing.)*
He sees,
has seen,
he has seen,
but Troy,
great city,
Troy's great city,
is no more.
Troy is no more.

HÊKABÊ: *(Sings.)*
OTOTOTOTOI!
Ilion is ablaze!
Pergamon's halls
rise up in flame!
Ilion's high towers,
Ilion's citadel,
devoured by fire!

CAPTIVE TROJAN WOMEN: *(Sing.)*
Like smoke on the wind,
our city fallen,
our city conquered,
drifts,
fades,
wastes away!

HÊKABÊ: *(Sings.)*
>Land, oh land
>that nursed my children!

CAPTIVE TROJAN WOMEN: *(Sing.)*
>É!
>É!
>É!

HÊKABÊ: *(Sings.)*
>My children,
>hear me,
>hear your mother's
>cry!

CAPTIVE TROJAN WOMEN: *(Sing.)*
>It is the dead,
>the dead
>you call with your
>cry of lament.

HÊKABÊ: *(Sings.)*
>And I cry as my
>old body
>sinks to the ground and
>with my two
>fists
>I beat, I beat the
>earth
>with my fists!

CAPTIVE TROJAN WOMEN: *(Sing.)*
>I kneel on the earth with you,
>old woman,
>and cry,
>cry to my husband,
>cry for him to rise up
>from Death's Dark Kingdom!

HÊKABÊ: *(Sings.)*
>   We are taken away,
>   dragged,
>   dragged—

CAPTIVE TROJAN WOMEN: *(Sing.)*
>   It is grief,
>   grief you cry out!

HÊKABÊ: *(Sings.)*
>   —to a house of
>   slavery!

CAPTIVE TROJAN WOMEN: *(Sing.)*
>   Away from my land,
>   my homeland!

HÊKABÊ: *(Sings.)*
>   IOOOO!
>   IOOOO!
>   Priam, oh Priam!
>   No grave for you,
>   my dear, no friend,
>   no way to
>   know
>   the end I suffer!

CAPTIVE TROJAN WOMEN: *(Sing.)*
>   Death,
>   holy death,
>   has closed his eyes,
>   death,
>   dark death amid
>   unholy butchery!

HÊKABÊ: *(Sings.)*
>   Oh temple of the gods,
>   city I love—

CAPTIVE TROJAN WOMEN: *(Sing.)*
 É!
 É!
 É!

HÊKABÊ: *(Sings.)*
 —yours the red,
 devouring
 flame,
 yours the murderous
 spear point!

CAPTIVE TROJAN WOMEN: *(Sing.)*
 You will fall,
 fall to the earth,
 the dear earth,
 and your name be
 no more!

HÊKABÊ: *(Sings.)*
 Listen!
 Listen!
 Did you hear?

CAPTIVE TROJAN WOMEN: *(Sing.)*
 Crashing!
 Crashing!
 Tumbling!
 The towers!
 Troy's walls!
 The sound!
 AIIIIIIII!

HÊKABÊ: *(Sings.)*
 Quaking!
 The earth!
 The whole—

CAPTIVE TROJAN WOMEN: *(Sing.)*
> city shaking!
> IOOOO!
> IOOOO!

HÊKABÊ: *(Sings.)*
> IOOOO!
> Trembling limbs,
> trembling,
> trembling!
> Onward, now!
> Forward!
> Into slavery!

CAPTIVE TROJAN WOMEN: *(Sing.)*
> IOOOO!
> IOOOO!
> TALAINA!
> Mourn,
> mourn the city,
> the unhappy city!
> Mourn,
> mourn the city
> that is no more!
> On!
> On to the ships!
> The Achaian ships!
> On!

(Exeunt all led off by TALTHYBIOS and the SOLDIERS.)

*

IPHIGENEIA IN TAURIS

(ΙϕΙΓΕΝΕΙΑ Η ΕΝ ΤΑΥΡΟΙΣ)

CHARACTERS

IPHIGENEIA *daughter of Agamemnon and Klytaimnêstra*
ORESTÊS *brother of Iphigeneia*
PYLADÊS *Orestês's friend*
CHORUS OF CAPTIVE GREEK WOMEN *slaves of Iphigeneia*
FIRST CAPTIVE GREEK WOMAN *leader of the Chorus*
HERDSMAN
THOAS *king of the Taurians*
SLAVE ATTENDANT *of Thoas*
ATHÊNA
SLAVE ATTENDANTS, TEMPLE SLAVES, GUARDS

IPHIGENEIA IN TAURIS

Tauris.
Early morning.
Outside the Temple of Artemis.
A blood-stained altar.
Enter IPHIGENEIA from the temple.

IPHIGENEIA: I am Iphigeneia, the daughter of Agamemnon and
Klytaimnêstra. The same Iphigeneia who was lured to Aulis as a bride
for the great Achilleus but sacrificed to Artemis by my father.

As it happened, my father's brother, Menelaos, had a wife,
Helen, who was abducted by Paris, a prince of Troy. And so, to
comfort Menelaos, and to punish the offending Trojans for the
outrage done to Helen's marriage, my father assembled in the famous
bays at Aulis a fleet of ships, one thousand strong. But a strange lack
of wind kept the expedition from sailing.

My father, resorting to divination from burnt offerings, was told
by the army's ancient seer, Kalchas, that fair winds to Troy would
come only if he honored a pledge made long ago to Artemis. My
father had vowed to sacrifice to the moon goddess the loveliest thing
that year brought forth. And since my mother Klytaimnêstra gave
birth to me that same year, I was, according to Kalchas, the victim in
question. It was wily Odysseus devised the lie to get me to Aulis
without raising suspicion. They told my mother I would be married to
Achilleus. And so, poor unsuspecting girl, I came to Aulis, decked out
in my bridal finery, eager to see my groom, the beautiful Achilleus.

But instead of marriage, I was lifted over the altar, and just as the
sword was about to pierce my throat, Artemis stole me away, and a
young doe was put in my place. And yet, to the eyes of the Greeks and
to my father's it was I, Iphigeneia, who was slaughtered.

In the meanwhile, Artemis conveyed me through the bright air
and settled me here in Tauris, a barbarous land ruled by Thoas, its
barbarous king. Being swift of foot got him his name, for "thoas"
means swift, and he runs as though with winged feet. Goddess
Artemis made me priestess in her temple. My duty here is ghastly,
unspeakable. Any Greek setting foot on this soil is sacrificed. But it's

not for me to wield the knife; my task is merely to consecrate the victim. The actual slaughter is done by others in the shrine.

Last night brought with it the strangest dreams. Perhaps if I speak about it, it will bring some healing. I dreamt that I was back home in Argos, sleeping in the room I had as a child, when suddenly the earth began to heave and roll. I ran from the house in terror, and once outside, I saw the cornice of the palace tumble down, and after it the whole house, down to the ground, in ruins. Only one pillar remained standing of the house of my fathers, and that pillar at its capital streamed with blond hair and spoke with a human voice. Then, my eyes flooding tears, and true to my duty of preparing foreign victims for sacrificial slaughter, I sprinkled it with water to prepare it for death. This, now, is how I interpret my dream.

Orestês, my brother, whom I consecrated with water, is dead. As for the pillars of a house, they are its male children, and those whom my lustral waters sprinkle are killed. I must now perform the last rites for my brother, far from him though I am. That much, at least, I can do; and my women, the Greek slaves the king has given me, will help.

But why aren't they here? They should have arrived. I'll wait inside. *(Exit into temple.)*

ORESTÊS: *(Enters with PYLADÊS.)* Be careful, Pyladês. Someone may be on the road.

PYLADÊS: I am, Orestês. I've looked everywhere.

ORESTÊS: Is this the temple we sailed from Argos to find?

PYLADÊS: Yes, I think it might very well be.

ORESTÊS: There's the altar, streaming with Greek blood.

PYLADÊS: Browned bloodstains. This has got to be it.

ORESTÊS: And here, look, trophies hung under the edge.

PYLADÊS: Spoils of dead foreigners. Shields, heads.

ORESTÊS: Apollo, what new trap are you leading me into, what new snare devised by your oracles? You ordered me to avenge my father's murder. I did so: I killed my mother who killed *him,* and I did this at your command. But then the Furies came, relentless, implacable, vindictive creatures of revenge for killing her, for spilling maternal blood. Attacking and attacking and attacking, they drove me from my land, an outcast, an exile. The races I've run, doubling back and back again on the course, I can't even count anymore.

I came to you then, desperate to escape this spinning, reeling madness that had gripped me, to end its hold on my mind and end my painful wandering the length and breadth of Greece. In reply, you commanded me here to Tauris, here to the altar and temple of your sister Artemis, to remove the statue of her, which, men say, tumbled down from the sky to this very temple. "Lay hold of it," you said, "seize it by luck or cunning, and when you have it, take it to the city of Athens." And that's where your orders ended. Having done this, you said, I could rest from my perilous labor and be at peace. And so I've done as you ordered, come here to this hostile, unknown land.

Pyladês, since we're partners in this labor, I need your advice. What should we do? The walls that circle the temple are high, too high to climb even with a ladder and not be seen. Do we march up the stairs to the great bronze doors and pry them open with crowbars—crowbars we don't have? Do that and we'd be caught and killed. I have a better idea. Rather than death, let's get back to the ship and leave this place.

PYLADÊS: Run away? No, we don't do that. Not and also honor the god's oracle. We'll leave the temple now and hide on shore in caves carved out by the sea's waves, far from the ship. If someone should discover it and tell the king, we'll be taken by force. Under cover of night, we'll scrape our courage together and steal the image using all the cunning we can muster.

Look up there. You see? That space between the triglyphs? We can slip ourselves in there. Brave men don't shirk danger. Only cowards amount to nothing. We haven't rowed all this way just to turn back.

ORESTÊS: Good advice. I agree. Let's find a place to hide. I have no intention to ignore the god's oracle. Let's be bold. Youth offers no excuse to shirk a duty.

(Exeunt ORESTÊS and PYLADÊS. Enter IPHIGENEIA from the temple, along with an ATTENDANT SLAVE carrying a golden bowl. Enter the CHORUS OF CAPTIVE GREEK WOMEN by a side entrance.)

(Music. Song. Dance.)

FIRST CAPTIVE GREEK WOMAN: *(Chants.)*
> Keep silence,
> keep holy silence,
> all you who dwell
> by the Clashing Rocks
> of the Hostile Sea!

CAPTIVE GREEK WOMEN: *(Sing.)*
> Child,
> child,
> daughter of Lêto,
> Artemis of the mountains,
> I come,
> to your court I come,
> your court with its lovely columns,
> its golden cornices,
> I come,
> come with soft and maidenly step,
> slave to your holy temple's warder,
> Iphigeneia.
> Like her,
> like my mistress,
> my lady,
> I am torn from my blessèd home,
> my Hellas,
> land of towers,
> land,
> land of ramparts,
> famed for horses,
> and Europe,
> land of wooded fields,
> pastures,

green glades,
my home where my father's fathers lived.

FIRST CAPTIVE GREEK WOMAN: *(Chants.)*

    Here I am, my lady,
    daughter of great
    Agamemnon who
    forced the fortress
    of Troy with his
    thousand ships.
    What news is there?
    Why have you called me?

IPHIGENEIA: *(Sings.)*

    Pity, women,
    pity me!
    I am burdened,
    weighted with heavy laments,
    elegies for the dead,
    music the muses do not love,
    sounds the lyre will not accompany.
    I have lost my brother.
    I saw it last night in a dream,
    a vision in the dark
    that only now has left us.
    My house is destroyed,
    house of my fathers,
    I am lost,
    lost,
    no family, no
    loved ones.

    OIMOI MOI!

    How painful are the sorrows of Argos!
    Cruel spirit,
    Fate,
    you have stolen my brother,
    my only brother,

sending him down to Hades.
To him,
to him I pour these libations
on the stony earth,
to him,
from the bowl reserved for the dead:
milk of young mountain cattle,
Bakkhos's gleaming wine
and the toil of the tawny bee.
These I pour to the dead.

(To an ATTENDANT.)

Give me the vessel of gold
and the libations for Hades.

(She pours.)

Son of Agamemnon,
Orestês,
brother now in the Underworld,
to you I pour these libations,
for you are no more.
Receive these in place of tears
I would shed at your tomb,
in place of a lock of golden hair
to honor you.
I will not see your grave,
for I am far from our land,
the land where all men
believe I lie buried,
slaughtered in my grave.

CAPTIVE GREEK WOMEN: *(Sing.)*
I will sing,
will sing you a song,
a song in answer to your song,
mistress,
a song in an alien mode,
an Asian dirge sung by barbarian women,

laments for the dead,
sung by Hades,
no song of triumph.
OIMOI!

I weep for the house of Atreus,
weep for its sons who are no more,
glorious kings who are no more,
fallen now,
perished,
all,
with the light of its radiant scepters.

OIMOI!

Disaster plagued its prosperous line,
sorrow on sorrow,
murder upon murder,
destroying the monarchs of Argos.
So great was the outrage,
so terrible,
so fearful the sight,
that radiant Hêlios,
sun god,
with his winged steeds,
shifted the fixed course of his chariot,
veered,
turned back his golden,
his holy face,
and rose from then forever in the east.
Pain after pain
fell on the house of our kings,
king after king,
fathers and sons,
from the golden lamb,
sacred symbol of kingship in Argos,
slaughter upon slaughter,
grief upon grief,
a curse on fathers,
a curse on sons.

And now, mistress,
our royal house destroyed,
vengeance for the long-ago death
of the Tantalid sons
seeks you out as the last of the line,
to suffer its curse.

IPHIGENEIA: *(Sings.)*
No, women, no,
not only now,
not now,
has my fate turned dreadful.
I was cursed,
cursed from the night
my mother conceived me,
my mother the luckless
daughter of Lêda,
wretched Klytaimnêstra,
I, the first of her offspring.

And the fateful goddesses,
they who attend on childbirth,
have spun out for me
a terrible destiny!
That mother bore me,
that mother
gave me her breast,
raised me,
only to honor a pledge of my father,
a vow to sacrifice to the moon goddess
the loveliest thing the year brought forth.
I was that beast for sacrifice,
that pledge for unholy,
bloody slaughter
at my father's hands,
my father's disgrace.

The Greeks sped me
by horse-drawn chariot

to Aulis's sandy shore
to marry the Nêreïd's son,
mighty Achilleus.

OIMOI MOIIIIIIII!

An ill-fated bridal
that was no bridal!

Here I now am,
an alien in an alien land
bordering the Hostile Sea,
without husband,
without child,
no city or friend,
a stranger in a barren land,
I who was wooed by the
noblest of Greeks!

I do not sing or dance for Argive Hera,
or weave with my shuttle
at the murmuring loom
colorful images of Athêna and the Titans.
No, my music is the harsh cry of strangers,
the bloody music of death and despair,
as I stain the altars with their
blood and piteous tears.
But now I forget all that,
those tears,
and shed my own tears
for my poor brother,
dead in Argos,
brother I saw last at my mother's breast,
a baby, a child,
all the world before him,
in his mother's arms,
heir to the radiant scepter of Argos,
Orestês!

(Music out.)

FIRST CAPTIVE GREEK WOMAN: Look, a herdsman come from the shore with news.

HERDSMAN: *(Enters.)* Daughter of Agamemnon, listen to me; I have strange news to tell!

IPHIGENEIA: What is it? How excited you are!

HERDSMAN: A foreign ship, mistress! On our shores! Sailed safely through the dark Clashing Rocks! Onboard, two men, two young men. Offerings to the goddess Artemis, mistress; welcome offerings to slaughter in her honor. Ready the preparations at once. There's no time to lose.

IPHIGENEIA: Where are they from? What country? What do their clothes tell you?

HERDSMAN: Greek. They're Greek. That's all I know.

IPHIGENEIA: Their names? Did you hear them speak?

HERDSMAN: One of them called the other Pyladês.

IPHIGENEIA: And his friend? What was he called?

HERDSMAN: We don't know. We didn't hear.

IPHIGENEIA: Tell me how you found them. How did you capture them?

HERDSMAN: At the shore where the waves of the Hostile Sea break.

IPHIGENEIA: The sea? What have oxherds to do with the sea?

HERDSMAN: We were there to bathe the cattle in salt water.

IPHIGENEIA: Go back to my earlier question. Where and how did you capture them?

HERDSMAN: We had driven our herds from the forest grazing land down to the shoreline. There's a cave there hollowed out by the beating

waves of the sea, where purple fishers take shelter. One of us saw two
godlike young men sitting in there and hurried back on tiptoe to tell
us. "Look," he said, "there are two young gods in that cave!"
Then another of us, a pious sort, looked in at them and raised his
hands in prayer. "Sea goddess," he whispered, "and guardian of ships,
be merciful to us! Or are you the Dioskouroi," he asked, "or the
darling boys of Nêreus?"

Another of us piped in, a brash, roughhewn sort, with little
religion: "They're sailors, you fools, shipwrecked on our shore and
seeking shelter. They're terrified! Look at them! They know we
sacrifice foreigners."

Most of us agreed, and so we decided to hunt them down as
victims for the goddess, as custom demands. But then, with no
warning, one of the strangers rushes from the cave, trembling head to
foot, head jerking up and down, groaning in insane delirium.
"Pyladês," he screamed, "don't you see her? There! Trying to kill me!
Aiming all the vipers of her hair! She dragon from Hades! And there,
another! Fire-breathing! Spouting murderous gore! Swooping on
pounding wings, my mother in her arms, all stone, to crush me!"
But there was nothing, nothing to see. He'd misheard the sounds of
our cattle and barking dogs for those most likely made by the Furies.

Thinking he was about to die, we shrunk back in a crouch and
were silent. But he drew out his sword, and rushing in like a lion
among the cattle, he thrust at their flanks and ribs, believing he was
beating off the Furies, and making the sea blossom blood-red.

When we saw our herds wasted by this slaughter, we armed
ourselves and blew on conch shells to summon our nearby neighbors
to help. We figured we herdsmen were no match for these strapping
strangers with their youth and well-knit bodies.

It wasn't long before a large group had gathered. But by then the
young stranger had escaped his fit and fallen to the ground, his mouth
spilling foam. When we saw his convenient collapse, we wasted no
time and began pelting and striking at him. His friend meanwhile
wiped the foam from the young man's chin and protected the body
from our blows with the heavy weave of his cloak, guarding and
helping his dear friend with loving attention.

In his right mind again, he leapt to his feet, aware of the present
danger and the ruin that was all but upon them. He groaned loud, but
that didn't stop our attack, pelting them with stones from this side and

that. It was then we heard his terrible cry to his friend: "Pyladês, we're going to die! Let's meet our death with honor and glory! Draw your sword! Follow me!" When we saw our enemies charge us with brandished swords, we ran back, or most of us did, to hide in the stone gullies. But for everyone who fled, others charged forward raining stones on them, and when they ran back, those who had just retreated rushed forward, pounding and pelting them with objects. But even so, it was a miracle. For all the flying missiles from all those hands, not one of them struck the goddess's victims.

We finally overpowered them, but not without difficulty, and not by any bravery on our part; for we came at them from every side and knocked their swords from their hands with stones so they sank to their knees exhausted. We then hurried them off to the country's king, and when he saw them he sent them at once to you for purification and slaughter.

Mistress, you have often prayed for such victims for the goddess. Offer up the lives of many such men, and Greece will have no choice but to give you satisfaction for the brutal attempt to sacrifice you at Aulis.

FIRST CAPTIVE GREEK WOMAN: This is a wild tale, whoever this man is.

IPHIGENEIA: Go now, bring them to us. I'll see to the ritual preparations. *(Exit the HERDSMAN.)* Once, poor heart, once, you showed compassion to strangers of your own race, pity, pity toward Greeks who made their way here, shed tears when you took them prisoner. But now no more, because dreams have told me that Orestês no longer shares with me the sun's dear light. And so my heart is hardened toward you who have come.

I have just learned, friends, the truth of the saying, that the unfortunate who suffer are no kinder to those who are more unfortunate than they. But no wind sent by Zeus has come, and no ship, no ship blown by Zeus's wind through the blue Clashing Rocks to bring Helen to me, Helen who was my ruin, nor Menelaos. If I had them in hand, those two, I would have punished them, taken my vengeance, made an Aulis here like that other Aulis, where Greeks seized me like a young calf and slit my throat, the sacrificing priest my own father.

How do I forget the agonies of that moment when I reached out many times to touch him, to cling to his knees, his chin, in supplication, babbling stupidly: "Father, how can you do this? You lured me here to a marriage that is no marriage, a marriage that is a shame to us both! Back home in Argos, my mother and the Argive women are singing wedding songs that resound through our halls with the high-pitched trill of flutes! And here you are, killing me, slitting my throat, my own father! The husband you deceitfully promised me was Achilleus! But you lied! My husband is Hades! The husband you give me to is the Lord of the Dead! And this marriage is a marriage made in blood!"

When I left Argos with him, my father, I hid my face behind a finespun veil. I failed to grasp my little brother in my arms, Orestês now dead, and to kiss the lips of my sister. I was blushing; I was going to the house of Pêleus, and I would see them, my sister, my brother, when I visited Argos and our palace. I would see them again. But now, my poor Orestês, if you are dead, how far, how far you have fallen, how far from the splendid heritage your father holds for you.

This goddess is too subtle, this Artemis, this goddess of hypocrisy. She condemns the man whose hand is stained with blood, who has touched a corpse, or even a woman in childbirth. Polluted, she cries, and keeps him from her altars. And yet what pleasure she takes in human sacrifice! No. Zeus and Lêto can never have given birth to such a creature. Nor do I believe the tale of Tantalos. Tantalos who served up his son for the gods' enjoyment. What gods could delight in the cooked flesh of a boy!

I believe now these Taurians, being murderous in themselves, impose their own cruel nature onto the goddess. For I cannot believe the gods are evil. *(Exit into temple.)*

(Music. Song. Dance.)

CAPTIVE GREEK WOMEN: *(Sing.)*
> Dark,
> dark the meeting of two dark seas,
> where Io,
> driven,
> sped on by Hera's sting,
> left behind Argos for the Euxine Sea,

crossing from Europe to Asia's coast.
Who are they,
who,
who are these men
who have left behind the reedy pleasure
of Eurotas's stream
or the holy waters of Dirkê?
Who,
who are they who have come here,
come to this savage land
where the virgin daughter of Zeus,
Artemis,
spatters her altars and porticoed temples
with human blood,
the blood of human sacrifice?

Or did they sail the surging sea,
dividing the waves with their sharp-nosed prow,
with pine oars plunging this side and that,
hefty breezes full-bellying their sails,
questing to cram their hulls with greater wealth,
greater treasure for their halls?

But hope is foolish,
a foolish delusion to men who want more,
who sail vast seas in search of greater riches,
riches from faroff barbarian cities,
riches that fail to quench the desire,
insatiable longing never fulfilled,
for what's had is never enough.
There are those who lust for riches
and never achieve it;
for others who never seek it,
it comes with great ease.

How did they survive
the Clashing Rocks?
How did they pass
the never-sleeping capes of Phineus?
Did they hug the shore

through the billows of Amphitritê,
there where the fifty daughters of Nêreus
sing their songs and dance in a circle?
Or did they steer their coarse,
their cradled oars singing at the stern
in the southerly breezes that bellied their sails,
or the winds from the west,
did they steer across the sea
to the land of many birds,
with its white coast gleaming,
where Achilleus runs his glorious courses
beside the Hostile Sea?

How I wish,
how deeply,
deeply I wish,
that my mistress's prayers were answered,
prayers that would bring Helen,
Lêda's darling daughter,
here to this land from the city of Troy,
for then,
then,
her hair wet with deadly lustral waters,
my mistress's hand would slit her throat,
paying the debt that is due.
But best of all,
best of all news
would be the arrival from home,
from Greece,
from Argos,
a ship with sailors to end,
end the misery,
the toil,
of my wretched slavery.
But now,
now,
it is only in dreams that I am at home,
at home in my father's city,
my father's house,
singing,

singing,
singing songs and joyous hymns,
for dreams,
dreams,
are gifts that night,
blessèd night,
gives to all in common.

FIRST CAPTIVE GREEK WOMAN: *(Chants.)*
But here they are, the two,
hands bound together,
leaning on each other,
fresh victims for sacrifice to the goddess.

Silence, my friends,
for these young men are choice offerings,
the finest and noblest of their land.
The herdsman was right.

Great Artemis, if the rites of this city
are pleasing to you, receive these men
as sacrificial victims,
a custom which in my country
would be an abomination.

(Enter ORESTÊS and PYLADÊS, hands bound, guarded by TEMPLE SLAVES; then IPHIGENEIA from the temple.)

(Music out.)

IPHIGENEIA: So. My first thought must be to please the goddess as custom demands. Unbind the strangers' hands. They are consecrate and must not be restrained. *(To the TEMPLE SLAVES.)* Go inside and set in order everything needed and customary for the business before us. *(Exeunt the SLAVES into the temple.)* How sad—how sad. Two such splendid young men. Who was your mother, your father? And your sister, if you had one, how I pity her. What a beautiful pair of young brothers she will have lost. But who can predict fortune? The gods work in dark and mysterious ways.

Unhappy strangers, tell me where you come from. Your journey by sea was a long one. And longer yet will be your stay in the Underworld.

ORESTÊS: Why this pity for us, lady, whoever you are, when it only makes our approaching pain the worse? What sense is there to combat the fear of death by sympathy, or comfort a man condemned but offer no hope of rescue? What a fool! Out of one evil he makes two, and the victim dies in any case. Let fate take its course. And as for us, don't waste your tears. We're well aware of the sacrifices practiced here.

IPHIGENEIA: Which one of you is Pyladês? Tell me that first.

ORESTÊS: He is. Does that please you?

IPHIGENEIA: What Greek city is he from?

ORESTÊS: What good would it do you to know?

IPHIGENEIA: The two of you—are you brothers?

ORESTÊS: Brothers in love, not birth.

IPHIGENEIA: What name did your father give you?

ORESTÊS: By experience my name is Unlucky.

IPHIGENEIA: That's your fate, not my question.

ORESTÊS: My body will die, not my name.

IPHIGENEIA: Why won't you answer? Too proud?

ORESTÊS: A nameless death bears no insult.

IPHIGENEIA: Will you tell me what city you're from?

ORESTÊS: No; what good would it do?

IPHIGENEIA: Not even as a favor?

ORESTÊS: I come from glorious Argos.

IPHIGENEIA: In the name of the gods, is that true?

ORESTÊS: Mykenê—once a prosperous city.

IPHIGENEIA: Your coming here is much longed for.

ORESTÊS: Not by me, I assure you.

IPHIGENEIA: You're an exile, then? What happened?

ORESTÊS: An exile by chance, not choice.

IPHIGENEIA: Will you tell me one thing more?

ORESTÊS: Why not? I have the time.

IPHIGENEIA: Well, then, have you heard of Troy?

ORESTÊS: I wish I'd never even dreamed of it!

IPHIGENEIA: They say the war destroyed it.

ORESTÊS: Yes; that's no idle tale.

IPHIGENEIA: Has Helen returned to Menelaos?

ORESTÊS: She has. Bad news for my family.

IPHIGENEIA: Where is she? She owes me a debt.

ORESTÊS: In Sparta with her former bedmate.

IPHIGENEIA: I hate her no less than Greece does!

ORESTÊS: I, too, am a victim of her marriage.

IPHIGENEIA: Have the Greeks come home as reported?

ORESTÊS: All these questions at once!

IPHIGENEIA: Tell me before you die.

ORESTÊS: Ask me; I'll try to answer.

IPHIGENEIA: Did a prophet named Kalchas return?

ORESTÊS: At Mykenê they say he's dead.

IPHIGENEIA: Thanks to Artemis! And Odysseus?

ORESTÊS: Alive, but not yet back.

IPHIGENEIA: Curse him! I hope he dies first!

ORESTÊS: No need. He's cursed enough.

IPHIGENEIA: And Achilleus? Is he alive?

ORESTÊS: No. His marriage was useless.

IPHIGENEIA: Deceitful, as everyone knows.

ORESTÊS: You know a lot about Greece.

IPHIGENEIA: I'm from there. I was lost as a child.

ORESTÊS: No wonder you ask such questions.

IPHIGENEIA: There's a general they called "The Fortunate."

ORESTÊS: Not the one I'm thinking of.

IPHIGENEIA: Agamemnon, son of Atreus.

ORESTÊS: I don't know. Let's drop the subject.

IPHIGENEIA: Tell me, you must, just to please me!

ORESTÊS: He's dead. And his death destroyed another.

IPHIGENEIA: Dead? How? Oh god!

ORESTÊS: Tears? For one not related?

IPHIGENEIA: I weep in memory of his greatness.

ORESTÊS: He died slaughtered by his wife.

IPHIGENEIA: Oh god, I weep for them both!

ORESTÊS: Stop! No more questions!

IPHIGENEIA: Just one. Is his wife alive?

ORESTÊS: No; she was killed by her son.

IPHIGENEIA: Unhappy house! Why?

ORESTÊS: He revenged his father's murder.

IPHIGENEIA: Yes! Yes, and he did well!

ORESTÊS: Not as the gods see it.

IPHIGENEIA: Are there any other children?

ORESTÊS: Êlektra, still just a girl.

IPHIGENEIA: And Iphigeneia who was killed?

ORESTÊS: No one speaks of her now.

IPHIGENEIA: I pity both father and daughter.

ORESTÊS: She died for a wicked woman.

IPHIGENEIA: And the dead man's son—where is he?

ORESTÊS: He lives—everywhere and nowhere.

IPHIGENEIA: He's alive! Oh farewell to my worthless dreams!

ORESTÊS: Worthless, yes, like gods who prophesy, and are no more truthful than fleeting dreams. The ways of gods and men are equally chaotic. But one thing alone hurts: to be wise and to believe in prophecy, and so to plunge into ruin so great that only one who knows can understand.

FIRST CAPTIVE GREEK WOMAN: But what about us? Our parents? Are they alive, are they dead? Who can tell us?

IPHIGENEIA: Listen! I have a plan. If I save your life, will you take a letter back to Argos? A prisoner wrote it for me. He knew my hand wasn't the hand that killed and pitied me. Since then I have had no one to carry it back to someone in my family. I look at you and see a man of honorable birth, a man who knows Mykenê and those I love. Carry this letter for me and save your life—no shabby reward: your life for this light letter. As for your friend here, he must stay—the state demands it—as sacrifice to the goddess.

ORESTÊS: I agree to all you say, except for one thing: that my friend must die. The weight of that would be too great. I alone steer this ship of sorrows, and he joined me out of pity. To do you a good turn and escape myself at the cost of his life is a move I can't endure. No, give *him* the letter. He'll take it to Argos and do as you ask. As for my life, whoever wants can take it. No man destroys a friend to save himself. I love this man as I love my own life.

IPHIGENEIA: What a great and noble heart. And such loyalty to a friend. I can only hope that the brother I have left is a man like you. Yes, friends, I have a brother—a brother I never see. But you have your wish. This man will go with the letter, and you will die. It's clear to me his safety comes first in your heart.

ORESTÊS: Who will perform this dreadful sacrifice?

IPHIGENEIA: I will. It's how I serve the goddess.

ORESTÊS: What a grim office for a woman.

IPHIGENEIA: I have no choice. The law must be obeyed.

ORESTÊS: Can a woman kill a man with a sword?

IPHIGENEIA: No. I sprinkle your hair with lustral water.

ORESTÊS: Who, if I may ask, does the killing?

IPHIGENEIA: People inside the temple whose business it is.

ORESTÊS: How will I be buried once I'm slaughtered?

IPHIGENEIA: A sacred fire inside, and then a great chasm.

ORESTÊS: How I wish my sister's hand could lay out my corpse!

IPHIGENEIA: I pity you, poor friend, whoever you are, but your wish was
a futile one. Your sister lives far from this savage country. But since
we're both Argives, I will do all I can that your sister would have done.
I will lay many rich ornaments on your bier, soften your body with
yellow olive oil, and extinguish your ashes with wine. And on the
place where your body was burned, I will pour sweet-smelling honey
from tawny mountain bees.
      I'll go now and bring the letter from the temple. Don't
misunderstand. I'm only doing my duty. Attendants! *(Several
TEMPLE SLAVES enter from inside.)* Guard these men. But use no
restraints. They're to remain unbound. *(To herself.)* Perhaps, now, I
can send unhoped for news to Argos, to a friend I love most of all.
This letter saying that one he thought dead is alive will bring him joy
beyond belief. *(Exit into temple.)*

(Music. Song. Dance.)

FIRST CAPTIVE GREEK WOMAN: *(Chants.)*
      I grieve for you, poor man,
      doomed by the deadly drops of purification.

ORESTÊS: *(Speaks.)* You have no need to pity me, friends. But I thank you for your kindness.

FIRST CAPTIVE GREEK WOMAN: *(Chants.)*
But you, young Pyladês,
we rejoice in your good fortune.
You will set foot on your native soil.

PYLADÊS: *(Speaks.)* What joy can there be when a friend must die for a friend?

FIRST CAPTIVE GREEK WOMAN: *(Chants.)*
This is a grim parting.
A cruel return.
OIMOI MOI!
Two men destroyed.
AIIIIII!
Which is the better fate?
My mind wavers this way and that.
Doubtful debate.
Which should I mourn?
You who must die
or you who must live?

(Music out.)

ORESTÊS: Pyladês, are you thinking the same thing I am?

PYLADÊS: I don't know what you're thinking.

ORESTÊS: Who is this young woman? She questions like a Greek. She knows about the sufferings at Troy, the return of the Greeks, Kalchas's prophecies, Achilleus. How? And then her pity for Agamemnon, for his wife, his children? She *must* be from Argos or why would she be sending a letter? Why would she question me as if she herself had a stake in Argos's fortune?

PYLADÊS: I agree except for one thing. Anyone not dead to the world will have heard about the misfortunes of kings. But there's one thing I'd like to add.

ORESTÊS: Tell me. Any thought helps.

PYLADÊS: I wouldn't want to live with you dead. I'd be shamed. I shared
your voyage, I should share your death. They'd call me a coward if I
sailed back to Argos and Phokis alone. Evil-minded people will say I
deserted or betrayed you, or even killed you for your throne. After all,
your sister would inherit your throne, and I as her husband would
share it. These are terrible thoughts and they shame me. No, we'll die
together. We'll be sacrificed and our bodies burned together. We're
friends, Orestês, and I love you.

ORESTÊS: No, Pyladês, you mustn't. My own misfortunes are enough to
bear, don't double them for me. If my death shames you, yours shames
me as well, because you've shared my troubles. Considering the life
the gods have dealt me, death comes as no evil. You're a happy and
prosperous man, Pyladês, and your heritage is pure, not stained and
godless like mine. Go back, have children with my sister whom I've
given to you in marriage, and my father's name would live on in your
children and not be blotted off the face of the earth. Go, Pyladês, live!
Live in my father's house!

 Come. Give me your right hand. Promise that when you get
home to Greece and horse-loving Argos, you'll raise a memorial
mound to me, and that my sister will honor it with her tears and a
lock of her hair. Let it be known that I died at the hands of an Argive
woman, consecrated at the altar for the sacrifice. And never desert my
sister because my father's house, yours now by marriage, is laid waste
by my own death.

 Dear Pyladês, dear friend, we grew up together, side by side in
your father's house, hunted in the mountains of Greece together as
boys, grew to manhood together: we were brothers in love, and
together we bore my terrible burden from Apollo—Apollo who
tripped me up with his evil cunning, prophet though he is, and drove
me as far from my native land as was possible, shamed at his earlier
prophecies to me. I gave him my all, trusted him, killed my mother at
his command, and now, now it's my turn to die.

PYLADÊS: You'll have your burial mound, Orestês, and I'll never abandon
your sister's bed, poor man. And in death, if it is possible, you'll be an
even dearer friend than in life. But Apollo's oracle hasn't killed you yet,

however close death may be. Sometimes, though, misfortune, by pure chance, takes an extraordinary turn.

ORESTÊS: Words are useless now, Pyladês. Apollo's commands have undone me. Here she comes from the temple.

IPHIGENEIA: *(Enters.)* Guards! Go inside, all of you, and help with the preparations. *(Exeunt the TEMPLE SLAVES into the temple.)* Here is the letter. But one thing still troubles me. A man with death hanging over him promises anything. But once safe, and the fear faded, he may forget or choose to ignore his promise. I'm afraid this letter's bearer, once safe in his own country, may not bother about it.

ORESTÊS: How can we reassure you?

IPHIGENEIA: Swear an oath to deliver it to my friends.

ORESTÊS: Will you swear an oath to *him*?

IPHIGENEIA: To do or not to do what?

ORESTÊS: To send him away alive from this barbarian land.

IPHIGENEIA: Of course. How else can he deliver the letter?

ORESTÊS: Will the king agree to this?

IPHIGENEIA: I'll persuade him and put this man onboard myself.

ORESTÊS: Take the oath, Pyladês; she'll tell you what to say.

IPHIGENEIA: Say: "I will deliver this letter to your loved ones."

PYLADÊS: I will deliver this letter to your loved ones.

IPHIGENEIA: And I will get you safely past the Clashing Rocks.

PYLADÊS: What god do you invoke to witness the oath?

IPHIGENEIA: Artemis, in whose temple I do her service.

PYLADÊS: And I swear by Zeus, the king of heaven.

IPHIGENEIA: And what if you break my oath and do me wrong?

PYLADÊS: May I never set foot on home soil. And you?

IPHIGENEIA: May I never see Argos again.

PYLADÊS: There's one thing we've overlooked.

IPHIGENEIA: Which is?

PYLADÊS: Allow me this one exception. If the ship should be wrecked, and the letter and cargo are lost, but I'm saved, let the oath be no longer binding.

IPHIGENEIA: Here's what I'll do, for the more precautions the better. I'll tell you myself the message the letter contains. That way, if the ship goes down and you're saved, you can deliver the message in words. At least it's safe. But if everything goes as planned, and the letter is not lost, by saving yourself you will also save my message.

PYLADÊS: Your suggestion does well by us both. Tell me who in Argos receives the letter and the message I should report.

IPHIGENEIA: Take this to Orestês, son of Agamemnon. Tell him: "Iphigeneia, slaughtered at Aulis, sends this. She is alive, though all of her friends think her dead."

ORESTÊS: Where is she, then? Has she come back from the dead?

IPHIGENEIA: I am Iphigeneia. Please let me finish. "Dear brother, save me from this place before I die. Bring me to Argos; save me from this barbarian land. Rescue me from this goddess's dreadful service, the slaughter of foreigners on her altar."

ORESTÊS: Pyladês, what can I say? Am I dreaming?

IPHIGENEIA: "Do this, Orestês, or I will haunt your house with this curse." I repeat his name only so you won't forget it.

ORESTÊS: Oh gods!

IPHIGENEIA: Why call on the gods? This is my concern!

ORESTÊS: It's nothing. Go on. Finish. I was thinking of other matters.

IPHIGENEIA: Tell him that Artemis saved my life. She substituted for me a doe, and it was that doe my father sacrificed, that doe he plunged his sword into, not me. The goddess then brought me here, Artemis, to this country and shore. So there it is. There's the message. And here's the letter.

PYLADÊS: Lady: this is the easiest oath I have ever been bound by.
And so, I make good that oath with this one gesture. Take it, Orestês, this letter from your sister.

ORESTÊS: And I accept, my mind stunned with the wonder of it! But before I read it, dear sister, let deeds do what words cannot! Let me hold you in my unbelieving arms.

IPHIGENEIA: You mustn't wrong me; my clothes are sacred to the goddess and not to be touched.

ORESTÊS: Dear sister, dear daughter of our father, Agamemnon, don't turn away. You have the brother you never thought to see again.

IPHIGENEIA: My brother? What are you saying? If my brother is here then this must be Argos, this, this must be Nauplia.

ORESTÊS: No, my dear, your brother is not in Argos.

IPHIGENEIA: Are you the child of Spartan Klytaimnêstra?

ORESTÊS: Yes, and Pelops's grandson.

IPHIGENEIA: Can you prove this?

ORESTÊS: I can. Ask me questions of our father's house.

IPHIGENEIA: Isn't it for you to speak and me to listen?

ORESTÊS: I'll tell you first what I heard from our sister Êlektra. Have you heard of the quarrel between Atreus and Thyestes?

IPHIGENEIA: I have. It was over a golden lamb.

ORESTÊS: And you wove that story in fine thread on your loom?

IPHIGENEIA: Dear man, what a chord you've touched in my memory!

ORESTÊS: And you also wove the sun turning back on its course.

IPHIGENEIA: Yes, I wove that, too, in the delicate fabric.

ORESTÊS: And the water your mother sent you for your wedding bath?

IPHIGENEIA: If the marriage had been happy, I would have forgotten.

ORESTÊS: You also sent a lock of hair to your mother.

IPHIGENEIA: I did; as a memorial for my tomb.

ORESTÊS: Now I'll tell you something I saw myself. Hidden away in your room when you were a girl, I saw the spear of Pelops, our ancestor, which he brandished when he killed Oinomaös and won Hippodamia.

(They embrace.)

(Music. Song. Dance.)

IPHIGENEIA: *(Sings.)*
    Oh my dearest man,
    for that's what you are,
    nothing, nothing dearer!
    I hold you, dear Orestês,
    now grown so big,

so far, so very far
from beloved Argos!

ORESTÊS: *(Speaks.)* And I hold you, dear sister, we all thought dead.

IPHIGENEIA: *(Sings.)*
> Let tears,
> tears of joy and mourning,
> flood our eyes.
> Here,
> here is the child,
> the baby, the boy,
> my dear newborn love,
> I left in his nurse's arms
> when last I saw him.
> My soul,
> my soul leaps up with greater joy
> than ever I can say!
> This day has dawned beyond
> wonder, beyond all hope!

ORESTÊS: *(Speaks.)* May our fortune be as happy in time to come.

IPHIGENEIA: *(Sings.)*
> Dear friends,
> dear, kind women,
> how frightened I am,
> frightened that this dream,
> this vision,
> will fly from my arms
> and climb the heavens.
> Great hearth built by the Cyclops,
> beloved Mykenê, city of my fathers,
> I thank you for his blessèd life,
> his nurture, my dear Orestês,
> Orestês that you have rescued and raised to manhood,
> dear, dear brother, beacon fire of our house!

ORESTÊS: *(Speaks.)* Our birth was blessed and from a noble house;
> but our destiny is cursed.

IPHIGENEIA: *(Sings.)*
> I know, I remember,
> I, Iphigeneia,
> the terrible,
> the terrible, dreadful day
> when my father lay his sharp
> blade at my throat.

ORESTÊS: *(Speaks.)* AIIIII! I wasn't there, not at Aulis, but I see it now in my mind's eye.

IPHIGENEIA: *(Sings.)*
> No song,
> no wedding song,
> led me to that deceitful bed, that
> bed, no marriage bed,
> no Achilleus for husband,
> but moaning and tears beside the altar
> that would flow with my blood,
> and the water for ritual purity.

ORESTÊS: *(Speaks.)* I groan for my father's dreadful deed.

IPHIGENEIA: *(Sings.)*
> Father, he was no father!
> I had no father!
> One misery follows another,
> great strokes of some divine power.

ORESTÊS: *(Speaks.)* But what a misery if you had killed your brother.

IPHIGENEIA: *(Sings.)*
> Terrible, terrible is the evil I would have done.
> Terrible the dreadful things I dared, dear brother.
> How slenderly you escaped destruction at my hands.
> But where, where will it end?
> Where?
> What fate will Fortune send me?
> What, what way, what means will I find

to return you from this murderous,
this bloodthirsty land,
to Argos,
to Argos,
before the sword seeks out your blood?
This, this is it,
this is my soul's task,
to search out a way of return.
Will you go by land on storm-swift feet?
No, that would mean death on trackless paths
at the hands of barbarous tribes.
Or by ship through the dark Clashing Rocks?
An endless flight, an endless odyssey.
Wretched, unhappy woman,
what can I do, what?
What god, what mortal, what unhoped for chance,
will find a way where no way is,
and find for us,
the last children of Atreus,
a release from this evil?

(Music out.)

FIRST CAPTIVE GREEK WOMAN: There are no words to express what
I have just seen!

PYLADÊS: Careful, Orestês! Now's not the time for embraces and tears,
even for loved ones. We have more immediate matters to see to;
like escaping this barbarous place.

ORESTÊS: You're right. Even with fortune on our side, it helps to help
ourselves.

IPHIGENEIA: No, Orestês, please, I have to know about Êlektra! Please
don't deny me. How is my sister?

ORESTÊS: She's married to Pyladês, and she's happy.

IPHIGENEIA: Where is he from?

ORESTÊS: From Phokis. The son of Strophios.

IPHIGENEIA: Then he's my cousin? Grandson of Atreus?

ORESTÊS: And my only true friend.

IPHIGENEIA: Then he wasn't even born when my father killed me.

ORESTÊS: He was a late child.

IPHIGENEIA: Dear Pyladês, how happy I am for you! And my sister!

ORESTÊS: He also saved my life.

IPHIGENEIA: Oh Orestês, how could you have done that to Mother?

ORESTÊS: I avenged Father! I won't talk about it!

IPHIGENEIA: But why did she kill him? Her husband!

ORESTÊS: Don't ask! You mustn't know!

IPHIGENEIA: I won't. Are you now king in Argos?

ORESTÊS: Menelaos is king. Our uncle. I'm in exile.

IPHIGENEIA: Surely he didn't betray us.

ORESTÊS: No; fear of the Furies drove me out.

IPHIGENEIA: Because of our mother, you mean.

ORESTÊS: My mouth is raw with their bridle!

IPHIGENEIA: So that was the fit they saw.

ORESTÊS: They weren't the first.

IPHIGENEIA: Why did you come here?

ORESTÊS: Apollo's oracle. I couldn't ignore it.

IPHIGENEIA: But why? Can you tell me?

ORESTÊS: I'll tell you. This is how it all began. When my mother's—when that evil I refuse to speak of became my responsibility to avenge—the Furies tracked me, tracked me ruthlessly on my flight. I had no place to hide. Apollo then led me to Athens and arranged a trial before the dreadful goddesses that no man names. A court had been established long ago by Zeus to try a blood-guilt case for Arês.

But when I arrived in Athens, no one in the city would give me shelter; everyone believed I was hated by the gods. And yet, there were some who pitied me, took me in and fed me. But just to be safe, they sat me apart, by myself, not with them, though under the same roof. No one spoke to me. The fear of polluting themselves, and their food and drink was too great. And instead of the communal bowl, they measured out equal servings of wine in individual bowls and so went at it. It didn't seem proper to criticize my hosts, so I let it pass, grieving silently that I was known by all as my mother's murderer. And yet, even so, I couldn't hold back my sighs. I now hear that my misery is a ritual in Athens. The Feast of the Bowls I think they call it.

The time came for the trial. I took my place on the platform. The eldest of the Furies on the platform opposite me charged me with my crime. I pled my defense, and Apollo presented evidence that finally saved me. When Athêna counted the votes and cast her vote, they came out even. And so I was acquitted. And so I left. Those Furies who were satisfied with the verdict, established a holy sanctuary near the court. But those who were not persuaded never relented and continued to pursue me night and day, dogging me relentlessly till I came once more to Apollo's holy precinct at Delphi.

I threw myself down before his temple, without food or drink, and swore aloud that I would take my life upon that spot if Apollo, who had destroyed me, refused now to rescue me. Then, his voice echoing from his golden tripod, he commanded me to come here to Tauris. I'm to rescue the wooden statue of Artemis that fell from the sky and set it up again in the land of the Athenians.

I beg you, beg you to help me. Apollo promised salvation, but I can't do it alone. Once I have the statue, I'll not only be freed of my blinding madness, but I'll take you back on my many-oared ship to our home in blessèd Mykenê. Oh dear, dear sister, save our father's house, save me, for I'm lost if we fail to rescue the goddess's statue!

FIRST CAPTIVE GREEK WOMAN: Some deadly wrath of the gods has fallen on this cursed house, plaguing its children with misfortune.

IPHIGENEIA: I agree with you, Orestês, but it terrifies me. How can we escape the goddess? And the king, once he discovers the missing statue? He'd kill me. If only we could do both at a single stroke. Rescue the statue and get onboard. It would be a noble risk. But if the statue goes, and I stay, it means my death. And yet you would be free and have carried off your mission and returned home. I'll do it if I must. I'm not afraid to die if it means saving you; a house that loses its last male heir is beyond hope. A woman's life is far less worth preserving.

ORESTÊS: No, I can't! I can't! I refuse to be your murderer as well as my mother's! I've shed enough blood! Dear sister, we're together in this all the way. If I go, you go with me; if you stay and die, I'll die with you. And yet, how can all this be displeasing to Artemis? Apollo sent me here to rescue her statue and take it to Athens. Why would he have done that? Why would he have sent me here as a victim for sacrifice, if not to reunite us? Everything considered, I know we'll get home again.

IPHIGENEIA: How do we steal the statue and not be killed? That's what stands between us and Argos. We surely don't lack the will.

ORESTÊS: Could we kill the king?

IPHIGENEIA: Kill the host who took me in? No.

ORESTÊS: But if it saves our lives?

IPHIGENEIA: I can't, I wouldn't dare.

ORESTÊS: Then hide me in the temple.

IPHIGENEIA: There are guards inside; they'd see us.

ORESTÊS: There's no way, then. We're ruined.

IPHIGENEIA: No. I'll say you're stained with your mother's blood—

ORESTÊS: How clever women are!

IPHIGENEIA: —and not fit for the goddess. I sacrifice only what's pure.

ORESTÊS: And the statue?

IPHIGENEIA: I'll ask to purify you in sea water.

ORESTÊS: But the statue's still in the temple.

IPHIGENEIA: I'll say I need to wash that, too, you'll have touched it.

ORESTÊS: Where? In some inlet of the sea?

IPHIGENEIA: Yes, near where your ship is tethered.

ORESTÊS: Who'll carry the statue?

IPHIGENEIA: I will. Only I can touch it.

ORESTÊS: And what will Pyladês do?

IPHIGENEIA: I'll say he's tainted, as well, with the same blood.

ORESTÊS: Will the king know of our plan?

IPHIGENEIA: I'll tell him. I'll persuade him. There's no way to hide this.

ORESTÊS: And the ship will be ready to sail.

IPHIGENEIA: Everything else I leave in your hands.

ORESTÊS: There's one other thing. Convince your women to keep this
secret. Arouse their pity. It's up to us now. May fortune smile on us.

IPHIGENEIA: Dear friends, dear women, I put my life in your hands.
Do I succeed, am I ruined, do I lose my country, my brother, my

beloved sister? It's all up to you. We're all of us women, and women are loyal to each other, we defend our common interests. We keep secrets when necessary and help each other when danger threatens. Do that for us now. Help us make our escape. Pledge us your loyal silence. You see before you here three dear friends whose fate is one: either they reach their native land, or they die. Do this for me and I swear to you that I will return and see that each of you comes safely home to Greece. I beg you by your right hand, and you by your cheek, and you, your knees, and your loved ones at home! Will you? Will you help? Who will not? Say it, say it now. Will you? If you refuse, then I and my brother are dead.

FIRST CAPTIVE GREEK WOMAN: Dear mistress, be brave!
Save yourself! That's all that's important! Zeus as my witness,
we'll keep your secret.

IPHIGENEIA: Bless you for that, and I wish you all happiness! Orestês,
Pyladês, it's your turn now. Go inside the temple. The king will be
here soon to see if the sacrifice has been properly carried out. *(Exeunt
ORESTÊS and PYLADÊS into the temple.)* Artemis, lady, who saved
me from a murderous father beside the bay at Aulis, save me now, too,
as well as these young men. Do so, and all the world will believe the
words of Apollo. Fail in that, and he will never again be believed,
and the fault will be none but yours. Be gracious, lady, to us and to
yourself, and leave this barbaric land and come to Athens. This is no
suitable place when you can live in a blessed city. *(Exit into temple.)*

(Music. Song. Dance.)

CAPTIVE GREEK WOMEN: *(Sing.)*
Halcyon bird,
bird by the waters,
by the rocky cliffs,
bird that sings your fate as a lament,
your sad fate,
a dirge without end,
for a spouse forever lost.
I,
I, too,

am a bird,
a bird without wings;
I,
I, too,
lament,
sing my sad fate in an endless dirge;
I,
I, too,
sing my song of mourning like you.
Oh how I long,
how I long for Greek festivals,
for people in the market,
my country's people;
how I long for Artemis,
goddess of birth,
dweller beside the Cynthian hill,
the slender palm,
the prospering laurel,
the gray-green shoot of the sacred olive
which sheltered Lêto in childbirth,
and the lake that whirls its waters
in a circle where the song the swan sings
honors the Muses.

How many the tears,
how many the streams of tears
that welled from my eyes
for the crash of my city's towers and walls,
the deafening pound of destruction that leveled my city,
and brought me onboard the enemy's ships,
plunder shoved between oars and enemy spears.
I brought a great price,
traded for gold by barbarian men,
brought to their hostile barbarian shores,
where I serve the virgin daughter of Agamemnon,
she who attends the hunter goddess,
Artemis who slays the deer,
whose altars run with the blood not of sheep,
but of men,

foreigners who reach these shores.
How fortunate the man who has
never known happiness,
but always,
ever,
only bitter Necessity.
He knows no pain when adversity strikes.
But to know,
to have known,
happiness and joy,
and then be dashed into grim disaster,
is too evil,
too unbearable
a fate for mortals.
But you,
you, my lady,
great goddess,
you will be sped on,
onward,
homeward,
sped home on an Argive ship of fifty oars,
with the shrill screech of the wax-bound reed pipe
of Pan of the mountains
to give the oars,
the splashing oars,
their rhythm,
and Apollo,
prophet Apollo,
plucking his seven-stringed lyre,
will sing and lead the way,
lead the way safely,
safely,
safely to gleaming Athens.
But me,
me,
you leave behind here,
behind on the shore,
as you speed like the wind
through the foaming waves,

and the breeze bellies out
the sails beyond the prow.

Oh if only,
if only I could follow the sun,
follow,
follow his radiant track
on his way to the west,
and over my room,
my girlhood's chamber,
fold my wings and still their beating.
I would join the swirling,
dancing choruses,
where once as a girl,
decked out in finery,
with luxuriant hair,
I left the side of my dear mother
and danced and sang at a noble wedding
with the joyous bands of my friends,
vying,
vying for who was most lovely,
whose veils the finest,
whose curls the loveliest
to cover and shade
our bright faces
from the sun's holy light.

(Enter THOAS with SLAVE ATTENDANTS and GUARDS.)

(Music out.)

THOAS: Where is Iphigeneia? Is the sacrifice over?

(Enter IPHIGENEIA from the temple with the wooden statue in her arms.)

FIRST CAPTIVE GREEK WOMAN: Here she is, my lord.

THOAS: What's this? What are you doing? Why have you moved the statue? It mustn't be touched.

IPHIGENEIA: King Thoas, stay where you are!

THOAS: What's happened in the temple?

IPHIGENEIA: I spit out the evil omen!

THOAS: Tell me.

IPHIGENEIA: My King, the captured victims are unclean.

THOAS: How do you know this?

IPHIGENEIA: The statue turned its back.

THOAS: By itself, or did the earth shake?

IPHIGENEIA: By itself. And it closed its eyes.

THOAS: The strangers' pollution?

IPHIGENEIA: They've done dreadful things.

THOAS: Who did they kill?

IPHIGENEIA: Their mother. The two of them together.

THOAS: Not even a barbarian would have dared that!

IPHIGENEIA: They've been driven out of every city in Greece.

THOAS: But why did you bring the statue?

IPHIGENEIA: To purify it in the holy light.

THOAS: What told you they were polluted?

IPHIGENEIA: As I questioned them, the goddess turned away.

THOAS: Greece made a clever girl, to see so well!

IPHIGENEIA: They tempted me with pleasant news.

THOAS: From Argos?

IPHIGENEIA: That my brother Orestês is well and thriving.

THOAS: A bribe so you'd let them escape.

IPHIGENEIA: And that my father was alive and well.

THOAS: But you were true to the goddess.

IPHIGENEIA: I hate everything Greek for destroying me!

THOAS: How do we handle these men?

IPHIGENEIA: First we purify them.

THOAS: In spring water or the sea?

IPHIGENEIA: The sea will wash away all pollution.

THOAS: And acceptable to the goddess.

IPHIGENEIA: It's also better for me.

THOAS: But the sea washes up against this temple.

IPHIGENEIA: I'll need privacy for other tasks.

THOAS: You have it. I mustn't see forbidden rituals.

IPHIGENEIA: I'll also purify the statue.

THOAS: Your piety and forethought are remarkable.

IPHIGENEIA: You'll give me what I need?

THOAS: You have only to ask.

IPHIGENEIA: Have them bound.

THOAS: But where could they escape to?

IPHIGENEIA: Never trust a Greek.

THOAS: Slaves! Go bind them.

IPHIGENEIA: And cover their heads from sight.

THOAS: Do as she says.

(*Exeunt several SLAVE ATTENDANTS into the temple.*)

IPHIGENEIA: I'll need the help of some slaves.

THOAS: These men are yours.

IPHIGENEIA: And send someone to inform the city.

THOAS: Of what?

IPHIGENEIA: To remain indoors.

THOAS: To avoid pollution?

IPHIGENEIA: Their pollution is highly infectious.

THOAS: You, go inform the city.

(*Exit a SLAVE ATTENDANT.*)

IPHIGENEIA: No one must come in sight of them.

THOAS: I marvel at your concern for the city.

IPHIGENEIA: I also look after my friends.

THOAS: I take it you mean me?

IPHIGENEIA: What else, my King?

THOAS: No wonder all the city admires you.

IPHIGENEIA: You must stay here at the temple and—

THOAS: Do what?

IPHIGENEIA: —purify it with a torch. And when they're brought out—

THOAS: Yes?

IPHIGENEIA: Cover your face with your cloak.

THOAS: To avoid their pollution.

IPHIGENEIA: And if I seem to be gone a long while—

THOAS: How long do you need?

IPHIGENEIA: Don't be concerned.

THOAS: Serve the goddess well and in your own time.

IPHIGENEIA: May the gods give us success in our enterprise.

THOAS: I join you in that.

> (Enter SLAVE ATTENDANTS from the temple with ORESTÊS and
> PYLADÊS, bound and with heads covered. They are followed by other
> TEMPLE SLAVES carrying paraphernalia for the ritual as well as
> sacrificial animals.)

IPHIGENEIA: They're coming now, bringing the goddess's sacred robe and
adornments, as well as newborn lambs whose blood will wash away
their guilt. And torches and all else I need to purify the strangers and
the goddess. To all citizens I say: If you come here to serve the temple,
or to offer sacrifice before marriage, or pray for safe delivery in

childbirth, escape the taint of pollution by avoiding this place.
Leave it as swiftly as possible.

Oh goddess, virgin Artemis, daughter of Zeus and Lêto, if I wash
away the blood guilt of these men, and reach the proper place for my
sacrifice, you will dwell in a house of purity, and fortune will have
blessed us! What remains to be said, I will not say, knowing that all is
known to the gods, and to you, beloved goddess!

*(Exeunt IPHIGENEIA, ORESTÊS, PYLADÊS, and the rest; then
THOAS into the temple.)*

(Music. Song. Dance.)

CAPTIVE GREEK WOMEN: *(Sing.)*
How beautiful,
how glorious the radiant child,
son of Lêto,
birthed in the fertile valleys of Dêlos,
golden-haired child,
Apollo,
Apollo,
skilled in the lyre,
Apollo who delights in the sure swift aim of his bow.
From hogback ridge,
the high mountain reef bound by the sea,
she took him,
his mother,
Lêto took him,
from his fabled birthplace
to the peak of Parnassos,
to Parnassos, mother of abundant waters,
Parnassos that leaps in frenzied dance,
ecstatic dance, with Dionysos.
There,
from the earth,
brought forth from earth,
a monstrous creature,
Python,
great snake,
back spangled with scales,

eye bright as fire,
lay coiled in the dark laurel covering of the grove,
guarding the primeval oracle of Earth.
A child still,
a still leaping child in your mother's arms,
you slew it, Apollo,
slew the earth's monster,
and sat, a conqueror of the sacred oracle,
on the golden tripod, where now, to this day,
now you sit in truth,
dispensing prophetic answers
to mortals at Earth's navel,
beside the flowing streams of Castalia.

But Apollo's coming,
Apollo's conquest of the golden tripod,
drove from her place,
her holy oracular place,
Themis,
Earth's daughter,
and in answer to Apollo,
in jealousy for her daughter,
her daughter goddess,
primordial Themis,
Earth from her earthly womb begot Dreams,
nightly apparitions,
visions of truth,
that revealed in the deep, dark dungeons of sleep
to all mankind things which once were,
and things, truths that are yet to be,
yet to find fulfillment.
And so,
Earth in anger,
indignant for her daughter,
stole from Apollo,
from Apollo's temple,
pride of place as the center of augury.
And Apollo sped off on lightning-swift feet,
sped off to his father Zeus on Olympos,
and coiling his infant arm,

grasping with his boy's hand,
Zeus's throne,
implored him,
his father,
to free the temple from the goddess's grudge.
Zeus laughed to see his son so eager,
so quickly to claim the worship,
and also the golden riches it brought.
He shook his mighty head, Zeus did,
waved his heavy curls and nodded,
and put an end to the truth of visions,
night apparitions and prophetic dreams,
and gave back to his son,
to his son Apollo,
his honor,
and to his throne the visitors from all the earth,
who flocked, who thronged, to hear his Truth.

(Music out.)

SLAVE ATTENDANT: *(Enters running and shouting.)* Guards, keepers of
the altar! Where is King Thoas? Open the temple doors! Open! Tell
King Thoas to come out!

FIRST CAPTIVE GREEK WOMAN: What is it? Why are you yelling?

SLAVE ATTENDANT: They've escaped! The two young foreigners! Fled
the country with the help of that traitor, Iphigeneia! And the goddess's
statue gone with them in their ship!

FIRST CAPTIVE GREEK WOMAN: I don't believe it! But the king just
left here in a great hurry.

SLAVE ATTENDANT: Where? He must be told!

FIRST CAPTIVE GREEK WOMAN: I don't know. But go look for him.
When you've found him, tell him.

SLAVE ATTENDANT: Women! Damn them! You had a part in this!
All of you!

FIRST CAPTIVE GREEK WOMAN: You're mad! We had nothing to do with the strangers! Go pound on the palace gates! Hurry!

SLAVE ATTENDANT: Not till I know if he's inside the temple. *(Pounding on the doors.)* Open, open! Tell the king I have news, bad news!

THOAS: *(Enters from the temple.)* What's the meaning of this?

SLAVE ATTENDANT: They lied, these women, saying you'd left!

THOAS: Why? What were they after?

SLAVE ATTENDANT: That can wait! This can't! She's gone, Iphigeneia, gone off on their ship with the two foreigners! And the goddess's statue with them! All this ritual was a plot!

THOAS: Do you know what you're saying? What could she possibly have—

SLAVE ATTENDANT: She's saving Orestês.

THOAS: Her brother?

SLAVE ATTENDANT: The man who was to be sacrificed.

THOAS: I almost don't believe—

SLAVE ATTENDANT: No, listen! Listen to me first! When you've heard, then you can plan how to get them back!

THOAS: I'm listening. They have a long journey ahead; they won't escape me.

SLAVE ATTENDANT: When we reached the shore where Orestês had hidden his moored ship, Iphigeneia waved us away, saying to stay at a distance. She had mysteries of fire and sacrifice to tend to. We did as she asked, and she walked along ahead, holding the shackles binding the strangers. We all thought this suspicious, but it didn't worry us much, so we let her go. Finally, out of sight, to make us believe something was being done, she broke into strange wild sacrificial shouts that made her sound like a witch washing away stains of blood guilt. We sat silent for a while, doing nothing; but then the thought came to us that the strangers might have slipped their bonds, killed the girl, and taken off. But the fear of seeing the forbidden was too great and so we did nothing. Finally, even though forbidden, we decided there was no other way, and we went.

There was the Greek ship, on each side winged with its sweep of oars, and fifty sailors sitting at the ready, oars in hand. And there, standing on the shore by the ship's stern, we saw the two youths, free of their shackles. Some of the sailors steadied the prow with poles and hurried to weigh anchor, while others lowered rope ladders into the sea for the three to climb aboard. But having seen her treachery, we had lost all respect and never thought twice about grabbing the girl, and the cables, and trying to drag the steering oars from the rudder-ports. Words flew back and forth then: "Who are you to think you can steal our statues and priestesses? Who are you? What's your name?" And he shot back: "Orestês, son of Agamemnon, and this girl's brother, come to take her home!" Still, we never let loose of the girl, which is how I got all these bruises and cuts. They may not have had swords, those two, nor did we, but they came at us like Furies with their fists, kicking us, ribs and stomach, till we were worn down with pain and exhaustion. Bloodied, we retreated to the cliffs where we thought to be safer and pelted them with stones. But archers at the stern held us off, forcing us to retreat even farther.

Meanwhile, the ship in the heavy surf is in danger of washing ashore, and the girl is afraid of stepping into the eddies, so Orestês, hoisting her onto his left shoulder, wades out and, leaping onto the ladder, sets down her and the goddess's statue safely on the ship's deck. From somewhere amidships a voice rings out: "Men of Greece! Grab your oars and churn the sea white! We sailed through the Clashing Rocks into the Hostile Sea, and we sail away with everything we came for!" A roar rose from the ship and all at once the sea is set foaming with slashing oars. As long as she's in harbor the ship is safe, but once she begins her move into open sea, she meets a monstrous wave. A sudden squall descends on the sails, bellying them backward, and driving the ship astern. Rowing like heroes, they struggle to keep the ship from foundering on shore.

Then Iphigeneia rises and prays aloud: "Artemis, daughter of Lêto, deliver me, your priestess, safely from this barbarian land and back to Argos! Forgive me my theft! You, too, have a brother you love!

Believe me when I say I also love mine!" Her prayer finished, the sailors, struggling, raise a song of praise to Apollo. Then, stripping their shoulders naked, they take up the rhythm of the coxswain's chant. But the ship is swept ever closer to the rocks. Some of us rush into the heavy surf with ropes to snare the vessel, and I was sent here to tell you all that has happened.

You must hurry down there now, King Thoas, with ropes and grappling hooks. Unless the sea dies down, these strangers have no hope of escape.

FIRST CAPTIVE GREEK WOMAN: Poor Iphigeneia, back again in the grip of the tyrant who will put you to death with your brother.

THOAS: Citizens! Men of this barbarian land! With the goddess's help we will snare these godless men by land or sea. And when we've caught them, they will be flung from the cliff to their death or impaled alive for all to see.

Down to the shore now on horseback! And sailors, pull our swift ships down to the sea! As for you women who were part of this plot, your punishment will come when time permits! *(Turns to leave as ATHÊNA appears above the temple.)*

ATHÊNA: Stop, King Thoas! Enough of this madness! I am Athêna! Listen to me and stop this insane rush to the shore; it will do you no good. It was Apollo ordered Orestês here to Tauris for three reasons. First, to escape the Furies for murdering his mother; second, to rescue his sister Iphigeneia and return her to Argos; and, finally, to remove the sacred image of Artemis and bring it to my country. This mission was to free him of his pain. So much for my message. Now to Orestês.

You're mistaken, Thoas. Orestês will not be captured and killed by you, as you expect, for I have asked Poseidon to calm the stormy sea and allow the Greeks a safe journey to their destination. He is doing so as I speak. As for you, Orestês, who I know can hear me, for being a goddess my voice may be heard at great distance, listen to me. Continue your journey with your sister and the sacred statue. And when you arrive at god-built Athens, you will find a place at the farthest reaches of Attika, before the border, near to the Karystian Rock—my people call it Halai. There you will build a temple and install the image. Name it after the land of Tauris, and in memory of your agonies as you fled across Greece, stung by the remorseless

Furies. For ever afterward, men will sing praises to her as Artemis Tauropolos. And establish this custom. When men gather to celebrate her festival, let the priest lay a sword to a man's throat and draw from it a single drop of blood as ransom for the blood that was not spilled here. In this way you satisfy religion and honor the goddess with her rights.

You, Iphigeneia, will be key warden of the goddess's temple on the sacred terraces of Brauron. You will be buried there when you die, and they will dedicate to you the finespun garments left behind by women when they die in childbirth. As for these Greek women, they must be freed and returned to their homes, for their hearts were loyal.

I saved you once before, Orestês, at your trial in Athens. The votes were even, and so I released you. That judgment is now law. When votes are even, the accused man is acquitted. So take your sister from this land, Orestês. And, you, Thoas, rein in your anger.

THOAS: Divine Athêna, no man who fights the gods' words is sane. I was angry with Orestês and his sister for deceiving me and making off with the statue; but no longer. What honor can there be in striving against the power of gods? I wish them good-speed to your country with the goddess's statue, and good fortune in establishing it there. As for these women, they will be returned to Greece and happiness. And, finally, I call back my troops and my navy as you have directed.

ATHÊNA: Good. Necessity rules both men and gods. Blow, winds, and carry this son of Agamemnon to Athens! I will go with him and keep safe my sister's image. *(ATHÊNA slowly disappears.)*

(Music. Song. Dance.)

FIRST CAPTIVE GREEK WOMAN: *(Chants.)*
Go in good fortune,
go as being among the blest,
as being among the saved.
Pallas Athêna,
revered goddess among gods and men,
we do as you command.
Our ears are full of joy.
Our joy beyond all hope.

*

ION

(ΙΩΝ)

CHARACTERS

HERMÊS

ION *son of Kreousa and Apollo, about seventeen*

KREOUSA *daughter of Erechtheus and queen of Athens*

XOUTHOS *husband of Kreousa*

CHORUS OF KREOUSA'S FEMALE ATTENDANTS

FIRST FEMALE ATTENDANT *chorus leader*

FEMALE SLAVE ATTENDANT *of Kreousa*

MALE SLAVE ATTENDANT *of Kreousa*

OLD SLAVE *male slave servant and tutor of Kreousa*

PYTHIA *priestess of Apollo at Delphi*

ATHÊNA *protecting goddess of Athens*

DELPHIANS

ION

Dawn, before sunrise.
Delphi.
Before the Temple of Apollo.
An altar on the porch, a laurel grove to one side.
Enter HERMÊS.

HERMÊS: Call me Hermês. I'm known far and wide as the servant of the gods, or, more specifically, their runner. But to pinpoint it with total accuracy you would have to call me their lackey, for, take it from me, that's just what I am. My father is Zeus the Great, and my mother, Maia, daughter of a goddess and the famous Atlas, the same Atlas who bears on his broad bronze back the weight of the heavens, the ancient home of the gods.

Now, I've come here to Delphi where Apollo sits upon the so-called earth navel, otherwise known as the earth's midpoint, and from which he delivers oracles to humans, forever prophesying what is and what is yet to be. But to my story.

There is a city, quite famous, really, a Greek city, named after Athêna, goddess of the gold-tipped spear, and it was there that Apollo "married," you might say, Kreousa, though more realistically speaking, he forced himself on her, Kreousa, the daughter of King Erechtheus. All this happened, you see, at the so-called Long Rocks in Athens, the northern exposure of Athêna's hill, and it happened without her father's knowledge—the god preferred it be that way—and she carried to term her belly's burden, Kreousa did. Her time come, she gave birth in the palace, and then carried the child to the very cave beneath the Akropolis where Apollo had raped her. There she left him in the shelter of a wicker cradle, left him, as it were, to die. And yet, she kept the custom of her forebears. At the birth of earth-born Erichthonios, Athêna wrapped two guardian snakes around his body before handing him for safe keeping to the daughters of Aglauros. And that is why to this day Athenians adorn their children with the image of two coiled snakes of beaten gold. But back to Kreousa. She wrapped and decorated the child with what she could and abandoned him there to die.

Now, Apollo, being my brother, said to me: "Go, brother," he said, "go to Athens, you know the city, its people sprung from the earth, famous Athens, the goddess's city, and find in a cave there a baby. Pick him up, swaddling clothes, cradle and all, and bring him to my seat of prophecy at Delphi. Place him at the temple's entrance where he can't help but be seen and I'll tend to the rest. I should tell you, by the way," he said, "he's mine."

All right, so I do him this favor; after all, we're brothers. I picked up the baby, cradle and all, and settled him directly on the front steps of this temple where no one could miss him. I even pulled back the lid to make him more visible.

Now, just as the sun began its trek across the heavens, the shrine's priestess appeared on her way inside, and she spotted the cradle, baby and all. Livid that some town girl had passed off her bastard onto the god, she rushed to save the temple from pollution and put the intruder beyond the sacred precinct. But pity suddenly took the place of cruelty—not without the god's interference, of course—and she ended up raising the child, quite unaware that Apollo was its father, and knowing nothing of the mother who gave him birth. Not even the boy knows who his parents are.

Growing up, he played and wandered freely among the altars. And when he reached young manhood, the lords of Delphi entrusted him with the stewardship of the god's gold. From that day to this he has lived a life of purity in service to the god's holy temple. As for Kreousa, his mother, she married Xouthos, and I'll tell you how that came about. It was like this.

War had broken out between Athens and Chalkis, and Xouthos came to the aid of Athens, and Athens won. As his reward, Xouthos was given Kreousa to be his wife, despite the fact that he's not Athenian, but Achaian by birth, the son of Aiolos whose father just happens to be Zeus—not a bad family to marry into.

Years have passed since their marriage, and yet they find themselves still childless. And that's why they've come here to Apollo's oracle, burning for children. Apollo, who may at times appear forgetful, is not so in this case, for he alone is directing these events to this conclusion. When Xouthos enters this shrine of Apollo's oracle, he, the god, will give him his own son, naming Xouthos the father. In this way the boy is received into his mother's house, and will later be revealed to her there. Apollo's liaison thus remains undercover, and the boy receives his rightful place and position in the bosom of the royal family. The god will name him Ion, and he will be known throughout Greece as the founder of Ionia.

Ah, but here he comes now, Apollo's son, with laurel boughs to sweep clean the temple's entrance. I'll call him Ion, his name-to-be, the first of the gods to do so. Meanwhile I'll stash myself in this laurel grove to see what fate has in mind for the boy. *(Exit into grove.)*

(Enter ION from the temple followed by several TEMPLE ATTENDANTS.)

(Music. Song. Dance.)

ION: *(Chants.)*
> Hail, bright sun,
> god Hêlios of the burning chariot,
> rising above dark earth,
> driving in flight lingering stars
> into the dismal vault of holy night!

> Parnassos's pathless peaks flame with your fire
> and receive for mortals
> the course of your chariot's fiery wheels.

> The smoke of waterless desert myrrh
> rises to the rooftop of radiant Apollo's
> holy temple, and Pythia, Delphian priestess,
> sits on her tripod, crying aloud to Greeks
> songs Apollo sings inside her.

(To the TEMPLE ATTENDANTS.)

> Delphian servants of Apollo,
> go to Castalia's silvery springs,
> bathe yourselves in the pure waters
> and return to the temple.
> But guard your words,
> keep holy silence,
> and to those who come to consult the oracle,
> speak only words of kindness and purity.

(Exeunt the TEMPLE ATTENDANTS.)

I'll sweep the temple now,
sweep it as I've done since childhood,
with twigs of laurel bound with holy bindings,
purify the entrance of Apollo's house,
and with drops of water tame the dust.
I'll also shoo away flocks of birds that
foul the sacred offerings,
frighten them off with my bow.
Without father or mother to watch over me,
I tend Apollo's shrine that has raised me.

(Sings.)

Come, trusty broom,
new-blooming branch
of lovely laurel,
sweeper of the steps
of Apollo's temple!
You grow in gardens,
immortal gardens,
where sacred springs
never cease their flow,
gliding,
rippling among holy myrtle.
From dawn to dark,
while the sun soars high,
together we sweep
the god's fair temple,
my daily task,
my day's sweet toil.

Oh Paian! Oh Paian!
Blest be you, blest,
great son of Lêto!

My labor is fair,
no labor fairer

than labor for you
and your place of prophecy.
Glorious the task
of my hands' labor,
not for man but
immortal gods;
I will never tire
of my holy toil.
Apollo, father,
I call you father,
father whose bounty
saved my life,
father,
Phoibos,
lord of the temple!

Oh Paian! Oh Paian!
Blest be you, blest,
great son of Lêto!

(Chants.)

But enough of sweeping with these laurel boughs.
Now for water from a golden ewer,
water straight from Castalia's springs,
Castalia's eddies,
water I sprinkle about for the dust,
water chaste as the hands that spread it.
May I always serve Phoibos,
may my toil never end,
except if Fortune sees fit to bless.

Here they come again!
Oh, no!
That rush of feathered friends from Parnassos!
You there! Up there!
Stay away from here,
Apollo's holy temple!
Go back to Parnassos where you came from!

All you do is foul and pollute!
You may be Zeus's herald,
eagle of the mighty beak that rules the skies,
but stay away!
And here's another!
Oh!
Swan, white swan,
red feet against your belly sailing the skies,
take those feet to another place!
Not even Apollo's lyre that plays to your song
can save you from my arrows!
Fly away, fly!
Away to Dêlos and its lovely lake,
or your song will have a bloody end!
Oh, and another!
What new one is this?
No nesting here, you, under our eaves,
nest of straw and twigs and—oh!
My bowstring's twang will make an end of you!
Have your babies by the gentle Alpheios,
or the groves,
the sacred groves of the Isthmus!
Just stop fouling the temple with your filth!
I don't like to kill you,
you announce the gods' will,
but I'll do my duty to Apollo's shrine,
to the god who sees to me and feeds me.

(ION *returns to his sweeping and sprinkling as the* CHORUS OF
KREOUSA'S FEMALE ATTENDANTS *enter admiring the area's
sculpted and painted decorations.*)

FIRST FEMALE ATTENDANT: *(Sings.)*
Look!
Then it's not *only* in Athens
the gods have fair-columned
temples to honor them!
And homage paid to Apollo,
Apollo Protector of Roads!

Loxios, too,
Lêto's son,
has a double-faced temple
fair to the eye.

FEMALE ATTENDANTS: *(Sing.)*

Over there!
Look!
Heraklês slaying the Lernian Hydra
with his golden sword.
There!
Look!
I see!
Who's that near him?
With the flaming torch?
I heard *his* story at my loom.
Iolaos who shared Heraklês's labors!
And here!
Bellerophon on winged Pegasos,
killing the three-bodied fire-breathing monster!
I see!
There's so much!
Look!
There!
The Battle of the Giants carved on the wall!
I see!
Yes!
Over there!
There she is!
Athêna!
Shaking her shield!
Her Gorgon shield!
At giant Enkelados!
And Zeus with his thunderbolt
fired at both ends!
Ready to strike!
I see! I see!
And Minas devoured by the heavenly flame!
And Dionysos!

His ivy-wound wand!
Unwarlike wand!
Killing another of Earth's giant sons!
Dionysos!
Dionysos!
Roaring god!

FIRST FEMALE ATTENDANT: *(Chants.)*
You there, boy!
You there by the temple!
May we enter the sanctuary with naked feet?

ION: *(Speaks.)* It isn't allowed to strangers.

FIRST FEMALE ATTENDANT: *(Chants.)*
Then will you tell me—

ION: *(Speaks.)* Tell you what?

FIRST FEMALE ATTENDANT: *(Chants.)*
Is it here?
The earth's navel?
Really here?
In Apollo's temple?

ION: *(Speaks.)* Yes, wrapped in fillets of wool and surrounded by Gorgons.

FIRST FEMALE ATTENDANT: *(Chants.)*
Yes, just as we've heard.

ION: *(Speaks.)* If you sacrificed a holy cake in front of the temple and want to ask Apollo a question, you may come to the altar but to enter the shrine you must also sacrifice a sheep.

FIRST FEMALE ATTENDANT: *(Chants.)*
I understand.
I would never transgress Apollo's laws.
What we see out here is delight enough.

ION: *(Speaks.)* Look at whatever you like as long as it's lawful.

FIRST FEMALE ATTENDANT: *(Chants.)*
> My mistress allowed me to come
> to visit the god's holy temple.

ION: *(Speaks.)* Whose house do you serve as slaves?

FIRST FEMALE ATTENDANT: *(Chants.)*
> Our mistress's house
> is Athêna's house, too.
> But here she comes now.

(Enter KREOUSA and a FEMALE SLAVE ATTENDANT.)

(Music out.)

ION: Your nobility shows in you, lady, whoever you are. Looks, they say, betray one's true character. But what's this? You amaze me! Why are you crying? The sight of Apollo's shrine makes people happy, but you shut your eyes and suddenly there are tears.

KREOUSA: You may be a stranger, my boy, but your amazement at my tears is a sign of true breeding. When I saw the temple, I was swept away by an old memory. Though I still stood here, my mind was far away. Oh the misery of women! How cruel the gods are! Where is justice, when the injustice that destroys us is at our masters' hands?

ION: Why are you so sad?

KREOUSA: Nothing. I've said what I had to say. Think nothing of it.

ION: But who are you? Where are you from? What shall I call you?

KREOUSA: Kreousa. Erechtheus was my father. My home is Athens.

ION: What a glorious city. And your ancestry is a noble one. It's an honor to know you.

KREOUSA: I'm fortunate there, yes, but in nothing else.

ION: But tell me, is it true, as they say, that—

KREOUSA: Goodness, so eager—but what are you asking, child?

ION: —that your father's father was born from the earth?

KREOUSA: Erichthonios, yes. That doesn't help much.

ION: And that Athêna lifted him out of the ground?

KREOUSA: With her virginal hands. But she's not his mother.

ION: And just as in the paintings, she gave him—

KREOUSA: —to the daughters of Kekrops, to guard but not to look at.

ION: But they opened the cradle and looked inside—

KREOUSA: —and bloodied the rocks when they jumped to their death.

ION: And the other story? True or false?

KREOUSA: What story is that? I have time to spare.

ION: That your father Erechtheus sacrificed your sisters?

KREOUSA: To save Athens, he found the courage.

ION: And you were the only one spared?

KREOUSA: I was a baby in my mother's arms.

ION: And a cleft in the earth is your father's tomb?

KREOUSA: Poseidon's trident killed him.

ION: At a place called the Long Rocks?

KREOUSA: Why do you ask that? The memory—

ION: Apollo honors it with lightning and thunder.

KREOUSA: Honor? I wish I'd never seen it.

ION: Why do you hate what the god most loves?

KREOUSA: Don't ask. That cave and I share a shameful secret.

ION: And which Athenian did you marry, lady?

KREOUSA: No citizen; he's from another country.

ION: Obviously a man of noble birth.

KREOUSA: Xouthos, son of Aiolos, descended from Zeus.

ION: A foreigner marry an Athenian?

KREOUSA: There's a neighboring city—Euboia.

ION: Across the waters; it's boundary the sea. I've heard of it.

KREOUSA: My husband helped Athens to conquer it.

ION: An ally, then. And then married you?

KREOUSA: My dowry was his war prize. I was won in battle.

ION: Have you come here with or without him?

KREOUSA: With him. He stopped off at Trophonios's shrine.

ION: To look around or to get an oracle?

KREOUSA: He has one question for both Apollo and the seer.

ION: Have you come about crops or some other issue?

KREOUSA: We're childless—after years of marriage.

ION: Never a mother? Childless?

KREOUSA: Apollo knows my childlessness.

ION: Poor woman, so much good fortune, and still unfortunate!

KREOUSA: But who are you? Your mother is blest in you!

ION: I'm called Apollo's servant, and that's what I am, lady.

KREOUSA: A city offering or bought as a slave?

ION: All I know is I'm called Apollo's.

KREOUSA: It's my turn now to pity *you,* stranger.

ION: True, for I know neither father nor mother.

KREOUSA: Do you live in the temple, or have you a house?

ION: Wherever I sleep, this is my home.

KREOUSA: Did you come as a child or as a young man?

ION: They say I was only a baby.

KREOUSA: And who nursed you, may I ask?

ION: No one; I never took the breast. I was raised—

KREOUSA: By whom, poor child? How your suffering mirrors mine!

ION: I call Apollo's priestess my mother.

KREOUSA: But how did you survive? How did you live?

ION: The altars fed me, and the kindness of the many visitors.

KREOUSA: I pity your poor mother! Who could she have been?

ION: Some wronged woman, perhaps, and I'm her son.

KREOUSA: You're certainly well off—and well-dressed.

ION: The clothes belong to the god I serve.

KREOUSA: And you've never tried to find them—your parents?

ION: How do I do that? I have no evidence.

KREOUSA: I know a woman who suffered the same as your mother.

ION: Who? I could share my troubles with her.

KREOUSA: I came here ahead of my husband for her sake.

ION: To do what? Tell me, I can help.

KREOUSA: To receive a secret oracle from the god.

ION: Tell me; I'll do everything I can.

KREOUSA: Yes—but it shames me.

ION: Shame is a lazy goddess; she helps no one.

KREOUSA: I have a friend—who says Apollo slept with her.

ION: Apollo? And a woman? No.

KREOUSA: Yes, and had a baby by him—kept it secret.

ION: Not the god. Some *man* wronged her, and she's ashamed.

KREOUSA: She says no. Her suffering has been a horror.

ION: Why if a god was her lover?

KREOUSA: Once she'd had the child—she abandoned him.

ION: This abandoned child—did it live?

KREOUSA: No one knows. I've come to Apollo to ask.

ION: If he's dead, how did he die?

KREOUSA: Wild beasts—

ION: Why does she think so?

KREOUSA: She returned to where she'd left him. There was nothing.

ION: No blood, no—

KREOUSA: Nothing. She searched everywhere.

ION: How long ago?

KREOUSA: If he were alive, he would be close to your age.

ION: What if Apollo took him to raise him in secret?

KREOUSA: How dare he not share that pleasure!

ION: The god was unjust. I pity the mother.

KREOUSA: She bore no other child.

ION: OIMOI! How like my own this story sounds.

KREOUSA: Somewhere a mother misses you, too.

ION: Don't force me to grieve what I've forgotten!

KREOUSA: I'll say no more. Just help me to an answer.

ION: I do what I can. But there's a weakness in your case.

KREOUSA: My poor friend's case? What weakness?

ION: Will Apollo reveal what he wants kept hidden?

KREOUSA: He will if the oracle is for *all* Greeks!

ION: He acted shamefully. Don't test him now.

KREOUSA: And she feels pain—the woman he violated!

ION: There's no one here who will deliver this oracle to you. If the god in
his own temple is shown to be evil, he would justly punish the one
who brought the answer. Forget your intention, lady. Avoid questions
the god opposes. We would be fools to try to force answers from
reluctant gods with sacrifices of slaughtered sheep or omens from birds
in flight. Answers won by force against their will are of little benefit.
Only what they give willingly is of any use.

FIRST FEMALE ATTENDANT: Disasters are all the same, only the form
changes. Look far and wide, you will find no true happiness in life.

KREOUSA: Unfair, Apollo! Twice unfair! Unfair in Athens and unfair here
to the absent woman I speak for! You should have saved your child!
You didn't! You should answer that mother's question! You don't! If
dead, she can honor him! If alive, she may—but enough of this, the
god refuses to answer, and so it is.
     But here's my husband coming from Trophonios's shrine. Tell
him nothing, stranger, nothing of what we've said, not a word. For I
would be guilty of operating secretly in my friend's cause and more be
learned than is good, secrets that would shame me by falling on
unwanted ears. Men are always ready to accuse women; the good and
bad lumped together, equally hated. It's the fate we're born to.

XOUTHOS: *(Enters with SLAVE ATTENDANT.)* First I greet you, Apollo!
And then you, dear wife! Has my coming so late frightened you?

KREOUSA: I had barely begun to worry, Xouthos. Not really. But what
oracle have you brought from Trophonios? Will we have children?

XOUTHOS: He preferred not to anticipate Apollo's response. But he did say this. Neither you nor I would leave the oracle without children.

KREOUSA: Oh Lêto, goddess, mother of Apollo, let us return home fortunate, and may our past dealings with your son turn out for the better.

XOUTHOS: So be it. But who speaks for the god here?

ION: I do, sir, here outside the temple; inside you will find nobles of Delphi, chosen by lot, seated near the tripod. They will tend to you there.

XOUTHOS: Good! I have all I need, then. I'll go in. I've heard the sacrifice made for all visitors has been slaughtered before the temple, and that the day is auspicious. A good sign for the god's oracles. Kreousa, go to the altars and surround them with laurel boughs, and pray I return from Apollo with a promise of children. *(Exit into temple.)*

KREOUSA: I will. I will. If Apollo is now willing to redress the wrongs he did—though he will never be wholly a friend—I accept. He is a god. *(Exit KREOUSA.)*

ION: Why is this woman always hurling barbs at Apollo, so dark, so mysterious? Does she so love the woman whose cause she defends? Or is she trying to keep hidden some secret she refuses to reveal? But what's that to me, that and the daughter of Eurystheus? No relation of mine, that woman. I'll go now and fill sacred vessels with pure water from golden pitchers.

Oh, but I really must have it out with Apollo. What's he thinking! Raping virgin girls and then abandoning them? Having children by them and then sitting idly by watching them die? Gods don't act this way! No, Apollo, not you! With all your power, you should use it to do what's right. When a man does evil, you punish him. So how is it right for you gods who make laws for man to break the same laws and not be punished? It's not fair.

But just for argument's sake, let's say—silly thought!—that you and Poseidon and Zeus who rules the heavens were ever to make restitution for your rapings and whorings, where would it end? Your temples would be stripped bare, empty, barren, and all in payment for your crimes. You think of your own pleasure only, no thought for the future, and that does great wrong. When men are punished for doing what the gods think good, then that's not right. Blame the gods who set the example for men! *(Exit.)*

(Music. Song. Dance.)

FEMALE ATTENDANTS: *(Sing.)*
    Here me, Athêna,
    blessèd goddess,
    blessèd Victory,
    born of no mother,
    born without pain,
    born,
    birthed from the head of Zeus
    by Titan Promêtheus,
    come, oh come,
    from golden Olympos,
    come,
    soar down,
    wing,
    wing your way,
    to the Pythian temple,
    come,
    from Zeus's radiant halls,
    to Delphi's streets,
    earth's hearth,
    world navel,
    Apollo's altar,
    where they dance,
    where they dance round his sacred tripod,
    tripod of unerring,
    unfaltering prophecy,
    dance and sing songs in praise of Apollo!
    Come, Athêna!
    Come, Artemis!
    Artemis,
    Lêto's daughter,

come,
and Athêna!
Goddesses both,
virgins both,
sisters,
holy sisters of Apollo!
Plead with him, maidens,
plead for us now,
that the house of Erechtheus,
ancient race,
have the clearest of prophecies:
the blessing of children.

Where children are,
there are riches,
riches uncountable,
and unspeakable joy,
for life abounds,
now and in future,
where youth,
fair youth,
shines like a beacon,
where youth,
golden youth,
gives life still to come,
fruitful issue to inherit from fathers,
wealth and joy unto many generations.
Sons are a father's strength in adversity,
sons his joy in times of good fortune,
and his land's protection in time of war.
Take away wealth,
gold and fine silver,
take away palaces,
princely and grand,
I will take in their place the children I nurture,
take in my arms the children I love,
for life without children is not to be borne.
Give me modest means,
but a life rich with children.

I see,
I see them,
see them there,
spectral daughters of Aglouros,
dancing,
dancing before Pallas's shrines,
dancing above your caves,
great Pan,
by the Long Rocks,
dancing,
dancing on green lawns,
to the wavering,
shimmering sound of your pipe
from your sunless cave.
It was there a poor girl
once gave birth to a child,
Apollo,
Apollo's child,
Apollo's son,
and exposed it for birds,
for beasts to tear in a bloody feast,
a bloody victim of a cruel love,
bitter marriage.
At my loom I have never heard,
nor heard in tale or song,
that the children of gods and mortals
are blest.

(Music out.)

ION: *(Entering.)* You've waited a long while for your master. Has he
   returned, or is he still inside asking about children?

FIRST FEMALE ATTENDANT: No, he's still inside. But wait, I hear
   doors closing. There he is. He's coming now.

XOUTHOS: *(Enters from temple and rushes to ION.)* Ah, dear boy, dear son,
   what a lovely beginning!

ION: What is this? I don't understand! What are you doing?

XOUTHOS: I want to hold you, dear boy, I want to kiss you!

ION: Have you lost your mind? Get your hands off me!

XOUTHOS: If love is madness then I'm mad! I want to touch you!

ION: No! I'm the god's property! You'll break the god's garland!

XOUTHOS: No, I know what's mine! I claim you! I love you!

ION: Another step and you'll claim an arrow in the ribs!

XOUTHOS: Why are you running away from the one you most love?

ION: Because I'm not fond of fighting off boorish strangers!

XOUTHOS: Kill me, then, burn me! You'll have killed your father!

ION: Father? What are you—? Father? Is this some joke?

XOUTHOS: I can explain. Just listen. It won't take long.

ION: What are you—!

XOUTHOS: I'm your father, you're my son.

ION: That's crazy! Who said such a thing?

XOUTHOS: Apollo, who raised you.

ION: So say *you*!

XOUTHOS: True, but informed by the oracle.

ION: Then you got the riddle all wrong.

XOUTHOS: My hearing is fine.

ION: And Apollo said *what*?

XOUTHOS: That the first person I'd meet—

ION: The first person you'd meet—

XOUTHOS: —as I came from this temple—

ION: And so?

XOUTHOS: —would be my son.

ION: You're joking! Your son, or a gift?

XOUTHOS: A gift, yes, but my son all the same.

ION: And I'm the first one you met?

XOUTHOS: No one else, dear boy.

ION: But how could this happen?

XOUTHOS: I'm as astonished as you.

ION: Then who is my mother?

XOUTHOS: I don't know.

ION: Apollo didn't say?

XOUTHOS: I was so happy, I forgot to ask.

ION: Then I guess I was born from the earth.

XOUTHOS: I rather doubt that, my boy.

ION: Then how can I be your son?

XOUTHOS: Let's leave that riddle to the god to puzzle out.

ION: No, we'll work it out ourselves.

XOUTHOS: If you say so.

ION: Have you ever had other women?

XOUTHOS: In the days of my wild youth, yes.

ION: Before Kreousa?

XOUTHOS: Never after.

ION: Could it have been then you had me?

XOUTHOS: The time is certainly right.

ION: Then how did I get *here*?

XOUTHOS: Don't ask *me*.

ION: Such a long way from Athens.

XOUTHOS: Quite a conundrum, I'd say.

ION: Were you ever in Delphi before?

XOUTHOS: Once, for the Bakkhic torchlight mysteries.

ION: Who did you stay with?

XOUTHOS: A Delphian—and there were—girls—from Delphi—

ION: You were, as they say, "initiated"?

XOUTHOS: Yes—there was lots of religious frenzy.

ION: You're saying you were drunk.

XOUTHOS: Oh, the god was with us that night.

ION: Then this explains my birth!

XOUTHOS: Fate has found you out, my boy!

ION: But the temple—how did I get here?

XOUTHOS: The girl abandoned you—?

ION: At least I wasn't born a slave!

XOUTHOS: And I'm your father. Accept me.

ION: I guess I shouldn't doubt the god—

XOUTHOS: That's my boy!

ION: What more could I want?

XOUTHOS: Now you've got it right.

ION: The son of a son of Zeus!

XOUTHOS: It's your fate, boy!

ION: And you're really my father?

XOUTHOS: If we trust the god, yes.

ION: Hello, Father—

XOUTHOS: I like the way that sounds, boy.

ION: What a day this has been!

XOUTHOS: Never better!

(They embrace.)

ION: Mother, whoever you may be, I long to see you now more than ever! And yet, if you're dead, I'll never do so.

FIRST FEMALE ATTENDANT: We all share in your happiness, but I might have wished my mistress could also have shared in this blessing of children as well as her house.

XOUTHOS: My son, Apollo acted well in allowing me to find you and bringing us together. You now have the father you never knew you had. I also understand your longing for your mother. I, too, want to know the woman who gave you to me. Time, perhaps, will help us find her together. I now want you to leave all this, the god's temple, your homelessness, and come with me to Athens where we will share purposes and your father's wealth and power will be your own. No one can accuse you of ignoble birth and poverty, for now you're rich and nobly born.

But why this silence? Why so downcast and troubled? Don't turn your father's joy to terror.

ION: Father, things seen close up look different than at a distance. I'm not saying I'm unhappy with this turn of fortune, my finding you, my father—nothing could make me happier. But when I think about Athens, it frightens me. They say the people are sprung from their soil and are native there. Where would that put me with my two disabilities—born of a foreign father and my own bastardy. Stained with this I would be powerless, nobody, a nothing.

And then here *I* come, a foreigner, to a house not mine, and a wife with no children. Before this you shared your sorrow equally, now the sorrow is hers alone, excluded from your joy. What else can she do but hate me? She has every reason, and you in your love for her would take her side and abandon me. Do otherwise and you throw your house into mad confusion. The truth is, I feel pity for her, Father. She's of noble birth, she shouldn't be made to suffer, growing old without children.

Listen to me, Father, listen to the good things I've had here. First of all, a life of peace and tranquility, a precious gift to any man, and no more trouble than is right. And I've never been bumped from the road. It's a terrible thing to have to give way to inferiors. I spend my time in prayer or talking to others, serving those who are happy in their lives, not heavy with sorrow. People come, people go, foreign visitors, and I welcome them all, everyone the same, always a fresh face meeting fresh faces. What all men should pray for, even reluctantly, is mine both by nature and habit, to be just and righteous in the eyes of the god.

Considering all this, Father, I think I'm better off here than in Athens. So let me stay. There's as much joy to be had in small things as in great.

FIRST FEMALE ATTENDANT: I like what you say; your choice allows my mistress to find happiness, too.

XOUTHOS: I've heard all of this I want; no more, now, hear? You must learn to be happy, son. And to start things off, I'll sacrifice and hold a common feast in the place where I found you. I failed that sacrifice at your birth, so this will make amends. I'll introduce you, for now, as a family friend, a foreigner I've invited to a meal. We'll do the same in Athens; they'll learn later you're my son. I don't want to grieve my wife with my good fortune, considering she's childless. In time, though, I'll win her consent to your having the throne.

But now I name you Ion, a name that suits your destiny. For as I left the god's shrine, it was you who first met me. Now gather your friends and invite them to the feast. After you've said your good-byes we leave Delphi.

I expect you women to say nothing about this. The penalty for doing so is death.

ION: I'll go. But there's one thing missing. Until I find my mother, my life is meaningless. Oh Father, I only hope she's Athenian! Then I could say what I want, speak what I feel! A foreigner in a city of pure blood may seem a citizen, except that his tongue is a slave and he hasn't the freedom to speak his mind.

(Exeunt ION and XOUTHOS with his SLAVE ATTENDANTS.)

(Music. Song. Dance.)

FEMALE ATTENDANTS: *(Sing.)*
Cries,
shrieks,
tears,
lamentation,
all, all,
when my mistress comes,
when my queen discovers her barren state,
barren life,
while her husband rejoices,
triumphant in his fatherhood,
his newfound son,
and she childless.
What song, Apollo,
what song did you sing,
son of Lêto,
prophetic god,
what oracle chanted,
wrapped in mystery?
And this boy,
who is he,
raised in your shrine,
tending your altar,
who,
whose belly bore him?
The oracle displeases me,
is it false,
is it treachery?
I fear what will come,
I dread where it leads,
for strange,
strange is the threat it brings;
and the boy is cunning,
clever in deception,
this child of trickery,
raised by the god but born where?

Friends,
shall I tell her,

shall I tell my mistress,
my queen,
tell her clearly where hope now lies,
stab her heart with news that her husband,
who was all to her,
sharer in all,
has done this deed,
has what he wants,
and she has nothing,
she who fades now to gray old age,
dishonored by neglect?
Curse him,
I curse him,
who came an alien,
outsider to Athens,
to grab up wife,
to grab up wealth,
and gave her back nothing!
I curse his treachery!
I wish he would die!
I pray to the god to turn back his prayers,
I pray to the god to turn back unsavored
the burnt offering!
Soon he will learn,
soon he will see,
my love for my mistress,
my queen,
as they go off,
new father,
new son,
to feast in celebration.

Hear me,
towering peaks of Parnassos,
Parnassos of the craggy ridge,
Parnassos throned high in the heavens,
where all night long Dionysos bounds,
the Bakkhic god leaps,
leaps high,

leaps nimbly,
with flaming twin torches,
leaps in the midst of his mountain-wild women,
his night-roving maenads,
never,
never let that boy enter Athens!
Let him die here!
Let him lose his young life!
But never come to Athens,
never!
What need have we of this foreign intruder?
Let Athens be ruled by the blood of Erechtheus!

(Enter KREOUSA and an OLD MALE SLAVE from different directions. She hurries to him.)

(Music out.)

KREOUSA: Old man, ancient tutor of my father Erechtheus while he still lived, come, come join me here at the god's shrine. Climb your slow way up the ascent and share with me the joy of Apollo's prophecy of the birth of children. The sharing of good news with friends is a pleasure. But if—and I hope it isn't—the news is bad, the sight of your gentle eyes is a calming rescue. I may be your mistress, but I take the same care of you as of a father, just as you once did for mine.

OLD SLAVE: Ah, dear daughter, yours is a noble spirit, no less so than your worthy ancestors sprung from Earth. But help me, help me up the climb, this holy ascent to prophecy, we might say. A little help goes a long way. Weary limbs need support, and youth is a wondrous cure.

KREOUSA: Follow me, then; watch where you step.

OLD SLAVE: Slowly, slowly. My mind is more spry than my feet.

KREOUSA: Lean on your staff; it's a winding path.

OLD SLAVE: This staff is as blind as I am.

KREOUSA: I know, but just don't quit on me.

OLD SLAVE: I'll try, but I'm not the old cocker I once was.

KREOUSA: Women that I often work with at the loom, trusted friends, what message did my husband have from the god concerning children? Tell me; it's what we came for. And if your news is good, you'll not find me unkind in my happiness.

FIRST FEMALE ATTENDANT: Oh god!

OLD SLAVE: This is no prologue to a happy tale.

FIRST FEMALE ATTENDANT: Poor lady!

OLD SLAVE: Bad news for us all.

FIRST FEMALE ATTENDANT: What do we do? To speak means death.

KREOUSA: What song is this? What is it you fear?

FIRST FEMALE ATTENDANT: Do I speak? Do I keep silent? What?

KREOUSA: Say what you have to say, however disastrous.

FIRST FEMALE ATTENDANT: I'll say it, yes, even if they kill me twice over. Poor, poor lady, you will never hold children in your arms or give them your breast.

(Music. Song. Dance.)

KREOUSA: *(Sings.)*
  Oh, let me die!

OLD SLAVE: *(Speaks.)* Dear daughter—

KREOUSA: *(Sings.)*
  My pain cries out!
  How can I live!
  The unhappiness!

OLD SLAVE: *(Speaks.)* Child—

KREOUSA: *(Sings.)*
> AIIII! AIIII!
> Straight,
> straight to the heart!
> The knife!
> The pain!
> Leave me!

OLD SLAVE: *(Speaks.)* You mustn't cry out so.

KREOUSA: *(Sings.)*
> The grief,
> the grief!

OLD SLAVE: *(Speaks.)* Not till we know—

KREOUSA: *(Sings.)*
> What more can we know?

OLD SLAVE: *(Speaks.)* —if your grief is your husband's grief, or only yours.

FIRST FEMALE ATTENDANT: *(Speaks.)* He has a son, old man, Apollo's gift, a joy he celebrates alone, apart from her.

KREOUSA: *(Sings.)*
> Your words,
> your words,
> like knives,
> rip through
> my heart!

OLD SLAVE: *(Speaks.)* This son, this child, is he alive, or yet to be born?

FIRST FEMALE ATTENDANT: *(Speaks.)* Born, the child is born, alive, grown, a young man. I saw it all.

KREOUSA: *(Sings.)*
>   I won't!
>   I can't listen!
>   I cannot!
>   Cannot!
>   Unspeakable!
>   Unspeakable!

OLD SLAVE: *(Speaks.)* Tell me, tell me clearly, how the oracle was fulfilled and who is the child.

FIRST FEMALE ATTENDANT: *(Speaks.)* The first one Xouthos saw on leaving the temple was the son Apollo gave him.

KREOUSA: *(Sings.)*
>   No!
>   Not true!
>   And my child?
>   Mine?
>   Where is mine?
>   Am I childless,
>   childless, barren,
>   empty?
>   Forever?
>   Alone,
>   alone
>   in my lonely house?

OLD SLAVE: *(Speaks.)* Who was meant? Who met him, this woman's husband? How did it happen? Where?

FEMALE ATTENDANTS: *(Speaks.)* The boy you saw sweeping the temple? Do you remember, mistress? He's the son Apollo chose.

KREOUSA: *(Sings.)*
>   If I could soar,
>   soar through the air,
>   the misty air,
>   from Greece,

as far as the
western stars!
So great is my
grief,
my friends!

(Music out.)

OLD SLAVE: What name did his father give him? Did he say, or isn't it decided?

FIRST FEMALE ATTENDANT: Ion, because he was the first to be seen.

OLD SLAVE: And the mother?

FIRST FEMALE ATTENDANT: That I don't know. I can only tell you, old man, that they've gone off in secret to make a birthday offering for the boy and celebrate their friendship. Your husband plans a great banquet in the sacred tent to feast his son.

OLD SLAVE: We have been betrayed, mistress, by your husband, and I share in your grief no less than you. He has devised matters to force us from the ancient house of Erechtheus, and so do good for himself and outrage to us.

   I say this not out of hatred for him, but because I love you more. He came to Athens an alien, a foreigner, and by marrying you received your house and all your inheritance. But now it appears there was another woman, a woman with whom, in secret, he has bred a host of children. And I'll tell you how he worked this deception. Once he knew you would never have children, and himself unwilling to share your affliction, he secretly takes to bed some slave woman and has a child by her—this same boy we have just now learned of.

   He removes him at once from the city and delivers him here to Delphi for some friend to raise. But to conceal this even further, the boy is quietly raised and educated in the temple's precincts, with the freedom to roam at will like some animal dedicated to the shrine. When Xouthos learns the boy is grown, he lures you to Delphi to question the god about your childlessness. So it's not the god who lied, but your husband, waiting patiently all this time for the boy to be raised. And what will he do now if his plot is detected? Blame it all on the god, of course. But if not detected, and he returns to Athens, he will pass the royal throne of Athens on to his son.

FIRST FEMALE ATTENDANT: I hate the clever man who anoints his villainy to smell like justice. My friends will be honest men too good to be clever.

OLD SLAVE: But this is not the worst to expect. Your house will now be ruled by a bastard slave woman's spawn with no mother, a nobody. If your husband had reasoned with you concerning your barrenness and convinced you that the house needs a noble-born heir to succeed and brought such a son, your shame would have been far less. And had you not agreed, he could have married a woman of his own kind.

As it is, you have no choice but to act as any woman would. Kill him. Kill your husband. Sword, deceit, poison, but kill him. And kill the boy, too. Kill them before they kill you. Hesitate and it costs you your life. Two enemies can never share a roof; one of them must suffer.

I'm with you in this. We'll share the deed, share the blood to be shed. I'll help you kill the boy. I'll go there now to where they're feasting and, live or die, I'll repay my masters the debt I owe for their kindness to me. Only the name of slave disgraces the slave. In everything else he's as honorable as a freeborn man.

FIRST FEMALE ATTENDANT: Whatever happens, we're with you, either to live nobly or to die.

(Music. Song. Dance.)

KREOUSA: *(Sings.)*
How can I be silent?
How?
But how,
how do I open the secret,
the dark bed,
the shadows,
to a blinding light?

(Chants.)

What stops me in the way?
Why defend virtue, my virtue, now?
Betrayed by my husband,
I am robbed of house,
robbed of children,
robbed of all hope,
hope to keep secret that dreadful rape,
hope to keep hidden that sorrowful birth,
but I could not,
could not.

By the starry throne of Zeus,
by Athêna who dwells on my home's high hill,
and by the holy shore of Triton's waters,
I'll hide it no more, my lover, my shame,
that evil marriage!

I'll lift my load,
and my life will be lighter!
With eyes dropping tears,
with a heart broken by the evil maneuvers
of men and of gods,
I will expose them now for what they are:
ingrates and betrayers of women's rights!
(Sings.)

Apollo, god,
Lêto's child,
who wake to life
the seven-stringed
lyre with music the
Muses sing,
I accuse,
I accuse you
in the light of day!

You came to me then
with your golden hair,
a sunburst of flame

to dazzle my sight,
as into my lap
I plucked soft saffron petals
reflecting your golden,
your radiant light.

You grabbed my wrist,
my pale white wrist,
and dragged me,
dragged me,
crying for my mother,
to that cave,
your bed, your
royal couch,
ravishing god,
where you played
Aphroditê's
shameless game
dear to her heart.

I bore you then,
bore you a son,
in misery bore him,
and in terror,
a mother's fear of
shame,
I brought him back to that
same cruel bed,
that bed where you yoked me,
that bed of sorrow,
and left him to die
on my dark bed of shame.

OIMOIIIII!

And now he's gone,
the food of vultures,
your child and mine,
hard-hearted god!

You! Son of Lêto!
Lyre-plucking god who
sing your own praises,
chanting,
chanting
from your golden throne
at earth's fertile navel
the future to all who
make their way here!
I say this in the light of day,
in the light of the day's great eye
I scream,
I scream,
I shout in your ear!
Evil, vile, seducing god!
Ungrateful lover!
What debt do you owe him?
What debt to my husband?
And yet you give him children,
children for his house,
and none to me!
And my son,
my son and, yes,
yours, hard-hearted god,
you leave a prey for birds to peck at,
stripped of the clothes his mother made him!

Dêlos,
where your mother bore you,
Dêlos and the young laurel hate you,
the laurel sprung up by the feather-leafed palm
when Lêto birthed you,
great seed of Zeus,
hates you, hates you!

(Music out.)

FIRST FEMALE ATTENDANT: OIMOI! What a hoard of evil is now
laid bare! Who could not weep for her!

OLD SLAVE: Dear child, my heart is so torn with pity I can't think. Threatened by one wave of evil, another washes astern to founder me. What is this new sorrow? What are you saying? What are these new charges against the god? This child. Who is it? Tell me, tell me again.

KREOUSA: I'm ashamed, but I'll tell you.

OLD SLAVE: I'll share your sorrow.

KREOUSA: Then listen. There's a cave at Athens, on the north slope of the Long Rocks.

OLD SLAVE: Pan's cave. I know it.

KREOUSA: I struggled with the god there. It was dreadful!

OLD SLAVE: Say it. I'm with you.

KREOUSA: He forced himself on me. My wedding of shame.

OLD SLAVE: Then I was right to guess—

KREOUSA: You guessed?

OLD SLAVE: Some illness you hid.

KREOUSA: I can tell you now.

OLD SLAVE: But how did you hide this "marriage" with Apollo?

KREOUSA: I delivered his child. Don't be shocked, old father.

OLD SLAVE: But where? Who? All alone?

KREOUSA: Alone in the cave that witnessed the rape.

OLD SLAVE: The child? Where is he? You're not childless!

KREOUSA: Dead. The victim of wild beasts.

OLD SLAVE: Then Apollo did nothing to help.

KREOUSA: Nothing. He's been raised in the house of Hades.

OLD SLAVE: But who exposed him? Not you, surely?

KREOUSA: Yes, I swaddled and left him in darkness.

OLD SLAVE: And no one saw? No one with you?

KREOUSA: Only grief and silence,

OLD SLAVE: How could you do that?

KREOUSA: With a flood of words. Words and pity.

OLD SLAVE: Hardhearted girl. But Apollo was harder.

KREOUSA: If only you'd seen him, his tiny hands, reaching—

OLD SLAVE: For your breast, or to lie in your arms?

KREOUSA: For everything I cruelly denied him.

OLD SLAVE: What could have made you do this?

KREOUSA: I thought the god would rescue his son.

OLD SLAVE: What a storm for your house!

KREOUSA: Old man, why hide your head and weep?

OLD SLAVE: To see you and your father so wronged.

KREOUSA: Life is change, nothing lasts.

OLD SLAVE: Let's dry our tears, then, my dear.

KREOUSA: What can I do? Misfortune paralyzes me.

OLD SLAVE: Revenge yourself on the god who wronged you.

KREOUSA: But I'm a human, he's a god.

OLD SLAVE: Burn down his temple.

KREOUSA: I'm afraid; there's trouble enough for me.

OLD SLAVE: Then dare the possible. Kill your husband.

KREOUSA: He was good to me once. I respect those times.

OLD SLAVE: Then kill the boy who's now your rival.

KREOUSA: How? Oh, I will! How do I do it?

OLD SLAVE: Arm your servants with knives.

KREOUSA: I will; but where will we find him?

OLD SLAVE: In the sacred tent where he's feasting his friends.

KREOUSA: No, it's too open; slaves can't be trusted

OLD SLAVE: That's the coward's way out. How would *you* do it?

KREOUSA: Oh, I have a plan, crafty and practical.

OLD SLAVE: And I can help you in both those ways.

KREOUSA: Then listen. You've heard of the War of the Giants?

OLD SLAVE: The Giants who fought the gods at Phlegra.

KREOUSA: And where Earth gave birth to the Gorgon monster.

OLD SLAVE: To help her sons antagonize the gods.

KREOUSA: And Athêna's daughter killed the monster.

OLD SLAVE: I know this story from long ago.

KREOUSA: Athêna who wears its pelt at her breast.

OLD SLAVE: Her armor that men call the aegis.

KREOUSA: Because she rushed into battle with the gods.

OLD SLAVE: What did it look like?

KREOUSA: A breastplate armed with coil upon coil of serpents.

OLD SLAVE: And how can this harm our enemies?

KREOUSA: You've heard of Erichthonios. Of course you must.

OLD SLAVE: Your house's founder. Born of the earth.

KREOUSA: At birth Athêna gave him—

OLD SLAVE: What? Don't hesitate to say it.

KREOUSA: —two drops of the Gorgon's blood.

OLD SLAVE: Which does what to men?

KREOUSA: One kills, the other cures.

OLD SLAVE: But how could the child—?

KREOUSA: In a golden bracelet passed from him to my father.

OLD SLAVE: And at death he passed it to you?

KREOUSA: Yes; here on my wrist.

OLD SLAVE: The goddess's double gift. How does it work?

KREOUSA: The drop that came from the hollow vein—

OLD SLAVE: What does it do?

KREOUSA: Wards off disease and nurtures life.

OLD SLAVE: And the second?

KREOUSA: It kills. Venom from the Gorgon's snakes.

OLD SLAVE: Do you carry them mixed or separately?

KREOUSA: Separately—bad and good don't mix.

OLD SLAVE: Dear child, you have all you need!

KREOUSA: The boy dies and you'll have killed him.

OLD SLAVE: Tell me where and how, I'll do it.

KREOUSA: In Athens, once he's come to my house.

OLD SLAVE: It won't work. Remember—you criticized me.

KREOUSA: Yes, I think I see.

OLD SLAVE: You'll be blamed for killing him, even if you didn't.

KREOUSA: The tale of the jealous stepmother—yes.

OLD SLAVE: Kill him here, you can deny the whole thing.

KREOUSA: And have my pleasure all the sooner!

OLD SLAVE: And hoist your husband by his own petard.

KREOUSA: Listen. You know what to do. Here. Take this golden bracelet
from my wrist and go to my husband's secret sacrifice. Once they've
finished eating and ready to pour libations to the gods, put a drop of
this poison in the boy's cup. No one else's. None but his. Reserve it for
the would-be master of my house. Once he's swallowed it, farewell

glorious Athens he will never know, for the earth will swallow him here in golden Delphi.

OLD SLAVE: Return to the house of your hosts; I'll see to everything here. *(Exit KREOUSA.)* Doddering, crotchety old feet, be young again in deed if not in time. You and your mistress now march against the enemy, allies in slaughtering this house-usurping boy. Virtue is a fine thing for the fortunate. But always kill your enemy before he kills you. There's no law to prevent. *(Exit.)*

(Music. Song. Dance.)

FEMALE ATTENDANTS: *(Sing.)*
    Goddess of crossroads,
    Einodeia,
    Dêmêter's daughter,
    queen who rules over nighttime assaults,
    guide by day, by daytime also,
    guide the cup of death to its end,
    to its destined end,
    its dark conclusion,
    filled with drops of Gorgon's blood,
    poured from Gorgon's knife-raw throat,
    earthborn Gorgon,
    to him guide it from my mistress's hand,
    to him who threatens the house of Erechtheus.
    Let no one,
    no foreigner,
    rule in my city
    but sons of the noble Erechtheids!

    If her plot should fail,
    her daring design,
    the boy's swift death,
    and the moment lost that gives her hope,
    my mistress will pierce her heart,
    or snap her neck with a cord,
    pain to end pain,
    and go down to death and a different world.

She could never live,
my queen,
my mistress,
in the light of the sun,
and see a foreigner rule
her noble father's house.

I feel shamed for the god of many songs,
Iakkhos,
Bakkhos,
Dionysos,
if this wandering boy, Apollo's bastard,
spies from beside the spring of Kallichoros
on the all-night torches of the Sacred Mysteries,
when the chorus of stars of Zeus's bright heaven
takes up the dance,
and the moon joins in,
and the daughters dance,
the fifty daughters of Nêreus dance,
in the sea,
in the eddies of ever-flowing rivers,
dance in praise of gold-crowned Korê
and holy mother Dêmêter.
It is here,
here,
he hopes to rule,
Apollo's boy, Apollo's bastard,
making his own the labor of others!

You poets who sing your slanderous songs
of women's lecherous lives and loves,
sing, sing for once, of men's brutal ways
and their evil, unholy treatment of women!
Behold how we excel men in piety!
Sing,
sing a different song of men's loves!
Sing of the son of Zeus's son,
of his ingratitude,
when he bedded another,

not his bed's partner,
sharing with another the blessing of children,
and getting for his labors a bastard son!

(Enter in haste a MALE SLAVE ATTENDANT of Kreousa.)

(Music out.)

MALE SLAVE: Women, where can I find our mistress the daughter of Erechtheus? I've looked for her everywhere in town and haven't found her.

FIRST FEMALE ATTENDANT: I know you, you're one of us. What's happened?

MALE SLAVE: They're after us! The city's rulers are out to kill her by stoning!

FIRST FEMALE ATTENDANT: What are you saying? Have they uncovered our plot to kill the boy?

MALE SLAVE: They have. And you're to be punished, too.

FIRST FEMALE ATTENDANT: But how do they know?

MALE SLAVE: Apollo exposed it; not wishing to have his temple polluted.

FIRST FEMALE ATTENDANT: How? Tell me. I beg you. Knowing the truth will make death easier.

MALE SLAVE: When Xouthos had left the god's temple, he took his new son to the place of the feast, telling him to raise a tent over the area, and if his sacrifice to Dionysos took too long, the boy was to begin the feast without him. He then gathered the cattle and set off for the twin peaks of Parnassos, where Bakkhic fires flicker all night, and where he would sprinkle the blood of victims as birth offerings for his son.

With the help of skilled carpenters, the young man raised pillars and posts to form a square one hundred feet on each side, large enough to hold the population of Delphi invited to the feast. He even took care to avoid the noon rays of the sun and its harsh glare in the dying of the day. And then for shade he took sacred tapestries from the god's treasury and hung them on the frame as walls, a glorious and splendid sight to see.

First, though, he threw across the frame a roof made of great bolts of cloth that Heraklês, Zeus's son, had plundered in his war with the Amazons and dedicated to Apollo. It appeared so grand as to be a second heaven, for woven in it was the panoply of the stars being marshaled in the great circle of the sky and Sun's chariot streaking toward the dying light, drawing in its train the sparkle of the Evening star! And then Night, black-robed, in her two-horsed tracerless chariot, slowly and stately making her way while the stars keep pace in her train. And the Pleiades next, fording the middle air, and Orion brandishing his sword, and the Great Bear, above, circling her golden tail around the polestar! And the moon's perfect white orb that divides the month, darts her beams on high, and the Hyades, surest sign for sailors, and Dawn, the bringer of Day, chasing down the stars.

He also hung the walls with other tapestries, stuff of Asia, barbarian design, strange sights. Stout-oared ships facing off ships of the Greeks. Creatures, half man, half beast, and horsemen chasing down stags and wild lions.

At the door of the tent hung an image of King Kekrops, first king of Athens, half man, half snake, coiling his tail near his daughters, a gift to the god from some Athenian. In the center of the feasting hall, the boy placed golden bowls for mixing wine. That done, a herald appears and announces so all can hear that any Delphian who wishes is welcome to the feast.

When the tent is full to capacity, the guests deck their heads with garlands and set to eating their hearts' fill. As they reach their limit, an old man suddenly appears in the center of the floor, a busybody of an old codger playing the role of wine steward, drawing much merriment from the crowd. Bustling about, he brings water to each guest to wash his hands, burns myrrh for incense, and personally delivers to each a golden drinking cup, having taken this duty on himself. When the feasting is finished, and the flutes begin, and the time is right for the common mixing bowl, the old man cries out: "These cups are too small, no, larger, bring larger ones, so our guests take their pleasures more quickly!"

Then among a great bustle servants fly about bringing cups of silver and gold. That done, he raises a special cup, as if honoring his new young master, and brings it to him filled with wine, but also with the poison, given to him, they say, by our queen, to kill her husband's newfound son. No one notices any of this, and as the boy and the rest of the guests raise their cups, someone, a slave most likely, says something that the boy, who has been raised among prophets and seers, takes for an ill omen and orders the bowls to be mixed again. That first libation to the gods he pours on the ground and orders the others to do likewise. Then there's silence while the new bowls are mixed with pure water and wine of Byblos. As this is being done, a boisterous cloud of doves bursts into the tent—the same as have free rein at the god's temple—and, swooping down, dip their beaks into the spilled wine to relieve their thirst as it trickles down their feathered throats. The libation does no harm to the others, except for one who settles at the new son's feet and begins to drink of the wine spilled from his cup.

All at once, its delicate form shudders with the force of a frenzied Bakkhant, uttering shrieks of distress that no seer could interpret. Everyone present stands around in astonishment, watching, as the poor thing gasps its last and dies, its red legs and claws grown limp. Immediately the young man leaps from his seat, naked arms flashing from his cloak, and shouts: "You're the one served me that cup, old man! Who's trying to kill me here? I'm asking you!" He seizes the old servant by the arm and in searching him finds the expected vial of deadly poison. It was a long while and after considerable torture before the old man confesses the plot and Kreousa's part in it.

Ion then rushes from the tent and calling together the rulers of Delphi addresses them: "Rulers of this sacred land of Delphi, a foreign woman, the daughter of Erechtheus, has tried to poison me!" The lords of Delphi then, by unanimous vote, order my mistress's death by stoning for the planned murder of one dedicated to the god and the added pollution of the sanctuary in the attempt.

The whole city is after her now, a woman whose longing for children forced her down a tragic path that now has cost her not only the hope for children but her life. *(Exit.)*

(Music. Song. Dance.)

FEMALE ATTENDANTS: *(Sing.)*

> Where to escape?
> No way out.
> No turning death aside,
> none.
> It is clear now,
> too clear.
> The death-mingled drink reveals it.
> The wine-god's libation,
> Dionysos's grape,
> mixed with the Gorgon's
> swift-working deadly gore.
> Too clear.
> The world below now demands its victims.
> Disaster for me,
> for my mistress,
> stoning,
> death by stones.
> Where can I flee?
> Where?
> Through the air on wings?
> Into earth's deep folds?
> Where?
> On a chariot moving swiftly like the wind?
> On the prow of a ship speeding to mid-ocean?

(Music out.)

FIRST FEMALE ATTENDANT: Only a god can hide us now by snatching us from view. Poor mistress, what suffering you still have in store. Are we to pay now with an evil end for the evil we planned for others?

KREOUSA: *(Enters.)* They're after me! They'll kill me! Slaughter me like a beast for sacrifice! I'm condemned!

FIRST FEMALE ATTENDANT: Poor lady, we know, we've heard the trouble you're in.

KREOUSA: I escaped from the house just in time! Slipped by without being seen! Where can I hide?

FIRST FEMALE ATTENDANT: At the altar. It's the only place.

KREOUSA: What good will that do me?

FIRST FEMALE ATTENDANT: There's a law. They can't kill suppliants.

KREOUSA: But it's the law has condemned me!

FIRST FEMALE ATTENDANT: They have to capture you first.

KREOUSA: They're right behind me! They can't be long! My enemies with swords!

FIRST FEMALE ATTENDANT: Hurry! To the altar! They're coming! If they kill you there, they'll be stained with your suppliant's blood. You have no other choice.

(Enter ION followed by an angry crowd as KREOUSA moves toward the altar.)

ION: Viper! Viper! Serpent spawned by the bull-faced river god, one look with the murderous fire of your eyes withers like the drops of Gorgon blood you would have used to kill me! Grab her! Throw her from the peak of Parnassos! Let the rocks and crags part her dainty hair as she tumbles down its sides! Fortune smiled on me before delivering me to Athens and the evil of a guileful stepmother! Here, among allies, I took stock of what you are, your mind, your menace, your hateful, criminal malice. Once trapped in the web of your house, you would have sent me packing to Hades in no time. And that altar you cling to won't help you any more than Apollo's temple. I have no pity for you. I pity myself, I pity my mother, who may not be here in body, but is never far off in thought.

Look at her! Look! No shame! Nothing! Weaver of lies with lies, guile with guile, cowering at the altar, as if that will wash her clean of guilt!

KREOUSA: Don't kill me! You have no right! I forbid you! In my name and the name of the god whose altar this is!

ION: What can you and Apollo have in common?

KREOUSA: My body is the god's; it's his to save.

ION: And yet you tried to poison his boy.

KREOUSA: Apollo's boy? No, your father's.

ION: No, Apollo's, when my father was absent.

KREOUSA: But not now. Now *I* am Apollo's.

ION: But my life was innocent; yours is guilt.

KREOUSA: I tried to kill my house's enemy.

ION: I didn't invade your country with weapons.

KREOUSA: You did! You'd have burnt the house of Erechtheus!

ION: Where were my torches, my flaring firebrands?

KREOUSA: You meant to take my house by force.

ION: So you try to kill me for what I "meant" to do?

KREOUSA: To save me once you'd *done* what you "meant" to do!

ION: You have no children, so you envy my father.

KREOUSA: Then you're taking my home because I'm childless?

ION: The land my father gave me he'd *won.*

KREOUSA: A son of Aiolos own Athenian land?

ION: He rescued your city with swords, not words.

KREOUSA: Allies don't own the land they help save.

ION: Do I have no share of my patrimony?

KREOUSA: A shield and a spear are your only inheritance.

ION: Leave that altar; it's holy ground.

KREOUSA: Advise your absent mother, not me!

ION: And not pay you back for trying to kill me?

KREOUSA: Slaughter me, then, but do it here.

ION: Would it please you to die at the god's altar?

KREOUSA: When Apollo does hurt to me, I hurt Apollo.

ION: FU! What can the gods have been thinking so to outrage common
    sense with the laws they made for man! The criminal has no right at
    the god's altar; he should be driven away. Polluted hands must never
    touch this shrine. The innocent deserve protection, not the guilty.
    Equal treatment for both is evil.

    *(As ION moves to grab KREOUSA, enter PYTHIA from the temple
    carrying a wicker cradle bound with wool fillets.)*

PYTHIA: Stop, child. Stop and listen to me. I have come to you here
    outside the temple, Apollo's priestess, who guards the sacred tripod's
    ancient law, I, chosen above all the women of Delphi.

ION: Dear mother.

PYTHIA: A name I love, though only a name.

ION: Have you heard how she planned to murder me?

PYTHIA: I've heard. But your savagery is wrong.

ION: Is it wrong to pay murder with murder?

PYTHIA: Wives are always hostile to stepchildren.

ION: And stepchildren to wives who mistreat them.

PYTHIA: No more. Leave the temple now for your home.

ION: What are you saying? Tell me what to do.

PYTHIA: Go to Athens with clean hands and good omens.

ION: All men who kill their enemies are clean.

PYTHIA: No, listen, I have something to say.

ION: What you say is meant kindly, I know.

PYTHIA: Do you see this basket I'm carrying?

ION: I see an old cradle bound with wool fillets.

PYTHIA: I found you in this, a newborn baby.

ION: What are you saying? Why wasn't I told?

PYTHIA: I kept them in silence; now I reveal them.

ION: But why did you hide it for so long?

PYTHIA: The god wanted you to serve his temple.

ION: And now he doesn't? How can I know that?

PYTHIA: He gave you a father and now sends you off.

ION: Did Apollo command you to save these things?

PYTHIA: The god caused me to think of it, yes.

ION: Why? Tell me. Don't leave me hanging.

PYTHIA: To keep it till the time was right.

ION: To help or to do me harm?

PYTHIA: Inside it are hidden the clothes you wore.

ION: Those clothes—they'll help me to find my mother—

PYTHIA: The god wills that now. He didn't before.

ION: Oh glorious day filled with such wonders!

PYTHIA: This is yours now, take it—and find your mother.

ION: *(Takes it.)* I will! I'll search all Asia and Europe for her!

PYTHIA: That's for you to decide, my dear. I raised you for Apollo's sake, and I restore to you now these things he wished me to save of my own accord. Why he did so, I can't say. No one knew I had them or where they were hidden. Good-bye now, dear child; I wish you the best, and kiss you as if you were truly my son. *(Exit into temple.)*

ION: I weep to think of it! How my mother, to hide her shameful love, cast me away, hid me, sold me, in secret, never fed me at her breast. I was resigned to a nameless life, a servant in Apollo's temple. The god was always kind, but my fate is a heavy load. Mother and son, suffering the same loss, both of them, the love, the comfort of each others' arms, the care, all those years.

But now, Apollo, I dedicate this cradle to you, so I may never know the secret it holds. If chance made my mother a slave, knowing would be worse than never knowing. Better to let matters be. Apollo, I dedicate this now to your shrine. But no. How can I do this? I can't. No. The god saved them for me, these tokens, for me to discover. To deny him is to fight his will. I'll be brave. I'll open it. My fate is here. *(He begins to open the basket.)* What are you hiding, you sacred bands and holy fillets, that have kept safe the secret of me? Look here, look!

The cover of this cradle is as new as it ever was, its wicker weaving as sound as ever, despite the years.

KREOUSA: No—I don't—I can't—what am I seeing?

ION: Quiet! You've caused me enough grief already!

KREOUSA: This is no time for silence. I'll say what I must and you won't stop me. That basket in your hand. I know it. I know because I once exposed you in it, long years ago. You're my son, my boy, my dear—a baby then, a newborn, and I abandoned you in the caves of Kekrops in Athens at the place called the Long Rocks. And I will leave this altar now, even if it means my life. (*She rushes from the altar and embraces ION.*)

ION: Seize her! Some god has deranged her mind, she's left the altar! Tie her hands!

(*Some DELPHIANS seize her.*)

KREOUSA: Kill me, then! Go on! Cut my throat! But I have you now, you and these hidden signs that tell me you're mine!

ION: How dare you! Who are you to claim what's mine?

KREOUSA: "Claim"? No, I know, I know! I've found you, you're mine, my son, my dear son!

ION: Dear son! You tried to kill me!

KREOUSA: How could a son not be dear to his mother?

ION: You're lying! I'll catch you up yet!

KREOUSA: Do, please do, son! There's nothing I want more!

ION: This cradle—is it empty, or what's inside?

KREOUSA: It holds the clothes I abandoned you in.

ION: Name them, then, sight unseen.

KREOUSA: And if I'm wrong, kill me.

ION: Continue. Your boldness almost frightens me.

KREOUSA: You'll find a piece of weaving I did as a girl.

ION: Describe it. All girls weave.

KREOUSA: An unfinished piece. My first attempt.

ION: What else? Or has your luck run out?

KREOUSA: There's a Gorgon's head in the very center.

ION: Oh Zeus, what fate is this hounding me?

KREOUSA: And fringed with serpents like Athêna's aegis.

ION: Look! Here it is! The weaving! Spoken like an oracle!

KREOUSA: The work of my girlhood, so long ago!

ION: What else? Or was this a lucky guess?

KREOUSA: Two coiled snakes. All gold.

ION: Athêna's gift to the family, I take it?

KREOUSA: Our children wear them in memory of Erichthonios.

ION: And what use do you make of this ornament?

KREOUSA: It's worn on the neck by a newborn infant.

ION: Yes, and here they are. Anything else?

KREOUSA: I placed a wreath of olive leaves on your head. If it's the same

one, it won't have withered but still be green and growing, for it comes
from the tree that Athêna first brought to the Rock.

ION: Dear mother, what greater joy can there be than this—to hold you, to
kiss your smiling face!

(Music. Song. Dance.)

KREOUSA: Oh child more welcome than light, than sun! The god, I know,
forgives me this extravagance!

(Sings.)

> But to have you in my arms,
> now, here,
> is something I never thought,
> never expected!
> You were dead to me,
> dead,
> in that place of darkness
> with Hades and Persephonê!

ION: *(Speaks.)* I once was dead, my dear, but now I'm alive, here in
your arms!

KREOUSA: *(Sings.)*
> Great Sky,
> great arch of heaven,
> radiant dome,
> what word,
> what shout,
> can say what I feel!
> How can such happiness be?
> How can there be such joy?

ION: *(Speaks.)* Nothing could have seemed more impossible than being
your son.

KREOUSA: *(Sings.)*
> I'm still trembling!

ION: *(Speaks.)* Fear that you have me, but it's only a dream?

KREOUSA: *(Sings.)*
>Yes, I had given up hope.
>Lady, priestess inside the temple!
>Who, who was it?
>Who brought my child to your arms?
>Whose hand brought my child
>to Apollo's house?

ION: *(Speaks.)* This was the god's work. Now, for all the evil we've suffered, let us enjoy our happy fortune.

KREOUSA: *(Sings.)*
>Dear boy, I wept when I bore you,
>and moaned when I tore you from my arms.
>But now, my face against yours,
>I'm alive and most blest in my joy!

ION: *(Speaks.)* Your song of happiness is mine, too, Mother.

KREOUSA: *(Sings.)*
>I'm childless no more,
>no longer barren.
>Our house has a hearth,
>our country a prince
>and a line of kings!
>Erechtheus is young again,
>and his house,
>his house of the earthborn,
>looks out on a sunlit,
>radiant landscape!

ION: *(Speaks.)* Mother, my father should be here, too; he should share with us the happiness I've brought you both.

KREOUSA: *(Sings.)*
>Child, no, you mustn't.
>How can I bear this disgrace?

ION: (Speaks.) Disgrace?

KREOUSA: (Sings.)
    Your father—
    your father is
    not who you think.

ION: (Speaks.) Then you weren't married?

KREOUSA: (Sings.)
    The marriage that made you
    had no torches or dancing.

ION: (Speaks.) A bastard, then? And my father? Who was he?

KREOUSA: (Sings.)
    I call as witness Athêna
    who slew the Gorgon—

ION: (Speaks.) What are you saying?

KREOUSA: (Sings.)
    —who sits on the high hill
    where the olives bloom—

ION: (Speaks.) I don't understand—

KREOUSA: (Sings.)
    —where the nightingales sing
    near the cliffs,
    Apollo—

ION: (Speaks.) Apollo? Why speak of Apollo?

KREOUSA: (Sings.)
    —forced me to his secret bed—

ION: (Speaks.) Don't stop; what you say will be a blessing to me!

KREOUSA: *(Sings.)*
> —and when nine months passed,
> I bore Apollo's secret child.

ION: *(Speaks.)* If what you say is true, your news is welcome.

KREOUSA: *(Sings.)*
> I feared my mother,
> I wrapped you in these,
> the unsteady weaving of a young girl.
> I didn't feed you at my breast,
> I didn't wash you as a mother should,
> but abandoned you in a desolate cave,
> a feast for birds,
> an offering to death.

ION: *(Speaks.)* How could you dare such a thing? You were my mother—

KREOUSA: *(Sings.)*
> Terror, my dear,
> awful terror forced me,
> forced me to throw you out to death.
> I never willed it,
> never wanted it.

ION: *(Speaks.)* And I was about to kill you—against my will—

KREOUSA: *(Sings.)*
> IOO! IOO!
> Tossed by Fortune,
> this way, that way,
> terrible past, terrible present,
> stormwinds lash us,
> fair winds bless us,
> there is no harbor forever safe,
> there is no peace forever sure,
> life's course changes,
> life's paths veer off,
> but peace is come now,

winds are fair, a harbor found,
and evils,
the evils we have suffered are enough.

Dear son, loved son,
let the sweet winds bless us.

FIRST FEMALE ATTENDANT: *(Chants.)*
We have seen here today that
hope is not ever beyond hope.

(Music out.)

ION: Goddess, mistress of Change, blind Chance, you who countless
times reverse man's luck on a whim, was it such a whim that brought
me close today to killing my mother, and my mother to killing me,
both of us to suffer in the slaughter? Is it possible, even in the sun's
encompassing radiance, to understand the sense of such things, here,
now, everywhere, at all times?

Dear Mother, to have found you is a joy that knows no words;
nor can I find fault with the father who gave me life. But there are
things I must say to you alone. Come, only you may hear this, and no
one must know. Mother, tell me who my father was, who he really is.
Young girls before have made mistakes, fallen into secret loves, and
shamed by the child, blamed it on a god. If my father was a mortal
man, tell me.

KREOUSA: I swear to you by Athêna Nikê, who fought beside Zeus's
chariot against the earthborn Giants, no mortal man is your father,
but Apollo who raised you.

ION: But he gave me to another father! Why? How could he do this, if I'm
his son?

KREOUSA: No, my dear, you're Apollo's son; and the god gave you to
Xouthos as a man might give his own son to a friend to be his heir.

ION: Tell me, Mother, you must. Is Apollo truthful? Does his oracle lie?
This troubles me deeply.

KREOUSA: All right, listen to me, I'll tell you what I think. I think it was as a great favor to you that Apollo placed you, his son, in a noble home. If you were known as the god's son, what would you have had? Nothing. No father's name, no inheritance. How could you, when I hid my relationship with him and did my best to kill you in secret? He couldn't have done better than give you to another father.

ION: No, I need more, more of an answer than this. I'm going into the temple to ask him directly if I'm his son or the son of a mortal father. *(ATHÊNA appears above the temple.)* What god is this facing the east in a cloud of incense? Mother! Come! We're leaving! We mustn't look at gods! *(ATHÊNA gestures for them to stop.)* Unless it's time for us to see—

ATHÊNA: No, stay. You needn't run. I'm not your enemy. I'm no less a friend to you here than I am in Athens, the city that bears my name. I am Pallas Athêna, and I've come—come in haste, may I say—to speak for Apollo. The god thought it best not to appear himself, in the event there be blame for past occurrences. And so he sent me to explain.

   You, Ion, are this woman's son, as you are also the son of Apollo. Father and mother. When Apollo gave you to a man who is not your father, he did so to establish you in a noble house. His design? To reveal to you and your mother your true parentage only when you had arrived in Athens. But the god's plan went awry, and all he had hoped to keep undercover burst in a blaze, and so he acted to save you both from destroying each other.

   I have come here now to bring this matter to a conclusion and to fulfill Apollo's oracle. So listen to me. Take this boy of yours, Kreousa, and return to Athens. There you will establish him upon the royal throne for he is sprung from the sons of Erechtheus, and it is right that he rule over my land and be renowned the length and breadth of Greece. He will have four sons, from one stock, who will give their names to the four tribes that live in the shadow of my high hill: Geleon, Hoplês, Argadês, and Aigikorês. And when the time is right, their sons will colonize the island cities of the Kyklades and the land along both coasts divided by the great sea, Asia and Europe. And they will be named Ionians, after this boy, and will know fame.

   As for you, Kreousa, you and Xouthos have been promised children together. Your first son, Doros, will name and bring the city of Doris to fame and great praise in the land of Pelops; and Achaios will rule the seacoast around Rhion, and its people find distinction in the name Achaian.

Apollo has managed all these matters well. First, he gave you a healthy birth and prevented your family and friends from knowing. He then ordered Hermês to bring the child from where you had exposed him in Athens, here to Delphi and his temple, where he nurtured and raised him and did not allow him to die.

Mum's the word, now, Kreousa. Tell no one that Ion is your son, allow Xouthos the sweet delusion of his belief, and go your way in the knowledge that you have been blessed. Farewell. You are a happy woman. The evils you have suffered are ended, and the future holds nothing but joy.

ION: Athêna, daughter of mighty Zeus, how can I not accept what you say? Accept it without question, no less! For I do believe now that I am the son of Apollo and this woman. But that, of course, was not unbelievable before.

KREOUSA: It's my turn now to make my declaration. I didn't praise Apollo before, but I praise him now, for he has given me back my son whom before he chose to ignore. I see these gates and this shrine as friendly now, that once were enemies. I greet them in farewell and with good grace, caressing them as I take my leave.

ATHÊNA: Very wise your change from blame to praise. We gods work slowly, though we win in the end.

KREOUSA: It's time, son; let's go home.

ATHÊNA: Yes, go, and I'll follow.

KREOUSA: A proper guardian for our journey.

ATHÊNA: And one who loves your city.

KREOUSA: Come, claim your ancient throne.

ION: As well I should; it's mine to possess.

(ATHÊNA disappears.)

(Exeunt ION and KREOUSA and the FEMALE ATTENDANTS.)

FIRST FEMALE ATTENDANT:
Apollo, son of Zeus and Lêto, farewell! *(To the audience.)* A house hard pressed by trouble and misfortune does well to respect the gods and take courage. In the end the good man is blessed with good, and the evil defeated by his own evil.

*

HELEN

(ΕΛΕΝΗ)

CHARACTERS

HELEN *daughter of Zeus and Lêda, and wife of Menelaos*
TEÜKROS *a Greek warrior, brother of Aias*
MENELAOS *husband of Helen*
THEONOÊ *sister of Theoklymenos*
THEOKLYMENOS *king of Egypt*
CHORUS OF GREEK SLAVE WOMEN *captives*
FIRST GREEK SLAVE WOMAN *leader of the chorus*
OLD MALE SERVANT *of Menelaos*
OLD WOMAN *palace servant of Theoklymenos*
MALE ATTENDANT *of Theoklymenos*
TWO FEMALE SERVANTS *of Theonoê*
KASTOR and POLYDEUKÊS *deified twin brothers of Helen*
ATTENDANTS, SERVANTS

HELEN

Egypt.
Outside the palace of Theoklymenos.
The tomb of King Proteus, father of Theoklymenos, is to one side.

HELEN: Here is Egypt. And here the Nile, river of fair nymphs fed by melted snows that flood the plains in place of blessèd rain from Zeus. Proteus, who was king here once, married Psamathê, a daughter of the sea's dark depths, when she renounced her husband Aiakos. She bore to Proteus two children: a boy, Theoklymenos, and a dear girl child named Eido, apple of her mother's eye. When she arrived at the tender age when it is proper for a girl to marry, she came to be known as Theonoê, because she had knowledge of all the present and future, powers of divination inherited from Nêreus, her mother's father, Old Man of the Sea.

As for me, I come from no obscure land myself. Sparta is my home and Tyndareos my father. There is, of course, the tale that Zeus in the form of a swan, pursued by an eagle, took refuge at my mother Lêda's breast, and through not very gentlemanly means, helped himself to what he sought. True or not true? Who knows. In any event, my name is Helen.

I'll tell you now of the misfortunes that have plagued my life. As it happened, three goddesses came one day to a glen on Mount Ida to visit the sheep-herding son of Priam, Alexandros, known also as Paris. They were Hera, Aphroditê, and Zeus's daughter, virginal Athêna. It was to be a contest of beauty. Their beauty. The three of them. Who was the most beautiful of all? And Paris was to judge.

Well. Aphroditê offered as a bribe to Paris, if she won, marriage to my beautiful self—assuming anything that causes misery can be called beautiful. And, yes, she won. So Paris abandoned his herds on Ida and arrived in Sparta to claim his prize, me, his bride.

Now, Hera, by no means amused with the loss of the contest, frustrated the love that might have been, by turning Aphroditê's substantial prize into thin air, a breathing image of me she fashioned from heavenly ether. And Paris? Well, believing he possesses me, he holds in his arms no more than an airy, vain delusion.

Zeus then made matters worse by engaging new plans. He pitted on opposite sides in a disastrous war the unfortunate Greeks and Trojans, and for what? To relieve Mother Earth's unholy glut of humanity and to raise to the heights Achilleus, the most valiant warrior of the Greeks. For all those years, the Trojans fought to defend and keep me, the prize, and the Greeks to win me as their spears' booty. And all that time it wasn't me, but an illusion, a name only.

As for me, my real self, Zeus had not forgotten me. Hermês swept me up, wrapped me in a sheath of cloud, and set me down here, in the house of Proteus, whom Zeus had judged to be the most honorable of men. I was here to keep pure my marriage bed for Menelaos. So here I am, while my poor husband goes off to rally an army, and arrives at Troy's battlements to win me back by force of arms. How many thousands, because of me, have lost their lives by Skamander's banks. And I, I who suffered miserably, am cursed by all as the woman who betrayed her husband and thrust all Greece into a devastating war.

Then why am I still alive, you ask? I've received a prophecy from Hermês that when my husband learns that I did not do those things, did not go to Troy, did not shame his bed with another man—that he and I would again one day live on the plains of Sparta.

While Proteus was still alive, marriage never threatened. But now he is dead, his son, Theoklymenos, has made it known he wants to marry me. And so, in honor of the husband I once had, I have come as a suppliant to this tomb of Proteus that my vows to Menelaos not be destroyed. My name may be reviled throughout all Greece, but my body here in Egypt is free of shame.

TEÜKROS: *(Enters with bow and arrows, at first unaware of HELEN.)* Whose house is this, I wonder? A house worthy the God of Wealth himself, with its royal circuit and corniced mass, and the splendid coping of its halls! *(Suddenly startled at the sight of HELEN.)* Ah! But what's this? What's this I see? The image, the loathsome, murderous image of that hated woman who destroyed not only me but all the Greeks! I pray the gods abhor you for your likeness to Helen! If this were not foreign soil, one of my deadly arrows would pay you for your likeness to Zeus's daughter!

HELEN: Poor man, who are you? Why do you shrink from me? Why hate *me* for *her* misfortunes?

TEÜKROS: I'm sorry! I gave way to anger. All Greece hates that daughter of Zeus. Forgive me.

HELEN: Who are you? What brings you to this country?

TEÜKROS: I'm one of those unfortunate Greeks, lady—

HELEN: It's no wonder you hate Helen.

TEÜKROS: —exiled from my native country.

HELEN: Oh, you poor man! Who did such a thing?

TEÜKROS: My father, Telamon—the last person you'd expect it of.

HELEN: But why? This suggests some calamity.

TEÜKROS: My brother Aias died at Troy. This caused it.

HELEN: Surely it wasn't you who killed him.

TEÜKROS: He killed himself—fell on his own sword.

HELEN: Was he mad? No sane man would have done so.

TEÜKROS: Do you know of Achilleus, the son of Pêleus?

HELEN: Yes. I hear he was once a suitor of Helen's.

TEÜKROS: He was killed. His comrades fought over his armor.

HELEN: And how did this cause Aias's death?

TEÜKROS: Another man won the armor, and Aias killed himself.

HELEN: And this was the cause of your exile?

TEÜKROS: Yes, because I didn't die with him.

HELEN: What are you saying? You, too, went to Troy?

TEÜKROS: And I who helped destroy it destroyed myself.

HELEN: Destroyed? Burnt to ashes? Troy is no more?

TEÜKROS: Not a trace. Not even where its walls stood.

HELEN: Poor, wretched Helen! It was for you Troy perished!

TEÜKROS: Troy? No, Greece, too! Unspeakable harm done!

HELEN: How long since Troy's destruction? Tell me.

TEÜKROS: The time of seven harvests.

HELEN: And how long were you at Troy?

TEÜKROS: Uncountable months—ten unending years.

HELEN: And the woman from Sparta? You captured her, too?

TEÜKROS: Menelaos, yes—dragged her off by the hair.

HELEN: Did you see the unhappy creature? Or is this hearsay?

TEÜKROS: I saw her as clearly as I see you.

HELEN: Could it be the gods made you all imagine it?

TEÜKROS: Talk about something else. Enough of Helen!

HELEN: So. Menelaos, then. Is he home with his wife?

TEÜKROS: At home? No. Neither in Argos nor Sparta.

HELEN: AIIII! Sad news—I mean, for those it touches.

TEÜKROS: Rumor has it he's vanished—he and his wife.

HELEN: Then all the Greeks didn't sail back together?

TEÜKROS: They did, but a storm scattered them every which way.

HELEN: Where were they when the storm came on?

TEÜKROS: Midway across the Aegean.

HELEN: And no word of him since then?

TEÜKROS: None. All of Greece says he's dead.

HELEN: *(Aside.)* Then this is the end of me! *(To TEÜKROS.)* Is the daughter of Thestios still alive?

TEÜKROS: Lêda? No. She died long ago.

HELEN: Was it Helen's shame that killed her?

TEÜKROS: So they say. She killed herself by hanging.

HELEN: And Tyndareos's sons? Alive or dead?

TEÜKROS: Depends on who you talk to. There are two rumors.

HELEN: Which is the truer? *(Aside.)* Ah, grief upon grief!

TEÜKROS: It's said they've become gods, turned into stars.

HELEN: Welcome words, at least. And the other?

TEÜKROS: That they killed themselves because of their sister's dishonor. But enough of this. I've wept once already over these tales. Now to my mission. I've come to see the prophetess Theonoê and need you to arrange the meeting. I want advice on how to steer my course for Cyprus. Apollo has decreed it's there I'm to live, and to name the city I'm to found Salamis, in remembrance of my far-off island home.

HELEN: The voyage itself will show you the way, stranger. You need no
help. Where you strike land, there you will found your city. But you
must set sail at once, before Theoklymenos, the land's ruler, catches
sight of you. He's off now hunting wild beasts with his hounds. If he
sees you, you're dead. He slaughters every Greek he catches. You needn't
ask me why, and I won't tell you. Besides, it would do you no good.

TEÜKROS: Thanks, I'll do as you say, dear lady. And may the gods
reward you for your kindness. For all the likeness you bear to Helen,
in your heart you're another entirely. No comparison. I pray she dies a
miserable death and never comes home to Sparta! *(Exit.)*

(Music. Song. Dance)

HELEN: *(Chants.)*
How do I sing my sorrows,
how do I sing my sorrows so great,
so many sorrows?
How make my sorrows heard?
Who will partner my cries of woe?

(Sings.)

Oh Sirens,
winged maidens,
daughters of Earth,
come, oh come,
come with Libyan flute,
with pipes or lyres,
bring music,
sad music,
to join my despair,
come with tears
to match my tears,
come with sorrow,
sorrow to match my
sorrow,
with songs of grief
to match my

grief.
Oh Persephonê, queen,
enthroned in Death's
dark halls,
send me your songs,
your singers,
and I will sing you
a song of sadness,
a deathly song,
a song of no joy,
sing you a song,
a song for the dead.

(Enter the CHORUS OF GREEK SLAVE WOMEN.)

GREEK SLAVE WOMEN: *(Sing.)*
By the waters of the deep blue pool,
where tender rushes grow,
I laid out my deep-dyed dresses on reeds
to dry in the sun's golden rays.
It was then I heard a cry,
a pitiful sound,
a song of lament not fit for the lyre,
a cry of pain,
a joyless moan,
anguished, despairing,
like a Naiad in flight,
fleeing in the mountains,
crying from a rocky cave,
protesting her rape by a brutish Pan.

HELEN: *(Sings.)*
Women of Greece,
captive plunder of
barbarian ships,
a sailor has come,
a Greek, a countryman,
come to add tears,
fresh tears to my tears.

Troy,
great Troy,
Troy is dead,
dead,
a smoking ruin.
And I, I,
I of the hated name,
I of the name men loathe,
must bear the guilt.
Lêda is dead;
my disgrace tied the noose;
too great a pain.
And my husband is dead;
lost at sea;
man of many wanderings.
And vanished are Kastor and Polydeukês,
brothers, twins,
my brothers,
vanished,
their country's glory.
Deserted are the plains
where their horses once galloped;
deserted the field by the reedy Eurotas
where once they wrestled
their bright young comrades;
a scene of youthful striving.

GREEK SLAVE WOMEN: *(Sing.)*
AIIIII!
AIIIII!
Mourn for Helen!
Weep, oh weep her doom!
Weep her destiny of many woes!
Your life, dear lady,
was a cruel mocking gift,
a life unlivable,
when swan-winged Zeus,
in a blinding flash,
sped through the air

and planted you in your mother's womb!
What evil have you not suffered?
What suffering have you not known?
Your mother is dead;
your brothers,
twin sons much loved of Zeus,
are favored no longer;
you will never again see your native land;
and in all of Greece, dear lady,
it is rumored you're partnered with a barbarian prince.
And Menelaos is dead at sea.
Never again
will you brighten your father's halls
or Athêna's Brazen Temple.

HELEN: *(Sings.)*
Who was it,
what man,
what Trojan,
what Greek,
cut down the pine
that brought
tears to Troy?
From that pine Paris,
son of Priam,
shaped a ship,
a ship of death,
ship that barbarian
oars sped forward,
bringing to Sparta
the shepherd prince,
to seek out,
to capture,
my ruinous beauty,
and shatter the peace
of my placid hearth.
And with him came
murder-dealing
Aphroditê,

trailing in her wake
death for Greeks.
But Hera,
high on her golden throne,
Hera,
who sleeps in the arms of Zeus,
sent down swift-footed Hermês.
As I gathered fresh roses
in the folds of my dress,
to bring to Athêna
in her Brazen Temple,
he swept me up and
sped me away
through the skies to this
unholy land—
making of me a wretched prize
in the war between Greece
and the sons of Priam.
Now by the streams of Trojan Simoïs,
my name is reviled by a false report.

FIRST GREEK SLAVE WOMAN: *(Speaks.)* Your suffering is great, I
    know. But it's best, I think, to bear one's burdens as lightly as possible.

(Music out.)

HELEN: Dear women, dear friends, what is this fate I am yoked to? What
    woman, Greek or barbarian, ever gave birth to a white-shelled bird's
    egg? And yet men say it's how Lêda bore me to Zeus. Was I born
    a monstrosity? A freak for men to stare at? And yet, my life *is* a
    monstrosity. I blame in part Hera, and in part my beauty. How I wish
    it had been wiped clean, like a picture, this beauty, and drawn again,
    plain, instead of this. They would have forgotten then, the Greeks,
    this evil fortune I'm burdened with, and remembered only the good,
    just as now they remember only the evil!
        Let a man set his hopes on one thing, and the gods cheat him of
    it, hard though it is, it must be borne. But my misfortunes are many,
    they come at me from every side. First, though I am guiltless, I am
    seen by all as evil. To be castigated for what one has not done is worse

than for what one has done! Even more, I am separated from my country, living among barbarians, deprived of those near and dear to me, a slave, though born of free parents. Among barbarians all men are slaves but one.

My one, my sole anchor, that has helped me keep an even keel, that my husband would come one day and rescue me from calamity, is cut from me now as well—for he is dead. And my mother is dead, and it was I who destroyed her. Unjust? Yes! Untrue? Yes! But it sticks all the same! My fate!

My daughter, once my pride and joy, glory of our house, is husbandless and grows gray in her virginal spinsterhood. Dead are my brothers, the Dioskouroi, twin sons of Zeus, and I am dead, dead in my heart, for all I've suffered. And still I endure.

Then why go on? Why live? What more is left to suffer? Do I choose marriage to escape my pain? Live with a barbarian husband? Preside at his richly spread table? No! A woman who marries an unloved husband begins to hate even her own body.

The best is to die. How is it not right? So deep is the depth of my despair. While other women rejoice in their beauty, it is this very beauty that has destroyed me.

FIRST GREEK SLAVE WOMAN: Whoever this stranger is, my dear, you mustn't assume that all he said is true.

HELEN: But he told me clearly that my husband is dead.

FIRST GREEK SLAVE WOMAN: Many things said clearly can also be false.

HELEN: And much that is unclear be true.

FIRST GREEK SLAVE WOMAN: You must stop dwelling on the dark side of things.

HELEN: Anxiety grips me and drives me to what I fear most.

FIRST GREEK SLAVE WOMAN: How much goodwill have you inside the palace?

HELEN: They're all friends, except the man who pursues me.

FIRST GREEK SLAVE WOMAN: All right, now, here's what you'll do. Leave this sanctuary and—

HELEN: Leave? How can you say that?

FIRST GREEK SLAVE WOMAN: —go inside to Theonoê, daughter of the sea, and ask her if your husband is alive or dead. Nothing is hidden from her. When the truth is known, then weep or rejoice accordingly. What good is it to grieve before you know? Do as I say. Take my advice. I'll even go with you myself to hear her prophecy. Women should help one another.

(Music. Song. Dance.)

HELEN: *(Chants.)*
    Friends, I accept what you say.
    Go into the house now, go,
    and learn the truth of what awaits me.

GREEK SLAVE WOMEN: *(Chant.)*
    I do as you say.
    You needn't coax me.

HELEN: *(Chants.)*
    IO! IO!
    Pitiful day!
    What words, what piteous words
    will I hear in my sorrow?

GREEK SLAVE WOMEN: *(Chant.)*
    Don't dwell on sadness, my dear,
    and grieve too soon.

HELEN: *(Chants.)*
    What has he suffered, my poor husband?
    What fate?
    Does he see the sun draw his four-horse chariot

across the bright sky?
The stars and moon in their nightly course?
Or does he share beneath the earth
the doom of the dead?

GREEK SLAVE WOMEN: *(Chant.)*
Accept whatever comes, my dear,
and hope for the best.

HELEN: *(Chants.)*
Eurotas, I call on you, be my witness,
river of my home, river green with reeds,
hear what I say: if the tale is true,
if my husband is dead—

GREEK SLAVE WOMEN: *(Chant.)*
What do these wild words mean?
What?

HELEN: *(Chants.)*
—I will hang by the neck in a deadly noose,
or drive a sword deep in my throat,
a bloody death, a sacrifice to that
trinity of goddesses and Priam's boy,
who tended his herds once on Ida's green slopes.

GREEK SLAVE WOMEN: *(Chant.)*
Let misfortune pass by
and leave you good hope.

(Exeunt the GREEK SLAVE WOMEN into the palace.)

HELEN: *(Chants.)*
Oh Troy, unhappy, piteous Troy,
destroyed by a deed I never did!
It was beauty, my beauty,
gave birth to much blood,
to grief and tears, tears and grief!
Mothers mourn their sons lost,

and for brothers slain young girls
shear their hair in sorrow
beside the weeping Skamander.

And Greece, Greece wails, too, in her pain,
striking her head in despair, scoring
her face with nails dripping blood.

Oh happy Arkadian girl of long ago,
Kallisto,
you left the bed of Zeus a shaggy-limbed bear
with a violent eye, how better by far
was yours than my mother's fate;
for you were saved from your burden of sorrows.
And you, too, daughter of Merops,
Titan maiden, you, too, were blest,
when Artemis, long ago,
chased you for your beauty from her chaste circle,
and turned you into a golden hind.

But my beauty, mine, has destroyed,
destroyed the citadel of Troy,
and the lives of many Greek men.

(Exit HELEN into the palace.)

(Music out.)

MENELAOS: *(Enters dressed in rags.)* Oh Pelops, old grandfather, you who
won that famous chariot race at Pisa against Oinomaös, if only you
had lost your life for good that day you were served up as a dish for
the gods! For then you would never have sired my father, and he
would never have sired Agamemnon and me, Menelaos. No shabby
partnership that, take my word for it! Nor do I boast when I say—
and you can take my word here, too—that the expedition I led to
Troy was top of the line! Not as a despot, mind you, not by force,
but leading the cream of the crop of Greek young manhood by their
willing consent.

Many of those men died, of course, and we know who they are,
as well as those who escaped the sea's terrors and arrived home safely

with the names of those who didn't. But I haven't been so fortunate in my homecoming. Since I laid waste the towers of Troy I have wandered incessantly the sea's surface, striving for return, longing, but the gods have different plans. I'm not worthy, it seems. What's more, I've sailed to every desolate, godforsaken landing place and port on the Libyan coast, and every time I near my country's coastline, gales force my retreat. I've never once engaged a favorable wind to drive me home.

And here I am now, here on this coast, a man with a boat shattered to pieces on the rocks, shipwrecked, my comrades lost almost to a man. Only the keel, a blessing of careful construction, stayed afloat, and it was with that, against every reasonable expectation, that I made it safely to shore, and with me my wife, Helen, whom I dragged by force from Troy. The name of this land, its people, I don't know; but I've kept out of sight, embarrassed by the shameful state of my dress, and to avoid questions. When a man of position falls onto bad times, he find himself in an uncommon state, all the worse for him than for a man long acquainted with misfortune.

The fact is, I'm very near the end of my rope. No food, no clothes—it's obvious they're bits and pieces salvaged from the sails— all my splendid garments swallowed by the sea. The wife I brought with me, the cause of all my pains, I've concealed in a cave by the shore, having compelled the few survivors to keep close guard, while I came here to seek out provisions that they sorely need. Seeing this house, its majesty, the coping all around, its grand gates, I decided to try my hand here. There's always hope of help from a rich man's house. The poor would give you nothing even if they wanted to.

Hello in there! Where's the gatekeeper? Come out and take in the news of my disaster!

OLD WOMAN: *(From inside the palace.)* Who's that out there? Who's at the gate? Go away, you hear? Go! Now! You're disturbing my master! You'll be killed! They kill Greeks here! You're not welcome!

MENELAOS: Ancient mother, threaten all you like, but speak more gently. Now, open up.

OLD WOMAN: *(Enters.)* Go away! Get! It's my job to keep Greeks from the palace!

MENELAOS: Don't you be pushing me about now with your arms waving and—

OLD WOMAN: It's your fault; you don't mind me!

MENELAOS: You're to go inside and deliver this message to your master—

OLD WOMAN: From you? A message? Oh, I'd smart for it, I would!

MENELAOS: —tell him a shipwrecked stranger under heaven's protection—

OLD WOMAN: I won't! No! Go to some other house!

MENELAOS: No, I'll go inside, and you'll do as I say!

OLD WOMAN: Stop being a nuisance! They'll force you to leave!

MENELAOS: God, where's my glorious army when I need it!

OLD WOMAN: You may have been great in your army, here you're nothing.

MENELAOS: Why am I made to suffer such indignities?

OLD WOMAN: You're crying? Why? Why this moaning?

MENELAOS: In memory of happier days.

OLD WOMAN: Then go and find some friends to cry for!

MENELAOS: What country is this? Whose is the palace?

OLD WOMAN: The house belongs to Proteus, and the land is Egypt.

MENELAOS: Egypt? What a disaster for me!

OLD WOMAN: What is it, you don't like the Nile?

MENELAOS: Not that, no—it was my fate I cursed.

OLD WOMAN: It isn't only you down on your luck.

MENELAOS: The king you mentioned, is he home?

OLD WOMAN: This is his tomb, Proteus; his son rules here now.

MENELAOS: Where is *he,* then? At home or away?

OLD WOMAN: Away. And he hates all Greeks.

MENELAOS: What have the Greeks done that I should suffer for it?

OLD WOMAN: It's all because Helen is here, Zeus's daughter.

MENELAOS: What—did you just say? Tell me again?

OLD WOMAN: Tyndareos's daughter, who once lived in Sparta.

MENELAOS: Where did she come from? What does this mean?

OLD WOMAN: From Sparta, of course, where else?

MENELAOS: When? *(Aside.)* Surely not from the cave?

OLD WOMAN: She came, my friend, before the Greeks sailed for Troy. But you must leave this house, now, for things in the palace are in a terrible state. You come at a bad time. And if the master catches you, your reward will be death. As for me, I like Greeks more than my words would make you believe. I spoke harshly in fear of my master. *(Exit into palace.)*

MENELAOS: Well, what a fine kettle of fish we have here! What am I to make of it? She tells me of new misfortunes coming on the heels of the old. I arrive here with the wife I took from Troy, deposit her under guard in a cave, and suddenly there's another woman living in this house with the same name as my wife! And what's more, she's said to be Zeus's daughter! Am I to think there's a man with the name of Zeus living on the banks of the Nile? No! Not likely! There's only one, and he's in heaven. And where in all the world is there another Sparta except beside the Eurotas with its lovely reeds?

I say again, what am I to make of it? Many men the world over, it seems, have the same names as other men—as do women and cities. But one thing's for certain, I won't run from the danger the old one spoke of. Can there be a man so uncivilized that, learning who I am, he'll refuse me food? The fires of Troy are famous, as famous as the man who lit them, me, Menelaos, known the world over.

All right, that's settled, I'll wait for him. And I have two choices. If he turns out to be a savage, I'll remain concealed and make my way back to the shipwreck. If he shows a gentle side, I'll ask for the necessities to meet our needs. This is the unkindest cut of all, that I, a king, should have to beg my bread from another king! But what must be, must be. In the words of some wise philosopher: Necessity is the strongest taskmaster. *(He remains half-concealed by the tomb as the GREEK SLAVE WOMEN enter from the palace.)*

(Music. Song. Dance.)

GREEK SLAVE WOMEN: *(Chant.)*
> I heard in the palace
> from the maiden of prophecy
> what I entered to hear, that Menelaos lives,
> that the earth has not covered him,
> that he has not descended to the
> dark-glowing cavern of death.
> He wanders the seas friendless, poor man,
> buffeted by waves from his native shores,
> blown to every port but home,
> since sailing from Troy.

(Music out.)

HELEN: *(Entering from the palace.)* Back now to my place of refuge at the tomb. Theonoê's words made my heart leap. My husband, she says— and she knows all things—my husband is alive, that he wanders every which way across the seas, here, there, through countless straits, and that, worn to exhaustion by his wandering, and when his troubles end, he will come here. One thing she failed to say, that when he returns, he will be safe. Nor did I ask, I was so joyous he was still alive. She also said that he had been shipwrecked somewhere very near, and that he had escaped with a few companions. When will you come, my dear? How I long for that moment! *(Catching sight of MENELAOS.)* Oh! Oh, no! Who are you? What do you want? Is this an ambush, some evil plot of Proteus's godless son? I'll run! I'll run to the tomb, like some filly or crazed bakkhant! He means to hunt me! How wild he looks!

MENELAOS: No, wait! Stop! Why this mad rush to the tomb? Stay! When I saw you I was struck speechless.

HELEN: Women, help me! He'll do me harm! He's keeping me from the tomb! He'll lay hold of me and take me to the king I refuse to marry!

MENELAOS: I'm no thief, and no hireling to do evil.

HELEN: But look at you! The rags you're wearing!

MENELAOS: Don't run. Stay where you are. No need for fear.

HELEN: Yes, stay where I am, now I've reached the tomb.

MENELAOS: Who are you, lady? Whose face do I see?

HELEN: And you? Who are you? Our questions are the same.

MENELAOS: I've never seen a more stunning resemblance!

HELEN: Oh god! For a god is present when we recognize our own!

MENELAOS: Are you Greek or native to this country?

HELEN: Greek. But tell me who you are, too.

MENELAOS: I've never seen a more perfect likeness to Helen.

HELEN: Nor I a more perfect likeness to Menelaos.

MENELAOS: Truth be known, I am that unhappy man.

HELEN: Here you are at last in your wife's arms!

MENELAOS: Wife? What are you saying? Don't touch me!

HELEN: The same wife my father Tyndareos gave you.

MENELAOS: Torch-bearing Hekate, send me kindly visions!

HELEN: I'm no phantom of the crossroads you see here.

MENELAOS: Yes, and I'm one man, and can't have two wives.

HELEN: Who is this other wife you say you're master of?

MENELAOS: The one in the cave, the one I'm bringing from Troy.

HELEN: I'm your wife; you have no other.

MENELAOS: Can I be in my right mind and my eyes are diseased?

HELEN: Doesn't just the sight of me convince you?

MENELAOS: How could I deny you look like her?

HELEN: Look at me! Use your eyes! What more do you want?

MENELAOS: My difficulty is I have another wife.

HELEN: That was a phantom. I never went to Troy.

MENELAOS: Yes, and who makes phantoms that live and breathe?

HELEN: The gods—out of air—to be your bride.

MENELAOS: Which god? Which god molded her? This is unbelievable!

HELEN: Hera—a substitute for me—so Paris wouldn't have me.

MENELAOS: And so, you were here and in Troy at the same time?

HELEN: A name can be many places, a body only one.

MENELAOS: Don't touch me! I had troubles enough when I came here.

HELEN: You'll leave me, then, to go with your phantom wife?

MENELAOS: Leave you? Yes. With blessings for your likeness to Helen.

HELEN: Oh god, I'm destroyed! To find a husband and then lose him!

MENELAOS: The misery I suffered at Troy is more convincing.

HELEN: AIIII! Was any woman ever more wretched? The husband I love
   deserts me, and I will never see Greece or my home again!

OLD MALE SERVANT: *(Entering.)* Menelaos, I've wandered this land of
   barbarians looking for you. The men you left behind sent me. It's been
   no easy search!

MENELAOS: What's happened? You've been raided by barbarians?

OLD MALE SERVANT: A miracle, sir, though miracle's too weak a word.

MENELAOS: Tell me. Your haste can only mean strange news.

OLD MALE SERVANT: It's this, sir: all your pains have been in vain!

MENELAOS: You're weeping over old sorrows. Tell me what's new.

OLD MALE SERVANT: Your wife is gone! Vanished! Into the heavens!
   Folded into air from the cave where we guarded her. On leaving, she
   said only: "I pity you poor Trojans and Greeks who lost your lives on
   my account because of Hera's trickery. You died at Skamander's banks
   thinking that Paris had Helen, when he never did. My task is now
   complete as fate would have it, the time allotted me here has run its
   course, and I return to Father Sky who begot me. I also pity Helen,
   daughter of Tyndareos, whose name all men abhor, though mistakenly.
   Her innocence is secure." *(Catching sight of HELEN.)* Ah! Daughter of
   Lêda! What a surprise! You were here all along! I was just saying that

you'd taken off into the blue. Little did I know you had sprouted wings. I assure you such mockery won't happen again. The trouble you gave us at Troy is more than sufficient.

MENELAOS: So this is what it was! I understand now! It fits! She spoke the truth. Oh day that I longed for! Day that my arms embrace you! *(They embrace.)*

(Music. Song. Dance.)

HELEN: *(Chants.)*
> My dear, oh my dearest of men,
> how long was this moment in coming!
> But now, dear friends,
> I greet my husband with joy,
> after so many dawns!

MENELAOS: *(Chants.)*
> So long and so much to say,
> where do I begin?

HELEN: *(Chants.)*
> Joy and tears, my dear,
> and you in my arms!

MENELAOS: *(Chants.)*
> Dear love, dear face, I find no fault!
> I have her, I have my wife,
> daughter of Zeus and Lêda—

HELEN: *(Chants.)*
> —whose brothers long ago in torchlight procession
> proclaimed blest, blest—

MENELAOS: *(Chants.)*
> Long ago? Yes. But now heaven leads you
> to another, a better fate.

HELEN: *(Chants.)*

    I praise the fate that brings you back.

    Let me live to enjoy my blessing!

MENELAOS: *(Chants.)*

    I pray you may, and join you in your prayer.

    Our fates are one:

    one cannot be happy and the other not.

HELEN: *(Chants.)*

    My friends, dear friends,

    I mourn no longer for the past and its miseries.

    I have the husband I longed for for so many years!

MENELAOS: *(Chants.)*

    How hard it was, those many days,

    but now I see the hand of Hera.

    My tears are tears of joy, not grief.

HELEN: *(Chants.)*

    What do I say? Who could have hoped it?

    To hold you close, hold you like this.

MENELAOS: *(Chants.)*

    And I hold you, you who I thought had

    fled to the ill-fated towers of Troy!

    How were you taken from my house that day?

HELEN: *(Chants.)*

    It's a bitter cause you seek!

    A bitter tale you ask me to tell!

MENELAOS: *(Chants.)*

    All that the gods give we must bear to hear.

HELEN: *(Chants.)*

    I detest the tale I'm made to tell!

MENELAOS: *(Chants.)*
> But to hear of troubles gone by is a pleasure.

HELEN: *(Chants.)*
> I never sought the bed of that barbarian prince,
> never sped on swift oars and the lust of desire
> to a lawless marriage!

MENELAOS: *(Chants.)*
> What divine power, what destiny,
> stole you from your native land?

HELEN: *(Chants.)*
> Hermês, son of Zeus, brought me to the Nile.

MENELAOS: *(Chants.)*
> A strange, a dreadful tale!
> At whose command?

HELEN: *(Chants.)*
> I have wept and wept, and now I weep again!
> It was the wife of Zeus destroyed me!

MENELAOS: *(Chants.)*
> But why should Hera curse *us*?

HELEN: *(Chants.)*
> There was danger in the springs,
> danger where the goddesses bathed
> till their bodies glowed
> and they stepped forward to be judged!

MENELAOS: *(Chants.)*
> But why should the judgment
> make Hera afflict you with evil?

HELEN: *(Chants.)*
> To take away from Paris—

MENELAOS: *(Chants.)*
    What?

HELEN: *(Chants.)*
    —me, whom Aphroditê had given him—
    his bride to be—

MENELAOS: *(Chants.)*
    Poor, poor woman!

HELEN: *(Chants.)*
    —and sent me, miserable, in misery, to Egypt!

MENELAOS: *(Chants.)*
    And then, as you say, gave Paris
    a phantom image of you.

HELEN: *(Chants.)*
    But you, my mother, you in your house,
    what sorrows you suffered!
MENELAOS: *(Chants.)*
    Tell me.

HELEN: *(Chants.)*
    She's dead. My mother is dead.
    Shamed by the disgrace of my lawless marriage,
    she hanged herself, with her own hands
    twisted the noose.

MENELAOS: *(Chants.)*
    OI MOI! And our daughter? Hermionê?

HELEN: *(Chants.)*
    Without husband, without child, my dear,
    she grieves for my unspeakable marriage.

MENELAOS: *(Chants.)*
    Oh Paris, how utterly you destroyed my house,
    root and branch, and yet your act

destroyed you, too, and the lives of how many
thousands of Greeks!

HELEN: *(Chants.)*
    And I was cast by the god from my country,
    my city, from you. In leaving my halls,
    in deserting your bed—
    though I never did, never—
    I was scorned and reviled by men
    for pursuing an evil love.

FIRST GREEK SLAVE WOMAN: *(Speaks.)* If good fortune attends you
now, it will make up for past sorrows.

(Music out.)

OLD MALE SERVANT: Let me share your joy, Menelaos. I begin to
understand, but not too clearly.

MENELAOS: Then share in our conversation, old man.

OLD MALE SERVANT: Is this not the woman who caused all our
sufferings at Troy?

MENELAOS: No. The gods deceived us. I held in my grasp a phantom
made of cloud, the source of all our misery.

OLD MALE SERVANT: All that blood and agony for a ghost?

MENELAOS: It was all Hera's doing. Rage over the Judgment of Paris.

OLD MALE SERVANT: And this is your real wife?

MENELAOS: She is. Take my word for it.

OLD MALE SERVANT: My daughter, how various and unpredictable are
the ways of god! However often he scrambles the pieces, somehow—
by chance, by design?—they always fall into place, into new patterns.
A man beset with misfortune is one day blest with fortune and the

god's good graces. Another, a fortunate man, is in the end cut down by terrible disaster and painful death. He discovers that fate is not to be trusted. You and your husband have had your share of troubles: you who fought off vicious accusations, while he battled Trojan spears in the heat of battle, which got him nothing then, whereas now, with no effort, he falls into fortune's lap.

And so you brought no shame on your ancient father, nor on your brothers, Zeus's sons, nor did the terrible things that rumor accused you of. I'm reminded of your marriage procession: I running beside your four-horse chariot with torches, you and Menelaos here in the coach, driving off from your father's splendid home to his. He's an unworthy servant who fails to honor his master's life, to rejoice with his good fortune and grieve along with his sorrows. I may be a slave, but at least I'm one of the good sort. Though I may not be known as a freeman, at least I have the heart of one. Better that than endure a double misfortune: to have an evil heart as well as a servile spirit.

MENELAOS: You're a good man, old friend. You've done me grand service on the field of battle, side by side, protecting me with your shield. I want you to go now and tell the friends I left behind where matters stand with us here. They're to go to the shore and wait for what trials I foresee for her and me, and be ready to join forces with us to escape, if possible, this barbarian land.

OLD MALE SERVANT: I'll do as you say, my lord. It's only now I see the truth about prophets and prophecy. Lies, rottenness, the whole business! Kalkas said nothing, not a word, while all around him men of his own country were being slaughtered by the thousands, and for what? For a phantom! And Trojan Helenos, why was he silent? It was his city we sacked and destroyed—for nothing! *(Exit.)*

FIRST GREEK SLAVE WOMAN: Where it's a matter of prophecy, I agree with the old man. Make the gods your friends, and you have more than a prophet in your house.

HELEN: So. Up to now, all has gone well. But tell me, my poor dear, how you escaped safely on your voyage from Troy? I know it will do me no good, but where a loved one is concerned, one wants to share every trouble.

MENELAOS: Your single question calls for a hundred answers. Am I to describe our many shipwrecks on the Aegean, of Euboia and the false beacons set by Nauplios, the cities visited in Krete and Libya, the lookout of Perseus? If ever I gave you your fill of tales, I should suffer in the telling no less than in the living and would be doubly grieved.

HELEN: Your answer is better than my question. I ask only one thing, leave out the rest. How long did your sea wandering last?

MENELAOS: Add to the ten long years at Troy seven more.

HELEN: Oh my poor dear, so long! And then to safely escape those troubles and come here to face death!

MENELAOS: Death? I don't understand. You make me shudder.

HELEN: The master who rules here now will kill you.

MENELAOS: What have I done to deserve this fate?

HELEN: Your unexpected arrival will block my marriage.

MENELAOS: Is someone planning to marry my wife?

HELEN: Yes, by force, if I hadn't escaped.

MENELAOS: Force? His own, or is he a king?

HELEN: He rules here, the son of Proteus.

MENELAOS: I now understand the woman who answered the gate.

HELEN: What barbarian gates have you been knocking at?

MENELAOS: These. And was driven away like a beggar.

HELEN: Surely not asking for food? Oh the shame!

MENELAOS: That's what it came to, but I didn't call myself that.

HELEN: Well, then, you know the whole story of my marriage.

MENELAOS: What I don't know is have you managed to elude him?

HELEN: Rest assured, your wife has never been touched.

MENELAOS: Sweet if true, but how can I believe that?

HELEN: Do you see the despairing place I sit—this tomb?

MENELAOS: I see a bed of leaves. What does it mean?

HELEN: I sit there as a suppliant, to escape this marriage.

MENELAOS: Is there no altar? Or is it a custom here?

HELEN: I'm as safe here as in our own temples.

MENELAOS: I can't take you aboard, then, and sail for home?

HELEN: Death is more likely than to have me again as your wife.

MENELAOS: Then I'm the most miserable of men.

HELEN: Don't be ashamed. Escape! Now!

MENELAOS: And leave you? I sacked Troy for you!

HELEN: Better than that your wife should cause your death.

MENELAOS: I'm not a coward! I'm the man who conquered Troy!

HELEN: Don't assume you can kill the king. You can't.

MENELAOS: Why? Is his body steel-proof?

HELEN: You'll see. But only fools attempt the impossible.

MENELAOS: What do I do, then? Hold out my hands to be bound?

HELEN: You've got yourself in a trap. Let's find a way out.

MENELAOS: Better to die in action than licking one's wounds.

HELEN: We've one single hope of safety, our only salvation.

MENELAOS: Bribery? Daring? Force? Persuasion?

HELEN: The king must know nothing of your arrival.

MENELAOS: Who'd tell him? How could he know me?

HELEN: He has an ally inside, powerful as a god.

MENELAOS: A private oracle in the palace?

HELEN: No, a sister. They call her Theonoê.

MENELAOS: An oracular name. What does she do?

HELEN: Knowing all things, she'll tell her brother you're here.

MENELAOS: Then this is the end. There's no other way of escape.

HELEN: We'll appeal to her as suppliants. The two of us.

MENELAOS: To do what? What hope are you opening for me?

HELEN: Not to tell her brother of your arrival.

MENELAOS: Assuming we win her over, could we escape?

HELEN: Easily, if we win her over. Without her there's nothing.

MENELAOS: This is your task. Women can handle women.

HELEN: I'll fall to my knees in supplication.

MENELAOS: And if we don't win her over?

HELEN: You'll be killed, and I'll be forced into marriage.

MENELAOS: False woman! Forced, you say! To get what you want!

HELEN: I swear by your life, by your head—!

MENELAOS: Swear? Swear what? To die? Never to marry again?

HELEN: Die, yes, by the same sword, to lie beside you!

MENELAOS: Seal the pledge. Take my right hand.

HELEN: I have it. I swear: If you die, I die, too.

MENELAOS: And I swear: If I lose you, I'll take my own life.

HELEN: How then do we die a death of glory?

MENELAOS: Here, on this tomb. I'll kill you and then myself. But first there will be a grand struggle for your love and marriage. Let any who dares come near. I will never dishonor the glory I won at Troy, nor return to Greece to shame my reputation! I who robbed Thetis of Achilleus, who saw Telemonian Aias fallen on his sword, and Nestor made childless. Am I not to think it worthy to die for my wife? It is, and I will. The gods, if they are wise, let the earth lie lightly on the brave man killed by his enemies. The coward they cast out unburied on a barren shore.

FIRST GREEK SLAVE WOMAN: I pray the gods bring good fortune on the race of Tantalos and be free of its sorrows.

(The great doors of the palace are being unbolted and opened.)

HELEN: AIIIIII! Will this misery never end! How is fortune so cruel! Menelaos, this is the end! We're ruined! The prophet Theonoê is coming out. The bolts are drawing back and resound through the house. Run! But why? Where? Whether she's here or there, she knows you've come. It can only be ruin for me now. But you, you who came safe from barbarian Troy, are now again to face barbarian swords!

(Enter THEONOÊ with two FEMALE SERVANTS, one carrying a stemmed bowl with a visible flame, the other a torch.)

THEONOÊ: Lead the way. Hold the torch high, and with its flame and sulfur from the inner temple cleanse the air, as holy rite ordains, that I may breathe the clear, pure air of heaven! *(To a FEMALE SERVANT.)* And you, if any unholy foot has polluted my path, cleanse it with purifying flame by striking the torch against it so I may pass! Once we have made our devotion to the gods, take the fire back to the hearth where it belongs.

Tell me, Helen, what of my prophecies? Have they come true? Shipwrecked, denied your phantom, isn't he come here as all can see? Poor man, to have escaped so many dangers, and not to know whether you will achieve a homecoming or stay here!

This very day in Zeus's court the gods will gather and argue just where you stand. Hera, once your enemy, now your friend, wants you brought safely back to Greece with Helen. The Greeks must learn, she says, that Aphroditê's gift to Paris was a false gift and the marriage a false marriage. But Aphroditê seeks to frustrate your return. It frightens her to think that Greece will learn that the fee she paid for the prize was false coin—a marriage that was no marriage.

The decision is mine whether to destroy or save you. Shall I stand with Aphroditê and tell my brother of your arrival? Or with Hera, and save you by concealing it, although specifically instructed to report? *(To the GREEK SLAVE WOMEN.)* Who will go and tell my brother that this man is here, and so assure my safety?

HELEN: *(Kneels quickly before THEONOÊ.)* Maiden. I kneel before you here in the despairing attitude of a suppliant. I beg not only for myself, but for him, my husband, the husband I have only now recovered and now am threatened with losing to death. Please don't tell your brother that my dear has returned to my loving arms. Save him. I beg of you. Don't sacrifice your piety to buy wicked and unjust tokens of your brother's gratitude. God hates violence, he commands us to seek possessions, but never to get them unfairly.

It was a timely decision, though no happy one for me, when Hermês gave me to your father in safekeeping for my husband. But that husband is here now and longs to have me back. Would the god and your dead father not want their neighbor's goods to be returned to them? How could they not? Don't give your headstrong brother more weight than your honorable father. If you, a prophet, who believes in the gods, are content to pervert your father's justice by honoring your brother's injustice, then it's shameful, shameful that with the help of the gods you know what is and what is to be, and yet fail to know the just from the unjust.

Save him, then, save him, my husband, and end the unbearable misery I am caught up in, and doing so grant an extra grace of fortune! All the world hates Helen. To all of Greece I'm the wife who betrayed her husband and went off to live in the golden opulence of Troy. But if I return to Greece, if I walk again the soil of Sparta, they will see and know that they were ruined by the scheming of the gods, and that I was never a traitor to my husband or family. They'll restore to me my virtuous name, and I'll give my daughter, whom no one now will marry, to a husband, and never again know the hateful beggary of exile, but live in my own home with what is mine.

If my husband had been killed and his mangled body placed on a pyre, I should have mourned him with my tears, however far away. But here he is, alive, returned safely to me, and must I then lose him again? No, maiden. Follow your father's honorable lead, and grant me this favor, I beg of you. The greatest renown for children is to be born of a noble father and to follow the example of his life.

FIRST GREEK SLAVE WOMAN: Your words evoke pity, as do you yourself. But I long to hear how Menelaos will plead for his life.

MENELAOS: As a warrior, I have no intention of falling at your knees in floods of tears. An act of such lowly cowardice would make the very dead beneath Troy's walls blush with shame. And yet it's said that the nobleman who meets disaster has the right to tears. But such "noble" behavior—if noble it is—is not for me. I choose not to play the coward. So. If you think it just to save a stranger justly attempting to save his wife, then give her back and help them both to escape. And yet if you judge otherwise, it won't be my first meeting with despair, nor the last, we've met often before. But it will show you to be an evil woman.

What I say now, words I believe both worthy and just of me, words most likely to move your heart—I say here at the tomb of your father. Ancient spirit of Proteus, old sir, you who inhabit this monument of marble, I ask of you the return of my wife, sent here by Zeus to be kept safe for me. You are dead, I know, and cannot yourself return her. But here stands a woman who would never allow her father, whom I now call upon in the depths of Death's Dark Kingdom, a father renowned for piety, to have his name reviled when once it was so splendid. The choice is hers. We are in her hands.

Hades, lord of the world below, I call upon you, too, for help! My sword has delivered you the bodies of dead young warriors in uncountable numbers—the price for this woman, my wife. You have your payment. So either return them to me now, these warriors, alive, or compel this oracular maiden to surpass even her father's godly nature by giving me back Helen. *(To THEONOÊ.)* But if you and your brother choose to rob me of her, then I must tell you what she has failed to say. We are bound by oaths, she and I. First, that I should fight your brother to the death of one or the other of us. And if he refuses and attempts to trap and starve us in our place of sanctuary, I will kill first her and then myself with the thrust of this sword, on the heights of this tomb, so that streams of blood will wash down its polished sides. We will lie here, two corpses, side by side, to your unending shame and your father's dishonor. Neither your brother nor any other man will have her, my wife. I'll take her with me; home, if possible; if not, then to the dead. *(His voice catches and his eyes fill with tears.)* What's this! What's the meaning of this! Tears? If I turn woman I'm pitiable, not a bold fighter! Kill if you think it best! But you will live in infamy. Or let my words persuade you, and you will be just, and I will have my wife.

FIRST GREEK SLAVE WOMAN: It's for you to judge, Theonoê, what has been said. Make a judgment pleasing to us all.

THEONOÊ: By nature and inclination I am given to piety. My self-regard is high, and I will not compromise my father's good name, nor do for my brother any kindness that will bring me dishonor. I hold in my heart a great temple to Justice, my inheritance, Menelaos, from Nêreus, my grandfather, and I will always keep it inviolate.

Since it is Hera wants to help you, it is with Hera I cast my vote. As for Aphroditê—who I pray will take no offence!—we have never been close, and I will remain a virgin to the end. The reproaches you leveled at my father's tomb, I quite agree with. It would be wrong not to return your wife. And were my father alive, he would never have hesitated reuniting you. But to be brief. I will do as you ask, and in saying nothing, refuse to aid my brother's wicked designs. In doing this, I render him true service by directing his evil intent to righteousness.

I leave it to you to find a way of escape. I'll stand aside, and be silent, and pretend to know nothing. I only ask you to consider the gods. Pray to Aphroditê to allow you a safe passage, and to Hera, who wishes both of you well, not to change her mind.

Dear dead father, I make you this promise: as far as lies in my power, your honorable name will never be tarnished. *(Exit into palace.)*

FIRST GREEK SLAVE WOMAN: The unjust man never prospers. Hope for safety depends on a just cause.

HELEN: As far as she's concerned, Menelaos, we're safe. We must now devise a plan of escape that will get us home safely.

MENELAOS: All right, then, listen. You've lived in the palace for many years and have come to know its servants.

HELEN: What are you getting at? Ah, yes, well, there might be some hope there for us. Tell me what you're thinking.

MENELAOS: We'll need a four-horse chariot. Could you persuade one of the grooms to get us one?

HELEN: I could. But we're on foreign soil. How would we escape by land, not knowing the way?

MENELAOS: You're right, of course. It makes no sense. All right, then, suppose I hide in the palace and kill the king with my sword?

HELEN: Theonoê would never hear of it. She'd break her silence if you planned to kill her brother.

MENELAOS: Even if we did reach the shore, we don't have a ship. Mine is at the bottom of the sea.

HELEN: I have an idea, Menelaos—even a woman, you know, might plan wisely. What would you say if I spread the news that you're dead?

MENELAOS: Unlucky omen, perhaps—but if we have something to gain, let's do it. I can play dead, as long as it's only a fiction.

HELEN: Good. Then I can mourn before this godless king, I can shave my head and keen laments, the way women do.

MENELAOS: But how will this help us escape? It seems rather pointless.

HELEN: I'll tell him you died at sea, and ask him to let me bury you in effigy.

MENELAOS: Suppose he agrees. Burying me in effigy still doesn't give us a ship to make our escape.

HELEN: I'll ask him for one, so we can cast your funeral offerings into the arms of the sea.

MENELAOS: Excellent, except for one thing. If he says to do the burial on land, your pretext is useless.

HELEN: I'll say it's not the Greek custom to bury on land those who died at sea.

MENELAOS: Very good! I'll join you onboard and help with the ritual.

HELEN: Yes, of course you'll be there, as well as your men who survived the wreck.

MENELAOS: Once I have a ship at anchor, my men will be there armed and ready to fight.

HELEN: Once onboard, you're in charge. I only pray we have a fair wind and a speedy voyage!

MENELAOS: We will. The gods are bringing my troubles to an end. But who will you say told you of my death?

HELEN: You. You'll say you sailed with the son of Atreus, saw him die, and are the sole survivor.

MENELAOS: Yes, and these bits of sail I've tied about me will be eloquent testimony to your story.

HELEN: What was a crisis then may soon be a blessing. An ill wind that might still blow fair.

MENELAOS: Shall I go in with you, or sit quietly by the tomb?

HELEN: Stay here. If he threatens you with violence, you have this tomb and your sword to protect you. I'll go into the house to shear my hair, exchange this white robe for black, and tear my cheeks with my nails till they draw blood. A great contest awaits us, Menelaos, and the scales can tip one way or the other. If my deceptions are discovered, I die. If not, I'll return to my native land and save your life.

> Great Hera, partner in the bed of Zeus, hear us, relieve us of our sufferings, we two miserable creatures who reach our hands to the skies where you live among the star-tapestried halls of heaven! And you, daughter of Dionê, Aphroditê, winner of the prize of beauty with the bribe of my hand in marriage, do not destroy me! You have dragged me through enough filth already by setting the name of Helen, though not her body, among the barbarians. If it is my death you want, at least let me die in my own land! Why does your appetite for evil know no bounds? You who traffic in passions, lies, treacheries, love-charm drugs that bring blood down upon houses! If you knew moderation, knew reason, there would be no god like you, I confess— the sweetest of gods to mortals. *(Exit into palace.)*

(Music. Song. Dance.)

GREEK SLAVE WOMEN: *(Sing.)*
> To you I call,
> to you I cry,
> you in your leafy haunts,
> sweet singer,
> sad singer,
> you who sit and sing and,
> singing,
> make of the shaded thickets halls of song,
> sad nightingale,

bird of tears.
Come,
come and,
trilling through your vibrant throat,
join me,
join my song,
my sad song,
share my lamentation
for Helen's grim sorrows,
and the mournful fate of the daughters of Troy
who faced the terror of Greek spears.
Sing,
sing of the shepherd prince,
skimming the sea with barbarian oar,
bringing to the sons of Priam disaster,
disaster,
you, Helen,
from distant Sparta,
you, fated bride,
disaster for Troy,
bride for shepherd-prince Paris,
dark lover,
sped on,
sped on by Aphroditê.
Swords thrust,
and stones sped downwards,
and many Greeks died,
many, many,
and now rest quiet
in Death's Dark Kingdom.
In sorrow,
despair,
in desolation,
their mourning wives,
their keening widows,
shear their long hair and
mourn empty beds,
beds where Love once played.
And more died,

more,
killed by their own:
Nauplios,
Nauplios,
solitary sailor,
rowed alone in his narrow skiff,
lit his treacherous,
dazzling false fire
there by sea-surrounded Euboia,
lying star,
star that dashed them on the rocks at Kaphêreon,
there at the headland of the vast Aegean.
Menelaos, then,
cast from Spartan shores by raging storm winds,
was blown to wretched,
harborless coasts,
on his ship,
the prize,
prize that was no prize,
but strife,
naked strife,
to the Greeks,
the phantom Helen
fashioned by Hera.
What is godly,
and what is mortal,
and what is in between godly and mortal?
Who can say?
Only he knows,
he who has broken through,
he who has seen god and then returned.
But what to say?
What words describe the ineffable,
the unknown?
Words are for reason,
not mystery.
What I know of god is confusion,
his way leads first this way,
then that,

then again this way.
Contradiction,
the always unexpected. And you, Helen,
you,
you who were born the daughter of divinity,
mortal and divine,
Zeus's own child,
Zeus who flew to your mother's lap
and sired you there,
planted the seed,
even you are reviled by your land:
Greece calls you
traitor, faithless, lawless, godless—
you, god's own child!
Is there an answer?

Men are mad
who find glory in war,
who seek to settle disputes with swords!
If battle and blood are needed for settlement,
Strife will never be swept from men's cities.
Strife tore the sons of Priam from their beds
and led them to beds of cramped damp earth.
But Strife would have spared them
had words done their work
in settling,
Helen,
the quarrel caused by you!
But they now wander Death's Dark Domain,
their mighty towers tumbled by flames,
as if Zeus had leveled his fiery bolts,
and yours is a life of pain and misery.

(Enter THEOKLYMENOS followed by ATTENDANTS with hunting nets and hounds on leashes.)

(Music out.)

THEOKLYMENOS: Hail, tomb of my father, I greet you! I buried you
here near my gates so that on leaving and entering my house I could

speak to you in passing, Father Proteus, I, your son, Theoklymenos. Servants, take the dogs and hunting nets into the palace. *(They do so quickly.)* Needless to say, I'm a stern critic of myself, and yet I've failed miserably in punishing criminals with death. I hear that a Greek has come ashore in broad daylight and slipped past my guards. Either he's a spy or has come by stealth to steal away Helen. Once we've managed to catch him, he's dead.

What is this? Have I returned too late and the deed is done? Where is she? Where is the daughter of Tyndareos? Left the shelter of the tomb and been smuggled away? *(He pounds on the doors of the palace.)* Servants! Open up! Open up in there! Unbar the doors! *(The doors open and several SERVANTS appear.)* Open the stables! Bring my chariot! Now! It will be for no want of effort on my part if my bride to be is spirited from the country! *(HELEN appears in the doorway.)* No, wait! No need! It appears my quarry hasn't fled after all. Why have you changed from white to black? And why have you shorn the hair from your noble head? And these tears, why, streaming down your cheek? Or has some news from home broken your heart?

HELEN: Master—for that is the name I must call you—I'm lost, undone, there's nothing for me now, I'm dead!

THEOKLYMENOS: What's happened? What is this catastrophe?

HELEN: My Menelaos—how can I say it?—is dead.

THEOKLYMENOS: How do you know this? Did you hear it from Theonoê?

HELEN: Yes, and one who was there when he died told me.

THEOKLYMENOS: There's someone here who can vouch for it?

HELEN: Yes, and how dearly I wish him somewhere else.

THEOKLYMENOS: Who? Where? I want a clear report!

HELEN: There! Crouching by the tomb.

THEOKLYMENOS: By Apollo! What a sight! The rags!

HELEN: AIIII! My husband must have looked like him!

THEOKLYMENOS: What's his country? Where did he sail from?

HELEN: He's Greek. He sailed with my husband.

THEOKLYMENOS: How does he say Menelaos died?

HELEN: The most pitiable of deaths—drowned at sea.

THEOKLYMENOS: Where did it happen?

HELEN: On Libya's harborless cliffs.

THEOKLYMENOS: He survived? And they shared the ship?

HELEN: Slaves are sometimes luckier than the highborn.

THEOKLYMENOS: Where did he leave the wreckage?

HELEN: There where I wish it cursed! But not Menelaos!

THEOKLYMENOS: Menelaos is dead. What ship brought him here?

HELEN: He says sailors found him and took him onboard.

THEOKLYMENOS: And the evil sent to Troy in place of you?

HELEN: The phantom made of cloud vanished into air.

THEOKLYMENOS: Oh Priam and Troy, destroyed for nothing!

HELEN: I, too, shared the disaster with Priam's sons.

THEOKLYMENOS: Did he bury your husband's body, or—?

HELEN: No, no, unburied. How I weep for that!

THEOKLYMENOS: So this is why you cut your long blond hair?

HELEN: Yes. He's as dear to me now as he was alive.

THEOKLYMENOS: You are quite right to weep.

HELEN: Life has nothing for me now!

THEOKLYMENOS: And yet, the news may be false.

HELEN: Can your sister be so easily fooled?

THEOKLYMENOS: No. And now what? Will this tomb be your home?

HELEN: By shunning you I stay true to my husband.

THEOKLYMENOS: Why taunt me like this? Let the dead be.

HELEN: Yes. I will. Prepare for the wedding.

THEOKLYMENOS: Your consent was long in coming, but thank you
for it.

HELEN: Let me tell you what we must do. Forget the past.

THEOKLYMENOS: On what terms? One favor deserves another.

HELEN: We'll arrange a truce. We'll be friends.

THEOKLYMENOS: I banish my quarrel to the winds!

HELEN: Then I fall to my knees to beg you as a friend—

THEOKLYMENOS: What is it? Say it.

HELEN: I want to bury my dead husband.

THEOKLYMENOS: What? A grave with no corpse? Will you bury a
shadow?

HELEN: In Greece there's a custom that if a man dies at sea—

THEOKLYMENOS: Tell me. The sons of Pelops are skilled in such matters.

HELEN: —we bury him in effigy with an empty shroud.

THEOKLYMENOS: Bury him, then, yes, raise a monument anywhere.

HELEN: That's not the way we bury drowned sailors.

THEOKLYMENOS: What then? I know nothing of Greek customs.

HELEN: We take out to sea the gifts we owe the dead.

THEOKLYMENOS: What can I offer for your dead husband?

HELEN: This man knows. I don't. My life has been fortunate till now.

THEOKLYMENOS: So, stranger, you have brought welcome news.

HELEN: Not welcome to me or the dead man.

THEOKLYMENOS: How do you bury those drowned at sea?

MENELAOS: The best their wealth allows.

THEOKLYMENOS: Whatever you want, take it, for her sake.

MENELAOS: First, the blood of an animal to the powers below.

THEOKLYMENOS: Tell me which and I will do as you say.

MENELAOS: The decision is yours. Whatever you choose is sufficient.

THEOKLYMENOS: In barbarian lands a horse or bull is the custom.

MENELAOS: Either will do. But make certain the beast is flawless.

THEOKLYMENOS: Our herds are rich with many splendid specimens.

MENELAOS: Bedding we'll also need, without the body.

THEOKLYMENOS: It shall be yours. What else does custom require?

MENELAOS: Arms and armor of bronze. He loved the spear.

THEOKLYMENOS: The arms you'll have will honor the line of Pelops.

MENELAOS: And fruits and beautiful flowers your earth brings forth.

THEOKLYMENOS: Yes, and what then? How do you give them to
the sea?

MENELAOS: From shipboard. We'll need a ship manned with rowers.

THEOKLYMENOS: How far out from land will the ship sail?

MENELAOS: To where the waves on shore can scarcely be seen.

THEOKLYMENOS: But why? What's the reason for this strange custom?

MENELAOS: To keep the victim's blood from returning to shore.

THEOKLYMENOS: You'll have what you ask, a speedy Phoenician vessel.

MENELAOS: Excellent, yes, and an honor to Menelaos.

THEOKLYMENOS: Will you need her with you? Can't you do it alone?

MENELAOS: No, it's a mother's duty—or wife, or child.

THEOKLYMENOS: Is it her duty, then, to bury her husband?

MENELAOS: Yes, the dead must not be robbed of their due.

THEOKLYMENOS: She may go. It's right to encourage piety in a wife.
Go inside now and choose what you need for the dead. And be
certain, you won't leave my country empty-handed after having done
her this kind service. For having brought me good news, you will leave

with proper clothing to replace those rags and food for your journey home. I can see what a sorry state you're in. As for you, unhappy woman, you mustn't grieve endlessly for Menelaos. He's met his fate and tears can't bring him back.

MENELAOS: Your task is laid out for you, lady. You must be content with the husband you have here and let go the other. Given the circumstance, it's the best course for you. And if I make my way safely back to Greece, I'll put an end to the slanders that vilified your name—but only if you prove a loving wife to your husband.

HELEN: I will. And my husband will have no complaint of me. You'll be very close and see for yourself. But now, poor man, you must go in and bathe and change to fresh clothes. As for me, you won't be kept waiting long for your reward. And knowing that, you will do your duty for my Menelaos with even keener interest, awaiting the very thing I so dutifully owe you. *(Exeunt into the palace, MENELAOS, HELEN, and THEOKLYMENOS.)*

(Music. Song. Dance.)

GREEK SLAVE WOMEN: *(Sing.)*
　　Long ago,
　　long ago,
　　the Mountain Mother,
　　Mother of All Gods,
　　sped swift-footed through wooded glens,
　　through rushing streams and the thunder-voiced roar
　　of the great salt sea,
　　frantic, frenzied,
　　in wild longing for her who had vanished,
　　the daughter whose name is not to be spoken.
　　Cymbals clashed their shrilly note,
　　bellowing,
　　crying,
　　crying loud,
　　as the goddess harnessed wild beasts to her chariot,
　　in search, in search
　　of the ravished girl

snatched from the maidens' circling dances.
In her wake,
on storm-driven feet,
sped bow-armed Artemis
and Athêna in battle dress.
But Zeus looked down from his eerie on high
and brought another fate to fulfillment.

When the Great Mother ceased her wandering,
futile, aimless,
far and near,
ceased the search for a daughter stolen,
search for the crafty, thieving abductor,
she crossed to where the Nymphs of Mount Ida
keep watch over snow-laden peaks,
and in grief hurled herself headlong
into rocky woods covered with snow.
In desolation she spread a great blight.
Fields, once green, withered and died,
lands, once sown, gave up no yield.
Her aim?
To destroy the generations of man.
For flocks and herds she gave no green nurture,
for man, no food,
and cities were dying,
sacrifice to gods had ceased,
no altars smoked with burnt offerings,
springs dried,
or choked at their source,
their fresh jetting water no longer sprang up,
and all,
all in grief,
unspeakable grief,
for a daughter lost.

When feasting had ceased for gods and men,
Zeus, to soften her wrath, spoke:
"Great Mother of Gods rages for her daughter.
Go, holy Graces,

and you, gentle Muses,
and with loud, ecstatic, and jubilant cries,
with music,
with dancing,
with dance and song,
banish black anger from Great Mother's heart!"
It was then for the first time that Aphroditê,
loveliest of goddesses,
took up the rumbling-voiced cymbal of bronze
and the skin-stretched round of the kettledrum.
And Great Mother laughed and held in her hands
the deep-sounding pipe
that thrilled her with its raucous clamor.

You failed, Helen, to observe her rites,
and lit an unholy flame in your chamber,
and so were cursed with the wrath of Great Mother
for neglecting to honor her holy godhead.
Great power resides in the dappled fawn skin,
in the sacred fennel stalk wreathed round with ivy,
in the clangor of the bull roarer high in the air,
whirling, whirling,
wild hair tossing in bakkhic ecstasy,
for Bromios,
Bromios,
and the goddess's all-night feast
when the moon shines bright in the gloom of darkness.
But you, Helen, gloried only in your beauty.
(Music out.)

HELEN: *(Entering from the palace.)* Friends, everything's gone well inside
the palace. Theonoê was questioned by her brother but said nothing
of my husband's arrival. She even said, only to help me, that he was
dead. As for Menelaos, he seized his opportunity well. The bronze
arms and armor he asked for to cast into the sea, he himself is
wearing, with his strong left arm thrust through the shield strap,
and in his right hand the spear. He's ready for any encounter while
pretending to do honor to the dead man. Once onboard, how can we
not be victorious against the Egyptians? Inside, when we entered,

I removed his rags, bathed his body with fresh, sweet water from the river, the first time in ages for him, and gave him new clothes.

But here he comes, the man who believes he has marriage with me in his grasp. I must keep silent. And you, dear friends, I beg you to say nothing and to take our side in this deception. Once we have rescued ourselves, it may be we can also help you to escape.

(Enter from the palace THEOKLYMENOS with MENELAOS dressed in full armor following, plus ATTENDANTS carrying the provisions for the burial ritual.)

THEOKLYMENOS: To work, men! Carry the provisions and offerings down to the sea, and do as the stranger instructs. Helen, listen to me, and don't take what I say amiss. Stay here. You honor your husband no less by not being there. My fear is you'll be seized by a fit of passion, recalling the love you had from him, and cast yourself into the sea. For even though his body is missing, you still mourn him too deeply.

HELEN: My newfound husband, what choice do I have but to honor my first marriage and the love I shared with him as his bride? My love for Menelaos is so great I would happily die with him. But what sense would it make to join him in death, what joy would it give him? So let me go now and bring him the funeral offerings the dead deserves.

I pray the gods grant you what I wish them to grant you, and the same to this stranger here for the help he's given us in this duty. And for all your kindness to us, Menelaos and me, I will be for you the wife you most deserve, since everything appears to point to a happy end. All we need now is a ship to fulfill our mission, and my pleasure will be complete.

THEOKLYMENOS: *(To an ATTENDANT.)* You, prepare a fifty-oared Sidonian galley with a crew of master rowers.

HELEN: Will the man in charge of the funeral command the ship?

THEOKLYMENOS: He will, and my sailors must obey him.

HELEN: Say it again, so there's no misunderstanding.

THEOKLYMENOS: I'll say it again and a third time. They must obey him.

HELEN: Blessings on you! And blessings as well on my plans!

THEOKLYMENOS: Don't waste your beauty with too much weeping.

HELEN: Today will show you how grateful to you I am.

THEOKLYMENOS: I'll be no worse a husband than Menelaos.

HELEN: How could I find fault with you? Wish me luck!

THEOKLYMENOS: That's up to you—as long as I have your love.

HELEN: I learned long ago to love my friends.

THEOKLYMENOS: Would you have me join you on the voyage?

HELEN: No, no, my lord, you must never serve your own servants!

THEOKLYMENOS: Very well. I need think no more about Greek rites. My house is unstained: Menelaos didn't die here. But go, someone, to tell my subjects to bring wedding decorations to the house! The land must ring with music and song so that all may envy the marriage of Theoklymenos and Helen! *(Exit a SERVANT into the palace.)* As for you, stranger, go and deliver into the sea's embrace these offerings to her former husband, then hurry back with my wife. You'll share our wedding feast today, then be off for home, or stay here and lead a happy life. *(Exit into palace.)*

MENELAOS: Oh Zeus, renowned by men as both father and wise, look down on us here and grant us an end to our pain. As we heave our troubles up a rocky slope, give us your goodwill. Reach out your hand, one touch of your finger rewards us with success. We have suffered an unbroken run of calamity for too long, a change is long overdue. Gods, I have called you many harsh and abusive names, I, Menelaos, but must I always know misfortune? Can I not again walk upright, like a man? Grant me this favor and I'm a happy man forever.

(Exeunt MENELAOS, HELEN, and ATTENDANTS with the offerings.)

(Music. Song. Dance.)

GREEK SLAVE WOMEN: *(Sing.)*
    Speed on,
    speed on,
    swift ship,
    speed on,
    swift vessel of Sidon,
    mother of oars loved by the waves,
    you lead the dance when the dolphins frolic,
    graceful in the waves when the sea is gentle
    and no wind blows,
    when the goddess of calm,
    Galeneia,
    gray-eyed daughter of the sea, sings:

FIRST GREEK SLAVE WOMAN: *(Sings.)*
    "Spread wide your sails
    to the salt-sea breeze,
    sailors, oh sailors,
    heave, heave,
    heave at the oars,
    the pinewood oars,
    as you steer Helen home
    to her fair-harbored shores
    and the city founded by Perseus."

GREEK SLAVE WOMEN: *(Sing.)*
    What will she find, Helen, at home?
    The daughters of Leukippos, perhaps,
    by the surging waters of Eurotas,
    or there,
    there at the temple of Pallas,
    in time to join once again in the dancing,
    or the all-night revel to honor Hyacinthos,
    killed by chance in the throw of the discus,

Apollo's challenge,
who could throw farthest,
Hyacinthos,
honored at Apollo's command
with revelry and a day of sacrifice;
or she'll see her daughter, Hermionê,
left behind in the house,
for whose marriage no pine torch has flared.

How dearly I wish I could wing through the air,
there where Libyan cranes in ordered flight,
row on row,
flee the rainy winter's storms,
following, following the raucous shriek,
the piping of their eldest,
shepherd who shrills as he flies
across rainless deserts and fruitful plains.
Oh long-necked streakers of the sky,
oh cranes, partners with the dancing clouds,
pass beneath the Pleiades at the zenith,
and Orion burning bright in the night sky,
trumpet the news as you settle on the banks of Eurotas,
that Menelaos who has taken the city of Dardanos,
will soon return home.

Speeding down the tracks of the air,
come, sons of Tyndareos, sky dwellers,
beneath the swirling sweep of stars,
Helen's brothers,
Helen's saviors,
ride the green salt swell of the sea's dark back,
and the froth of cresting waves,
bringing soft breezes from Zeus to the sailors;
and free her from that infamous shame,
marriage to a shepherd prince,
barbarian son of Troy,
the stain she suffered on the tongues of men,
punishment for that quarrel on Ida,
though she never saw Troy
or Troy's tall towers.

(Music out.)

MALE ATTENDANT: *(Enters in disarray from the side.)* Where is the king?

FIRST GREEK SLAVE WOMAN: In the palace.

MALE ATTENDANT: I must see him at once.

FIRST GREEK SLAVE WOMAN: He's preparing his marriage—

MALE ATTENDANT: *(Pounding on the palace doors.)* Open! Open! I must see the king! Bring him! Now! *(The doors to the palace open and a SERVANT appears.)* The king! Where is he?

SERVANT: He's coming now.

THEOKLYMENOS: *(Entering from the palace.)* What's the meaning of this?

MALE ATTENDANT: My lord, I have news, from the seashore!

THEOKLYMENOS: The funeral rites?

MALE ATTENDANT: It's all gone wrong, my lord! News so disastrous you won't believe it!

THEOKLYMENOS: Say it.

MALE ATTENDANT: Look for another bride, my lord! Helen has fled the country!

THEOKLYMENOS: Ah! On wing or by foot, I wonder?

MALE ATTENDANT: By ship, Menelaos commanding—the man who brought word of his own death!

THEOKLYMENOS: The shame! The disgrace! I still can't— What ship?

MALE ATTENDANT: The ship you gave him, the foreigner, Menelaos. In short, he killed or cleared out your crew and took off.

THEOKLYMENOS: But how? How? It makes no sense! One man against
so many?

MALE ATTENDANT: After Zeus's daughter had left the royal palace
for the seashore, she carried out a most cleverly arranged deception.
Mincing along in little steps, she keened, lamenting her husband,
keeping her step and in time with her song—her husband not only
not dead, but there beside her. When finally we arrived at the
dockyard, we hauled down a new Sidonian galley outfitted for fifty
rowers. Each man was assigned his own task. One man set the mast in
place, another the oars, then the white sails were furled and the rudder
lowered.

As they went about their chores, some Greeks appeared on shore,
Menelaos's crew, though little did we know it at the time—they'd
been lingering nearby awaiting this moment. Disheveled and grimy,
caked with brine from the sea and dressed as castaways, they were
nonetheless handsome men.

Then, for our benefit, the son of Atreus played his own little
scene. Pretending surprise at their arrival, he called to them pityingly:
"Men," he cried, "what Greek vessel are you from? Where did you go
down, and how did you get here? Come, join us, we're burying the
son of Atreus, Menelaos. His wife Helen here is burying him in
effigy."

Coming onboard, they shed false tears for the dead man,
carrying in their hands offerings they deemed proper. We were at
once suspicious, and murmured to each other at how many passengers
we'd taken on. Still, we remembered your order and said nothing.
The foreigner was in command, you'd said it yourself; and yet it was
that command that caused the disaster.

The remainder of the provisions being light, we easily got it
aboard. Except for the bull. He had ideas of his own, stomping and
pawing the earth, refusing to set foot on the gangplank, humping his
back, rolling his eyes, looking at us treacherously down his horns, till
finally Helen's husband calls out: "Up and at him, men who tumbled
the walls of Troy, do it the way we Greeks do, get him atop your
powerful young shoulders and heave him onto the prow, a sacrifice
offering for Menelaos dead!"

Here he pulled his sword and raised it high. They did as he

ordered, lifted the bull, got it onboard, and set it down on deck. Finally, all cargo stored, Helen mounted the ladder with her dainty feet and sat on the quarter-deck beside her supposedly dead husband. The remainder of the Greeks sat in close order, right and left, along the bulkheads, swords concealed beneath their clothes.

When we had reached a point neither too near nor far from shore, the steersman asked: "Should we keep sailing, sir, or is this far enough? You're in change of the ship." "Far enough," said Menelaos, and lifting his sword in his right hand, he strode to the prow, prepared for the bull sacrifice, but in his prayer said nothing about any dead man as he slit its throat. "Oh Poseidon, great lord who dwells in the sea, and you, holy Nereïds, daughters of Nêreus, deliver me safely, and my wife with me, from Egypt to the shores of Nauplia!" A good omen for the Greek, the spurts of blood from the beast's neck jutted into the sea.

At this, one of us said aloud: "There's treachery onboard! Let's get back to land! Steer to starboard! And you, the rudder, turn it!" But the son of Atreus, the slaughter of the bull completed, called out to his men from where he stood: "Men, the flower of all Greek manhood, no delay now! Kill them! Kill! Cut down the barbarian dogs and cast them into the sea!"

The boatswain then shouted orders to your sailors to counter his. "Fight with whatever you find! A spar, a bench, an oar, but crack the heads of these enemy bastards!" Every man leapt to his feet, we with oars and broken timber, they with swords! The ship was slick with blood! And there at the stern stood Helen, urging them on: "Show me those men of steel that sacked Troy! Show them, show these barbarians!"

They all fought like demons. Some kept their feet, others staggered, but any man down was sure to be dead. Menelaos, looking out for his men in trouble, rushed to their side with his sword slashing and cleared the deck of oarsmen who leapt terrified into the sea. Turning then to the helmsman, he ordered the ship steer straight for Greece. His men hoisted sail and a favoring breeze blew up.

They're gone, fled the country. I escaped death by lowering myself into the sea by the anchor line. I was near exhaustion when a fisherman pulled me out and set me ashore to bring you the news. I've learned one thing for certain: never be overtrustful. *(Exit.)*

FIRST GREEK SLAVE WOMAN: Who'd have thought it, my lord, that Menelaos could have been in our midst and no one know, neither you nor us!

THEOKLYMENOS: Tricked, outwitted by a woman's treachery! My bride fled, my bride escaped! If pursuit could have caught those foreigners, I'd have spared nothing! But as it is, I'll avenge myself on the sister who betrayed me! She knew, she knew Menelaos was here, in the house, and said nothing, nothing! She'll never again deceive another man with her prophecies!

(He starts into the palace but is blocked by the chorus of GREEK SLAVE WOMEN.)

FIRST GREEK SLAVE WOMAN: My lord, where are you going? What are you planning? What murder?

THEOKLYMENOS: Where justice calls! Out of my way!

GREEK SLAVE WOMEN: *(Clutching at his robes.)* Monstrous! This is a great wrong you're doing! We won't let go!

THEOKLYMENOS: How dare you order me!

FIRST GREEK SLAVE WOMAN: We have your good at heart!

THEOKLYMENOS: My good! No! Let me go—

FIRST GREEK SLAVE WOMAN: No!

THEOKLYMENOS: —to kill my vile sister—

FIRST GREEK SLAVE WOMAN: Vile? No! God fearing!

THEOKLYMENOS: —who betrayed me—

FIRST GREEK SLAVE WOMAN: Betrayal, perhaps, but for good!

THEOKLYMENOS: —and gave my bride to another!

FIRST GREEK SLAVE WOMAN: To another with a greater right!

THEOKLYMENOS: Over what is mine?

FIRST GREEK SLAVE WOMAN: The man who had her from her father.

THEOKLYMENOS: And then Fortune gave her to me.

FIRST GREEK SLAVE WOMAN: And then Fate took her from you.

THEOKLYMENOS: It's not for you to judge me.

FIRST GREEK SLAVE WOMAN: It is, if I am right.

THEOKLYMENOS: Who's king here, you or I?

FIRST GREEK SLAVE WOMAN: Royalty acts for the right, not the
wrong.

THEOKLYMENOS: I'd say you're in love with death.

FIRST GREEK SLAVE WOMAN: Then kill *me,* but you won't kill your
sister! A good slave never questions dying for her mistress.

*(The DIOSKOUROI, KASTOR and POLYDEUKÊS, appear in the air
above the palace on horseback.)*

KASTOR: Control your rage, Theoklymenos, King of Egypt! We are the
Dioskouroi, the twin sons of Zeus, whom Lêda once gave birth to
with the Helen who has fled your house. Your wrath over your
marriage is misplaced, it was never to be; and Theonoê, the daughter
of Nêreus, did you no wrong in honoring the will of the gods
and of your father.

It was not destined that Helen should live forever in your house,
but only to the present. When Troy's foundations lay in ruins, and she
had finished lending her name to the gods, this was to end and she
would return home to her old marriage and share again her husband's
noble roof.

Sheathe your sword now, and banish the thought of blackening it with your sister's blood. What she did was done wisely, an act of virtue; you must understand this. Except for one thing, we would have saved our sister long ago. But Zeus made us gods, and we found that fate and the other gods together were more powerful than we and willed to happen what has happened. Those are my words to you.

And now to my sister I say: Sail on, you and your husband—the winds will be fair—and we, your two brothers, coursing beside you over the shimmering sea, will bring you safely home. And when you have come full circle in your life's passage, you will be made divine, and with your brothers, the sons of Zeus, will share libations and gifts from the hands of mortals, for that is the will of Zeus.

As for the island where Hermês first set you down on your sky flight from Sparta and shepherd-prince Paris—that island that lies off and guards Attika—it will be known as *Helen* for its part in sheltering you.

For Menelaos, the intrepid wide wanderer, the gods and Fate have reserved a life after death on the Isle of the Blest. It's not that the gods hate the nobly born, and yet they're given more hardships than the faceless multitude.

THEOKLYMENOS: Sons of Lêda and Zeus, I forego my earlier quarrel with you over your sister, and if the gods so will it, let her return home. As for my sister Theonoê, I hereby pardon her. But I must say one thing more, which I'm certain you know. You are brothers to the bravest and most virtuous sister the world can know! Rejoice in her noble heart; for not many women are so blest!

(Music.)

(KASTOR and POLYDEUKÊS disappear. Exeunt THEOKLYMENOS and the GREEK SLAVE WOMEN into the palace.)

*

CYCLOPS

(ΚΥΚΛΩΨ)

CHARACTERS

SILÊNOS *old, grotesque, fat satyr, father of the chorus of satyrs*
CYCLOPS *Polyphêmos, one-eyed giant*
ODYSSEUS *famous Greek war-hero*
CHORUS OF YOUNG SATYRS *captured by the Cyclops*
FIRST YOUNG SATYR *chorus leader*
SHIPMATES *of Odysseus*
SLAVES *of the Cyclops*

CYCLOPS

Sicily.
At the foot of Mt. Aitna.
Outside the cave of Polyphêmos.
Enter SILÊNOS from the cave, grumbling and carrying a rake.

SILÊNOS: Oh Dionysos, the troubles I've gone through for you, the pains, the labors—as many now as when I was young and fit! I remember that first time, the time Hera drove you raving out of your mind, and off you took, deserting the mountain nymphs, your nannies, and I went after you. And then the war with the Giants, that earth-born brood, and I never left your side, flank to flank all the way, me on the right, covering you with a spear in one hand, shield in the other. And I struck that ugly mountain of a Giant Enkelados right through the button of his shield, and guts all over place! Hmm. Did I or didn't I? Am I dreaming all this? Have I begun to believe my own tales? No, by Zeus, I even showed my war spoils to Dionysos himself! But not all those labors can hold a candle to the trouble I'm in now.

You remember, master, when Hera sicked that band of Tuscan pirates on you, and they set out to sell you into slavery in a foreign land? Well, when I got wind of that, I and my satyr sons set sail in a second. There I stood at the stern, steering the double-oared ship, while my boys heaved at the oars either side, plowing the gray sea white with their effort, and all in search of you, lord.

Ah, but then as we rounded Cape Malea, a monster east wind knocked us off course and straight into this craggy land near the foot of Aitna. And we know what that means, don't we? Cyclopes! Sons of Poseidon! It's where they live, in caves far off the beaten track. One-eyed monsters with a preference for men—they eat them raw. And one of this brood caught us, satyr sons and all, and keeps us now as slaves in his house. Polyphêmos he calls himself; and he's our master now. So instead of the dancing reels of Dionysos, we now herd this godless Cyclops's flocks. And because my satyr sons are young, they're shepherding young sheep on far-off hillsides. OIMOI! As for me, my duties take a more domestic turn. I fill up his troughs, I sweep out his cave, and I play chef for this Cyclops's disgusting meals. Which reminds me—duty is duty—and that cave needs sweeping of a lot more than dust before the master returns with his—sheep and goats. *(Sounds of singing SATYRS are heard from off.)* But here come my satyr sons now, driving on their flocks. But what's this, boys, what's this? Dancing? Lively, too, it looks like! Leaps and bounds! Like the old days! Young then! And Bakkhos and his lyre! And us dancing our lewd way to Althaia's house for an all-night revel!

(The CHORUS OF YOUNG SATYRS with SLAVE ATTENDANTS bursts in dancing a lively and energetic dance as they sing and drive on their flocks of sheep and goats.)

(Music. Song. Dance.)

YOUNG SATYRS: *(Sing.)*
> You there, fair goat of the fine pedigree,
> where are you off to, little scamp, where?
> That path you're treading leads off to the crags!
> Just see how lovely it is here.
> Look around!
> What more do you crave?
> Gentle breezes and green, green grass!
> Grass for grazing and breezes for lazing!
> And water purling its way to your trough
> near the cave where your babies bleat. Baaaa!

> And you there, master horny head!
> The dewy grass is good here, too!
> Why wander off?
> Over here, now,
> before I persuade you with a stone!
> In you go,
> in, go in,
> into the sheepfold, you guardian of guardians,
> while your master-shepherd Cyclops wanders!

> You, Madam Ewe,
> relieve those old tits!
> Get on back in where your babies bleat. Baaaa!
> They slept all day while you were off munching,

crunching fresh green grass, dewy grass.
They're baaing you,
baaaa! baaaa! baaing you, ewe,
their bellies distressed,
calling their mama to come back, do!
Back to your cave, mama ewe!

There is no Bakkhos,
no Bakkhos here,
no Bakkhos,
no dancing,
no twirling, swirling,
the god's Bakkhic wand,
no shouts, no ecstatic cries of Maenads,
or erotic beating,
beating of drums,
drums beating,
throbbing drums,
pounding as the earth spurts jets of god's wine,
our god's holy wine.
Where,
where is Dionysos?
God, where is your wine?
And Nysa's Nymphs?
Not here!
Where?
I want to shout,
to join in their song!
IAKKHOS!
IAKKHOS!
And chase down Aphroditê like the wind,
the wind,
in hot pursuit with barefoot Bakkhants!
Ah, Bakkhos!
Dear god Dionysos!
Dear Bakkhos, dear friend!
Where are you now?
Where are you running?
Your sun-bright hair tossing,

tossing in the wind!
Where are you now without your companions?
Without me,
who was once your happy servant,
who now slave for a one-eyed Cyclops,
dressed in filthy, stinking skins
and without you, lord,
without your friendship,
without your love.

(Music out.)

SILÊNOS: Enough of that for now! Silence! Into the cave with the beasties! Hear?

FIRST YOUNG SATYR: You heard him! Move! *(Several YOUNG SATYRS enter the cave with the animals.)* What's the rush, Father?

SILÊNOS: There's a ship, down there, pulled up on the beach! Greek, I think. And they're coming this way, sailors, oarsmen, and someone who looks like their captain! Who could they be? Why are they here? For supplies? Yes. Must be. Bags around their necks for food, vats for water. Oh those poor men! Little do they know what they're in for in Cyclopes country. Our master's no friend to man except as hors d'oeuvres. But sit on your tongue and we'll find out who they are who've landed here on Aitna's craggy lip.

ODYSSEUS: *(Enters with his crew.)* Strangers, friends, can you tell us, is there a stream nearby? We're out of water and near dying of thirst. Or someone to sell provisions to my starving sailors? *(To his men.)* By god, what's this? We seem to have stumbled onto an orgy! All these satyrs! Dionysos must be somewhere near. Look at them, milling around near the cave! I'll address the old one first. *(To SILÊNOS.)* Greetings!

SILÊNOS: And greetings to you, sir! Who are you and where from?

ODYSSEUS: Odysseus of Ithaka, king of Kephallênos.

SILÊNOS: Ah, the chatterer, bastard son of Sisyphos.

ODYSSEUS: That I am. But spare me your aspersions.

SILÊNOS: Where did you start from to end up in Sicily?

ODYSSEUS: Troy. We fought a war there.

SILÊNOS: And lost your way back home?

ODYSSEUS: Wind storms drove me here against my will.

SILÊNOS: Oh, no! The same bad luck drove *me* here!

ODYSSEUS: You, too? Against your will?

SILÊNOS: I was chasing pirates who'd kidnapped Dionysos.

ODYSSEUS: What is this country? Is it inhabited?

SILÊNOS: This is Mt. Aitna, Sicily's highest.

ODYSSEUS: But the walls, where are they? The city towers?

SILÊNOS: There are none, stranger. Men don't live here.

ODYSSEUS: What *does* live here? Wild animals?

SILÊNOS: Cyclopes, stranger. In caves, not houses.

ODYSSEUS: Who's their king? Or do they rule themselves?

SILÊNOS: It's live as live can. There's no order here.

ODYSSEUS: What do they eat? Do they plow and plant?

SILÊNOS: Milk and cheese, and the flesh of animals.

ODYSSEUS: And a bit of wine, I imagine, from the vine?

SILÊNOS: Sad to say, no! It's why they don't dance.

ODYSSEUS: Do they fear the gods and welcome strangers?

SILÊNOS: They're especially fond of male tartare.

ODYSSEUS: Surely they don't eat human flesh!

SILÊNOS: Your foot touches land, you're down the hatch.

ODYSSEUS: Where is he now, this Cyclops, in the—house?

SILÊNOS: Hunting wild beasts. On Aitna. With his hounds.

ODYSSEUS: Do you know how to help us escape this place?

SILÊNOS: You'll tell me, I'm sure. I'll do what I can.

ODYSSEUS: Sell us some bread. Our larders are bare.

SILÊNOS: I told you, all we have is meat.

ODYSSEUS: Not a bad way to strangle an appetite.

SILÊNOS: And then there's curdled cheese and cow's milk.

ODYSSEUS: Bring them out. Let's see what we're buying.

SILÊNOS: How much in gold is it worth to you?

ODYSSEUS: In gold? Nothing. But I have wine.

SILÊNOS: Oh, it's been *years* since we had it!

ODYSSEUS: I got it from Maron, the wine-god's son.

SILÊNOS: Maron? The child these arms once coddled?

ODYSSEUS: The son of Dionysos, if that helps you any.

SILÊNOS: Where is it? Onboard? The wine?

ODYSSEUS: The wine? Why, the wineskin's right here!

SILÊNOS: That? But *that's* not enough for a swallow!

ODYSSEUS: You couldn't drink this dry if you tried.

SILÊNOS: Something hocus-pocus about it?

ODYSSEUS: For every swallow, the flask gives two.

SILÊNOS: Ah, how lovely to hear! Two!

ODYSSEUS: Will you taste it now? Try it neat first.

SILÊNOS: Oh, I thought you'd never ask!

ODYSSEUS: Here, I've brought a cup for you, too.

SILÊNOS: Just to hear you pour it excites me!

ODYSSEUS: Done!

SILÊNOS: Oh! Oh my! What a fine bouquet!

ODYSSEUS: You saw that, did you?

SILÊNOS: No, but I smelled it.

ODYSSEUS: Then have a drink and know for sure.

SILÊNOS: Oh! It puts wings on my feet! I'm dancing!

ODYSSEUS: Went down nicely, did it?

SILÊNOS: All the way down to my tippy-tip-toes!

ODYSSEUS: And, yes, you'll have some money with it.

SILÊNOS: Just never stop pouring! Money be damned!

ODYSSEUS: Then bring out the cheese and the lamb.

SILÊNOS: It's yours! And I will! And my master can go hang! Gods, I'll do anything for one cup of this wine! I'd give it, give it all, give it all away! Every sheep, every goat, of every herd of every Cyclops! I'd plunge off Lovers' Leap in Leukadia, bobbing about in the bubbling brine, drunk as a skunk, happy as a hermit! Ohhhhh! The man who doesn't tipple is mad! One swig of the stuff'll make you stand tall! Then on to a basket of bouncing boobies, and down and down to the promised gland where there's dancing all night and who gives a damn! What a *kiss* I'd give a drink like this! And farewell, Cyclops, you one-eyed bastard, take a long look where the sun don't shine! *(Exit into cave.)*

FIRST YOUNG SATYR: Odysseus, we'd like a word.

ODYSSEUS: Why not? We're friends.

FIRST YOUNG SATYR: When you took Troy, did you take Helen, too?

ODYSSEUS: We wasted Priam's whole house and family.

FIRST YOUNG SATYR: Yes, but, I mean, did you "take" her, you know? All of you there, lined up for miles, bumping each other to be the first. Gang-banging Helen round the clock. I mean, she liked men by the barrel, the bitch. And then *he* comes along, drop-dead cute Paris, in his rainbow britches, needlework crotch, and legs, oh god, legs to die for! What a rage and fashion's slave was he! And pitter-pat goes her traitor's heart to see those twin pillars give proof to the pudding! And good Menelaos, left behind, poor man, for a trick. Ah, women, women! Down with them, down with them all, down to Hades— or at least down on me, the bitches!

SILÊNOS: *(Enters from the cave, loaded with cheeses and leading lambs.)* Here you are, my lord Odysseus, the pick of the flock, young succulent lambs, nurslings, even, baaing their way to your arms, and cheeses, cheeses from curdled milk. Take them. They're yours. Leave the cave now while you can, hurry, but first, maybe, if you could, another drink of that glorious wine? Oh, no! What will we do? The Cyclops!

ODYSSEUS: We're done for now, old man! Where can we run?

SILÊNOS: Into the cave. You won't be seen there.

ODYSSEUS: Are you insane? Into the trap?

SILÊNOS: It's safe. There are lots of places to hide.

ODYSSEUS: What are you saying! Never! Odysseus, who with his shield, single-handed, stood up to ten thousand Phrygians at Troy, flee from a single man? I'd be shamed! If I die, I'll die with honor. If I live, I'll live with my rightful reputation.

CYCLOPS: *(Enters carrying a club and with his hounds.)* Make way! Make way! What's all this? What's going on here? Your idea of a Bakkhic holiday, boy? I don't see your Dionysos about. Where's your clacking castanets, where's your drums? And why are you just standing around? How are my lambs? The newborns? Nursing at their mother's teats, hmm? And my cheeses. Has the milk been poured in buckets to curdle? Answer me, you hear? Or this club of mine will make you do more than talk! Look up when I'm talking to you, not down!

FIRST YOUNG SATYR: There you are! There! Looking up! Looking up at you! Looking right up at Zeus himself! God, I can see Orion!

CYCLOPS: How's my lunch coming along?

FIRST YOUNG SATYR: You've a real delicacy in store today.

CYCLOPS: And the mixing bowls? Filled with milk?

FIRST YOUNG SATYR: You can drink a whole vat full, if you like.

CYCLOPS: Cow's or sheep's milk? Or a blend of the two?

FIRST YOUNG SATYR: Whatever—as long as you don't drink *me*.

CYCLOPS: That'll be the day. You and your fancy footwork leaping inside me would be my death. Hey! What's this? Those people near my cave, who are they? Have pirates come ashore to rob us? And why are my lambs outside the cave, their bodies tied together with willow ropes? Eh? And cheese buckets scattered here and everywhere? And the old man, his bald head swollen red with bruises—

SILÊNOS: OMOI! OMOI! Pain, pain! I'm all a-fever with all their blows!

CYCLOPS: Who did it? Who beat you, old man? I'm asking!

SILÊNOS: They did! There! Because I wouldn't let them rob you!

CYCLOPS: But don't they know I'm a god? Don't they know I'm descended from gods?

SILÊNOS: I told them, but nothing stopped them plundering your property. First the cheeses, and then the sheep, and I tried to stop them, but nothing. They said they'd leash you like some dangerous dog and right under your very eye pull out your guts and lay them in your lap, and then whip your back till it was raw, and then, then tie you hand and foot and toss you into the darkest part of the ship, and, and then sell you off to hard labor, to lift heavy rocks or work a mill.

CYCLOPS: Oh, is that so? Well, you just get on in there, and fast, and sharpen up my carving knives and get a good fire blazing on the hearth. *(SILÊNOS starts in but stops.)* I'll slaughter them now and fill my belly with a feast fit for a king. I'll have one of them hot from the coals as a splendid barbecue, and the others boiled to a turn, nice and tender. I've had my fill of mountain meat—lions and stags and the like, and haven't had a man dinner in ages.

SILÊNOS: And quite right, too, master; variety's the spice of the proper table. Too much ordinary fare is tedious business, and we haven't had guests for a meal in far too long.

ODYSSEUS: Cyclops, fair play is fair play. It's only right to listen to your visitors. Now, we left our ship and came here hoping to buy food. We're all out. And this fellow here, once he'd had a drop of wine down his gullet, decided he'd sell us these sheep in exchange for a full cup of wine. Oh, and he was willing, too, no question there, no twisting *his* arm in the bargain. And as for what he says, you can't believe a word of it. He's lying because he's been caught red-handed peddling your property behind your back.

SILÊNOS: Who, me? Oh damn you!

ODYSSEUS: Yes, if I'm lying.

SILÊNOS: I swear, Cyclops, I swear by your father, mighty Poseidon, by Triton and great Nêreus, by Kalypso, and by Nêreus's dear daughters, and the holy swell of the ocean and every kind of fish in the sea, I swear—oh dear, dear master, most handsome Cyclops, dear, sweet master—never, I'd never sell your property to strangers! And, and if I'm lying, may destruction drag these sons of mine off to hell, my sons, the apple of my eye!

FIRST YOUNG SATYR: The hell with that! I saw you selling them food! And if *I'm* lying, may destruction drag my *father* off to rot in hell! Just don't hurt the strangers.

CYCLOPS: And who are you, that I should listen to you? I'd trust old Silênos here more than Rhadamanthys himself. So why should I think he's lying? But you, strangers, I have a few questions I'd like answered. Where are you coming from? What's your country? And what city are you from?

ODYSSEUS: By birth, we're Ithakan, and we're on our way home after sacking Troy. We were driven off course by storms at sea.

CYCLOPS: So it was you who tore down Troy-on-Skamander to pay for the theft of the worthless Helen.

ODYSSEUS: Indeed, one and the same who endured those terrible wars.

CYCLOPS: Shame on you, shame! Disgraceful mission! Go to war with Phrygia for the sake of a single woman!

ODYSSEUS: It was a god did it; don't blame us mortals. But you, Cyclops, you who are the son of a noble sea god, you should not—and we beg this of you—you should not do harm to innocent men of goodwill, not kill them in cold blood, men who simply by chance happened upon your house. What dignity is there in making a godless meal of us? Especially as you have us to thank for safeguarding your father's temples throughout all Greece. His harbor at Tainaron, and his caves at Cape Malea, are inviolate; Sunion's rock, so rich in silver and sacred to Athêna, is safe; as are the sanctuaries of Geraistos. Not once did we disgrace ourselves, or Greece, by surrendering Greek possessions to the Trojans. And you have a share in all this, Cyclops, living as you do at the far reaches of Hellas, here, under Aitna, where rock runs liquid fire.

But if it so happens you disagree, then consider the law among men that says that shipwrecked sailors must be fed and clothed, given gifts, and treated with the respect and hospitality of the suppliant, not be spitted like any piece of raw beef and roasted for the rude host's delectation and the satisfaction of his flabby paunch. Priam's land has already treated us to a mountain of bereavement, its battlefields soaked with the blood of thousands. Wives have been widowed and countless old women and gray-haired fathers sent childless to the grave. If you roast us and wolf us down for dinner, where will Greece turn when she's in need?

Change your mind, Cyclops, and forget your belly's gluttony. Be like the god you are, and do right, not evil. I beg you. Base profits have their price.

SILÊNOS: My advise, Cyclops, is gnaw the flesh off every bone of this braggart and don't forget the tongue. One good chew and you'll be as clever and glib as your guest.

CYCLOPS: Listen to me, little man, the only god the wise man worships is wealth. Everything else is babble and purple patches, and we've just now heard enough of that from you. As for my father's temples, I don't give a damn. I do very well without them. Why mention them in the first place? As for Zeus and his fabled thunderbolts, I couldn't be less afraid if I tried. Nor do I recognize Zeus a greater god than I am. I've never bothered about him before, why should I start now? And now I'll tell you why.

When Zeus sends down his rain from the heavens, I'm snug in my well-sealed little cave. And after a feast of roasted calf, I lie back and down a whole vat of milk, and, belly up, I pound my pud while Zeus farts out his thunder. And then when Thracian winter winds whip down from the icy north and wrap us in snow, I cover my body in soft skins and furs, bank the great blazing fire, and forget its snowing outside. And like it or not, the earth grows grass to feed my flocks all year long.

And as for sacrifices, I sacrifice to no god but the god of my own belly, the only, the greatest god of all. To eat, to drink, day in, day out, and to give oneself no pain, no worry—this is all the Zeus any man of sense needs.

As for lawmakers and complicators of men's life, they can go stuff it, while I satisfy the urge of my heart's delight, which, as I live and breathe at this very moment, is to gobble you up in one gulp.

As to the gifts to guests you mention, you'll have them in profusion and not find fault with me there. A fine fire to warm you, sea salt sent specially by my father, and a sturdy bronze cauldron to wear as armor, which when brought to the boil will render you a succulent dish.

So inside with you now and worship at the altar of the god of the cave where you are all invited to the feast.

ODYSSEUS: Oh by all the gods on Olympos, have I escaped the tribulations of the war at Troy and the sea's angry gales, only to end up here, washed ashore on the stony heart of this godless creature? Oh Athêna, Pallas, great daughter of Zeus, now, now, if ever you have helped me, I need it most! My danger at Troy was nothing compared to this.

And you, Zeus, Zeus Guardian of Guests, who live on high, throned among the bright stars, look down on me now, look kindly, on me and on these evil doings! For if you do not, if you ignore this calamity, what a waste of worship men have spent on your godhead!

(CYCLOPS herds ODYSSEUS and his CREW into the cave. SILÊNOS follows.)

(Music. Song. Dance.)

YOUNG SATYRS: *(Sing.)*
Open up, Cyclops,
open the gates,
open the fleshy O of your
gaping gullet;
your guests are boiled and basted and
broiled to a turn,

hot,
hot from the coals,
hot,
hot and ready to gnaw,
to rend,
to rend and tear as you
lounge in fine furs,
munching the flesh from their limbs.

But count me out,
count me out of your pleasure.
Eat away,
stuff your belly,
suit yourself!
Just let me keep away from this cave.
I've had enough of your dirty dealings,
your sacrifice of men,
your godless greed
for the flesh of your guests!

Damn your cruelty!
Damn your heartlessness!
Pitiless sacrificer of helpless strangers!
Enemy of guests who seek shelter!
Evil devourer of human flesh!

(Music out.)

ODYSSEUS: *(Enters from the cave.)* My god, what have I seen? What
horrible, disgusting evil have I witnessed? Evil I thought possible only
in myths, not in the workings of men!

FIRST YOUNG SATYR: What is it? Tell us, Odysseus. Has the godless
Cyclops bolted down your precious shipmates?

ODYSSEUS: He has—he searched out the plumpest two, the most
strapping of my men, then lifted them to his palm and ran his hand
all over their bodies, testing their firm flesh.

FIRST YOUNG SATYR: Poor men! But tell me what happened.

ODYSSEUS: We had no sooner entered the cavern when he built a fire by
tossing onto the hearth great logs from a giant oak, so heavy it would
take three wagons to pull them; then he set on the fire the bronze
cauldron to boil.

Not far from the blaze he spread on the ground a bed of fir
branches and set about milking the cows till a vat that held ninety
gallons had been filled and placed beside it an ivywood cup, four feet
or more from brim to brim, and what looked like six feet deep. Spits
of buckthorn came next, whose ends he burned in the fire and
trimmed down the rest with an ax.

When this was completed, and the cook from hell satisfied with
his labors, he grabbed up one of my men and with a single swipe slit
his throat and drained the blood into the cauldron. The other he
seized by the tendon of one heel and dashed his brains out on the
sharp ridge of a rock. He butchered them then, hacking away at their
fleshy parts with a terrible knife and roasting them on the fire. The
arms and legs he threw in the cauldron to boil.

Tears streaming down my face, I stood nearby him in my
wretchedness, no choice but to watch him work. The others, their
faces gray as ash, cowered farther off in crannies of the cave, terrified.

He finally fell back, the gluttonous demon, bloated with his gory
meal of my companions, and belched a staggering, foul stench from
his maw. It was then that some god inspired me! I filled a cup with
Maron's wine and offered it to him. "Come, Cyclops," I said, "son of
the sea god, come taste this drink from the grapes of Greek vines, a
godly drink, a ruby cup of Dionysos!"

His belly about to burst with his abominable meal, he downs
it in a single draught, and raising a hand in admiration says: "Oh
best of guests, dear friend, to follow a noble meal, you offer me a
noble drink!"

Seeing his pleasure, I filled another, knowing the wine would be
his undoing and make him pay the price. Eventually, the wine fired
him to sing, and I continued pouring cup after cup, enough to make
even his stony heart beat a bit more fondly.

So there we are, he, inside, blasting the air with his blasted airs till
the cavern echoes, and my crew not far away, wailing hot tears. You
can hear the noise out here. But I slipped out quietly to escape, and
take you all with me if you agree.

So tell me, are you ready to be free of this monster and live with
the Naiads in Dionysos's halls? Your father back there in the cave

agrees, but he's so oblivious from enjoying the wine too much, he's stuck to the cup like a bird caught in lime, flapping its feeble wings in vain.

But you, you're young, you're strong! Get out of here! Get back to Dionysos, not at all like this savage Cyclops of yours!

FIRST YOUNG SATYR: Dear, good friend, if only we could see that day of freedom from this godless creature! Besides, this piteous pole of mine has lived the bachelor life too long and needs a place to put its head.

ODYSSEUS: Then listen to the revenge I've planned for the beast, and how to set you free.

FIRST YOUNG SATYR: I'd rather hear of the Cyclops's death than all the lyres in Asia!

ODYSSEUS: Cyclops is so infatuated with the drink, he wants to take it to his relatives for a party.

FIRST YOUNG SATYR: I see. Oh, yes, yes! You'll ambush him in the woods, and slit his throat or—or push him off a cliff.

ODYSSEUS: Thank you, but no—I work with cunning.

FIRST YOUNG SATYR: Tell us, we're all ears! We've heard about your cleverness.

ODYSSEUS: First of all, I want to keep him here, stop him from visiting his brother Cyclopes. I'll tell him he has a life of pleasure ahead, but only if he doesn't share the drink. Then when he falls asleep—and he will, for Bakkhos knows his business—I'll take the olive stake I saw in the hall, sharpen it to a point with my sword, and when that's done place it in the fire. Once it catches and is burning well, I'll take it hot as coals from the flame, and lifting it high ram it home into the monster's face, into his eye, his only eye, and melt that eye with fire. Then, like a joiner with his auger and belt, I'll twirl the stake round and round, deeper, deeper, till the jelly is dry as dust.

FIRST YOUNG SATYR: Bravo! Bravo! Such inventions drive me mad with joy!

ODYSSEUS: That done, you and my friends and your old father will board my ebony ship and set sail from this godforsaken Sicily.

FIRST YOUNG SATYR: Is there a way I could share in this ritual? My hand on the stake when you put out his eye, as men do with libations to the gods? I want a part in this bloody business.

ODYSSEUS: You must. The brand is immense. You'll help to hold it.

FIRST YOUNG SATYR: I could shoulder the weight of a hundred wagons if only I could smoke out that wasps' nest of this Cyclops's eye!

ODYSSEUS: You know my plan. Say nothing. Not a word. But do as I say. I'm not about to leave my friends behind in the cave and save only myself. *(Exit into cave.)*

(Music. Song. Dance.)

YOUNG SATYRS I: *(Sing.)*
    Tell me, tell me,
    who'll be first,
    who'll be first with his
    hand on the shaft,
    the flaming poker
    to put out his eye,
    and who,
    who second,
    who comes second,
    and then, and then,
    in with it,
    in,
    under the eyebrow,
    fizzle his eye,
    sizzle his sight,
    but how do we hold it,
    how,
    who'll tell me?

YOUNG SATYRS II: *(Sing from the cave.)*
>   Shhh!
>   Shhh!
>   He's coming,
>   here he comes,
>   stinking drunk,
>   sloshed,
>   from his rocky home,
>   singing,
>   braying,
>   flaying some terrible tune!
>   He should be made to pay for it dearly,
>   this offense to sense,
>   this awful offense!
>   Let's sing him a song,
>   a proper song,
>   a reveler's song,
>   to teach him good taste,
>   the tasteless buffoon!
>   Just a while,
>   a little while,
>   and he will be blind.

(Enter the CYCLOPS from the cave, followed by SILÊNOS carrying the wineskin and cup, and ODYSSEUS carrying a pitcher and mixing bowl.)

YOUNG SATYRS: *(Sing.)*
>   That man is happy,
>   that man who shouts,
>   who shouts the Bakkhic,
>   the Bakkhi's cry,
>   EVOHÈ!
>   EVOHÈ!
>   Off to the lusty revels,
>   EVOHÈ!
>   EVOHÈ!
>   heart's delight,
>   the god's loved juice,
>   the lord's sweet nectar,
>   EVOHÈ!

the master's liquid fire in his veins,
sailing,
driving him,
EVOHÈ!
EVOHÈ!
onward to conquest,
on to adventure,
EVOHÈ!
on the flower-laid couch,
adventure,
conquest,
EVOHÈ!
EVOHÈ!
one hand toying,
playing, caressing,
his strapping friend's treasures,
EVOHÈ!
the other,
other,
in the soft, dewy cleft
of his other dear.
With hair agleam with
sweet oil and myrrh,
he cries from between them:
EVOHÈ!
EVOHÈ!
from between them he cries:
"Who will open the gates to me first?"

CYCLOPS: *(Sings.)*
PAPAPAPAI!
PAPAPAPAI!
I'm filled,
oh I'm filled,
filled high with wine!
Filled to the tip-top
decks of my belly!
What a lovely feast!
What lovely cheer!
I'm off to bring cheer,

springtime cheer,
to my brothers' house,
spring cheer
to my brothers,
my brother Cyclopes.
Come, friend, come,
give me the wineskin.

YOUNG SATYRS: *(Sing.)*
Behold the groom,
the lover,
the handsome,
comes,
he comes,
eye a-sparkle!

CYCLOPS: *(Sings.)*
Who will love me?
I long! I long!

FIRST YOUNG SATYR: *(Sings.)*
Watch out,
I think he's
out for my ass.

YOUNG SATYRS: *(Sing.)*
In the cool,
cool of the cave
a lad,
a tight lad and a dewy lass,
await his coming.
Why wait for the night?
Bring on the torch!
Lead him on!
Blood will flow soon
in the cool of the cave.

(Music out.)

ODYSSEUS: Listen to me, Cyclops, because I know quite well this Dionysos you've been drinking.

CYCLOPS: Dionysos? You mean the god's the wine?

ODYSSEUS: Nothing less. The source of all joy.

CYCLOPS: At least I can say I belch him with pleasure.

ODYSSEUS: That's the god, all right, and he harms no one.

CYCLOPS: What kind of god lives in a wineskin?

ODYSSEUS: Wherever he is, he's at his ease.

CYCLOPS: Gods shouldn't dress in wineskins.

ODYSSEUS: Why not, if you like him? Or don't you?

CYCLOPS: Hate the wineskin, love the wine.

ODYSSEUS: In that case, stay and drink your fill.

CYCLOPS: I think I should share the drink with my brothers.

ODYSSEUS: Keep it for yourself and your honor is greater.

CYCLOPS: But I'd be a better brother if I shared.

ODYSSEUS: But partying often ends in brawls.

CYCLOPS: Sloshed I may be, but they wouldn't dare touch me.

ODYSSEUS: Old friend, you should stay at home when drunk.

CYCLOPS: But the man who drinks alone is a fool.

ODYSSEUS: Yet it's wise to stay at home when you're drunk.

CYCLOPS: What do you say, Silênos? Do we stay?

SILÊNOS: Stay? Why not? Who needs more drunks?

ODYSSEUS: Besides, the ground here is flowery and soft.

SILÊNOS: And what can be better than a drink in the sun? Take a load off, Cyclops, it's good to lie down.

(The CYCLOPS lies down, and SILÊNOS puts the mixing bowl behind him.)

CYCLOPS: Hey! Why'd you put that bowl behind me?

SILÊNOS: So nobody tips it over, Cyclops.

CYCLOPS: I know you! You're out to steal a drink! Put it there between us. *(SILÊNOS does.)* So, stranger, what's your name?

ODYSSEUS: My name? My name's Nobody. But what gift will you give me so that I can thank you?

CYCLOPS: Gift? Well, I'll eat you the last of your crew.

SILÊNOS: Fine gift you've given your guest, Cyclops! *(He sneaks a drink.)*

CYCLOPS: You! What are you doing? Drinking on the sly?

SILÊNOS: Me? No! No-no! The wine just had an urge to kiss me— says I'm cute.

CYCLOPS: It's you love the wine, not the wine you!

SILÊNOS: Not true! It finds me irresistible! I'm drop-dead gorgeous, it says.

CYCLOPS: You're here to pour, now pour! When it's full, give it to me!

SILÊNOS: Hmm. How's the mixture? Just a taste, to see.

CYCLOPS: You're driving me out of my mind! Just give it here now, slave!

SILÊNOS: Not before I see you crowned—*(Puts a flowery wreath on the CYCLOPS.)* and taken a little nip. *(He empties the cup.)*

CYCLOPS: This wine pourer's a thief!

SILÊNOS: Yes, but how sweet the wine is. Here it comes—just wipe your mouth first.

CYCLOPS: There! Clean as a whistle.

SILÊNOS: Your arm, crook it gracefully, yes, and then drink—as you see me doing, so far, so far back you can't see me anymore.

CYCLOPS: What the hell's going on here?

SILÊNOS: There, like that! And happily down the hatch we have it!

CYCLOPS: Stranger, be my pourer!

ODYSSEUS: At least I'm not unacquainted with the substance.

CYCLOPS: All right, all right, pour!

ODYSSEUS: I'm pouring, I'm pouring, just don't get excited.

CYCLOPS: That's easy to say when you're sober.

ODYSSEUS: There! Skoal! Bottoms up! And don't say die till the cup is dry!

CYCLOPS: *(Drinking.)* PAPAPAPAIIIIII! What a plant this grapevine is!

ODYSSEUS: Drink deep after stuffing your belly to bursting and you'll sleep like a baby. But leave even a dribble and the wine god makes a desert of your gullet. *(Pours another and the CYCLOPS drinks it dry in a single gulp.)*

CYCLOPS: IOOOOO! IOOOOO! I almost drowned in there! Such pleasure! Ah! Heaven—heaven and—heaven and earth, heaven and earth are all swirling, swirling—together—swirling together—swimming—all, all mixed up! And there, there's Zeus's throne—his throne—and the reeling wheeling whirling of the holy gods! *(The SATYRS dance around him with taunting suggestiveness.)* Do I give them a kiss? No, no, not you, not you or not you. I feel so seduced. No, no! Screw you, you taunting little Graces? What are you— no, that's enough, enough! Here's my Ganymede. My own little prick tease. Off to bed, off to bed with him now. He's better than all you Graces in a bundle. And cuter, cuter, my own sweet Ganymede. I've always hankered after boys more than girls.

SILÊNOS: What, Cyclops, I'm Zeus's Ganymede?

CYCLOPS: By Zeus, you are, and I'm abducting you from Dardanos.

SILÊNOS: Oh, I'm done for, sons! Something foul's in the offing!

CYCLOPS: What, you don't like your lovers drunk?

SILÊNOS: AIIII! The bitter wine I'll have to suck now!

(Exit the CYCLOPS, dragging a protesting SILÊNOS, into the cave.)

ODYSSEUS: Noble sons of Dionysos, the time has come. He's in the cave, and soon, when he's sleeping, he'll belch up his foul meal of my men's flesh. The brand we'll use is ready, and our task is set: to smoke out the eye of the Cyclops. Let's show the stuff you're made of.

FIRST YOUNG SATYR: Our hearts are hard as stone. But hurry on in, or my father'll be the one gets shafted. Everything here is GO!

ODYSSEUS: Hephaistos, fire god and lord of Aitna, rid yourself of this plague of a neighbor! Burn out the eye of this ungodly pest! And you, child of Night, black Night, Sleep, come with all your power and overwhelm this god-detested beast! After his glorious victories at Troy, do not desert Odysseus and his crew to an inglorious end at the hands of a creature who respects neither gods nor men. For if you do, we have no choice but to think Chance a god, and the gods as less than Chance. *(Exit into cave.)*

(Music. Song. Dance.)

YOUNG SATYRS: *(Sing.)*
>Soon,
>soon-soon,
>the tongs,
>the grim tongs,
>will grip the great neck of the
>guest-eating monster!
>Soon fire
>will put out his great, shining eye.
>The tree-large torch
>waits hidden in the coals.
>Wine do your work,
>work,
>do your work,
>gouge out his eye,
>bore it out,
>bore,
>let the blood of the raving
>Cyclops flow!
>Make him pay for his
>drunken pleasure.
>And then I long,
>I long for the god,
>the ivy-crowned god,
>god Dionysos.
>Will I ever know
>the joy of that day?

(Music out.)

ODYSSEUS: *(Enters from cave.)* For god's sake, you animals, shut your mouths! Quiet! I don't want to hear a word. Not a breath, not a blink, not a cough. If he wakes before his eye is gouged with fire it's over, everything, all in vain.

FIRST YOUNG SATYR: We're quiet. We're whispering. Our lips are sealed.

ODYSSEUS: All right, then, to work. Inside with you, and all hands on the stake. It's glowing nicely, red as coals.

FIRST YOUNG SATYR: Where do we stand? Who grabs the stake first? That way we all have our share in searing the Cyclops's eye.

SATYR 1: Over here by the cave mouth we're too far away to stick his eye.

SATYR 2: And I've just got leg cramps.

SATYR 3: Me, too, me, too! Just standing around here I sprained my ankle. Can't think how.

ODYSSEUS: Sprained your ankle? Standing around?

SATYR 3: Looks like. And now my eye's filled with dust.

ODYSSEUS: Worthless cowards! Every one of them! Not worth a damn!

FIRST YOUNG SATYR: Coward, am I? Coward because I value my neck? My back? My spine? Because I like my teeth intact? Well, I know a spell of Orpheus so grand it'll make the stake rise up on its own, march on over to that one-eyed bastard's skull, and bang! light that son of the earth like a torch!

ODYSSEUS: I've always known you for what you are, it's just that now I know it better. At least I have my friends in there to bank on, and if you're too weak to lend a hand, the least you could do is cheer us on. *(Exit into cave.)*

FIRST YOUNG SATYR: I will, I will! As long as his mercenaries run my risks, I'll shout myself hoarse with encouragement! Burn the Cyclops! Burn the Cyclops!

(Music. Song. Dance.)

YOUNG SATYRS: *(Sing.)*

Go! Go!
Stick it to him!
Stick it!
Give him the shaft!
Down with the bastard!
Burn, burn,
burn out his eye!
Burn out the guest eater!
Burn the herdsman,
the shepherd of Aitna!
Burn him,
torch him,
fry him to a crisp!
Burn him to a cinder!
Go, men, go!
Burn out his lights!
Bugger his eye!
Ram it home!
Shaft him!
Twist and pull,
twist and pull!
Careful,
he's in pain!
Don't let him hurt you!

(Music out.)

CYCLOPS: *(Enters from the cave with a bloodied face.)* AIIIIIIII! AIIIIIIII!
My eyeeeeee! My eyeeeeee! Scorched to a cinder!

FIRST YOUNG SATYR: That's a catchy tune, Cyclops, sing it again.

CYCLOPS: IOOOOOOO! IOOOOOOO! You've killed me, murdered
me, what a miserable end! Undone, undone! But you won't escape me,
never escape this cave, I'll get you, I'll punish you! Evil bastards, evil!
I'll bar the entrance, stand in the doorway, spread out my hands, block
the way! Like this, like this! *(He blocks the cave mouth.)*

FIRST YOUNG SATYR: What's all the shouting for, Cyclops?

CYCLOPS: I'm ruined!

FIRST YOUNG SATYR: You certainly do look a fright.

CYCLOPS: And miserable! Miserable!

FIRST YOUNG SATYR: What? Were you drunk? Did you fall in the fire?

CYCLOPS: Nobody destroyed me!

FIRST YOUNG SATYR: Then nobody has wronged you.

CYCLOPS: Nobody blinded me.

FIRST YOUNG SATYR: So, then, you're not blind.

CYCLOPS: I'm blind, can't you hear!

FIRST YOUNG SATYR: But how could nobody blind you?

CYCLOPS: Don't make fun of me! Where is he? Where's Nobody?

FIRST YOUNG SATYR: Nowhere, Cyclops.

CYCLOPS: It was him, that abominable guest, destroyed me.
     Did me in with his drink.

FIRST YOUNG SATYR: When wine gets a hold, he's not easy to
     grapple with.

CYCLOPS: For god's sake, tell me, have they left, or are they still here?

FIRST YOUNG SATYR: Still here. Standing. Quiet as mice. Under the
     overhang.

CYCLOPS: To my left? To my right?

FIRST YOUNG SATYR: Your right.

(The CYCLOPS stumbles right; ODYSSEUS, his CREW, and SILÊNOS emerge silently from the cave.)

CYCLOPS: Where?

FIRST YOUNG SATYR: Next to the cliff. Got them yet?

CYCLOPS: No, but I've broken my head on the rock! AIIIIIII!

FIRST YOUNG SATYR: And while you were doing that, they gave you the slip.

CYCLOPS: Which way? This way? Where'd you say?

FIRST YOUNG SATYR: No, over here.

CYCLOPS: And where the hell's that?

FIRST YOUNG SATYR: Turn. Turn around. This way. Your left.

CYCLOPS: You're laughing at me, mocking my pain!

FIRST YOUNG SATYR: No, not now. He's right there in front of you.

CYCLOPS: Fiend! Demon! Where the hell are you hiding?

ODYSSEUS: Far enough away to keep Odysseus safe.

CYCLOPS: What's that? Hmm? What's this new name?

ODYSSEUS: Odysseus, the very name my father gave me. This payment you've made, Cyclops, is your destiny for the evil meal you made of my men. And my burning Troy to the ground would have been nothing if I hadn't punished you for murdering my companions.

CYCLOPS: AIIII! AIIII! The ancient oracle is now fulfilled! On your way from Troy I would be blinded by you, it said, as now I am. But it also prophesied that you would pay for this outrage by drifting and wandering the seas for what would seem an eternity.

ODYSSEUS: And I say, go stuff it! What you say *will* happen has already happened. But I'm off to the beach now, Cyclops. I have a ship there waiting to set sail, to take me across the Sicilian sea and home.

(Exeunt ODYSSEUS and his men carrying the provisions and leading the lambs. SILÊNOS follows.)

CYCLOPS: Oh, no you won't. You'll see. As for me, blind or not, I'll make my way to the top of this cliff through the tunnel in the back of my cave, tear off a piece of this rock, and hurl it after you till you're smashed to smithereens, all of you, you, your crew, your men. You wait— *(Exit into cave.)*

FIRST YOUNG SATYR: We're off now to be shipmates with Odysseus, and then to be the best of slaves to Dionysos.

(Exeunt the YOUNG SATYRS.)

*

ACHAIANS: another designation for Greeks or Hellenes.

ACHAIOS: son of Xouthos and Kreousa.

ACHILLEUS: greatest of Greek warriors in the war at Troy; killed Hêktor; was killed by Paris.

AEGEAN: the sea between Greece and Turkey; an arm of the Mediterranean.

AGAMEMNON: king of Mykenê; brother of Menelaos; leader of the Greeks against Troy; husband of Klytaimnêstra; killed by his wife.

AGLAUROS: wife of Kekrops.

AIAKOS: king of Aigina; judge of souls; keeper of the keys of Hades.

AIAS: Greek hero from Salamis at Troy; killed himself when he was denied the arms of Achilleus.

AIGIKORÊS: son of Ion.

AIOLOS: son of Zeus; father of Xouthos; king of the winds.

AITNA: volcano in eastern Sicily; Cyclopes live on its slopes.

ALEXANDROS: another name for Paris.

ALPHEIOS: river that flows past Olympia in the Peloponnesos.

ALTHAIA: daughter of Dionysos and Dêianeira.

AMAZONS: nation of warrior women of legend who lived around the Black Sea; Heraklês battled them.

AMPHITRITÊ: goddess; wife of Poseidon.

ANDROMACHÊ: daughter of Priam and Hêkabê; wife of Hêktor; mother of Astyanax.

APHRODITÊ: goddess of sexual love, beauty, and fertility; wife of Hephaistos and lover of Arês; said to have been born out of the sea foam; also known as Kypris after the island that was the seat of her cult; one of the three goddesses in the beauty competition judged by Paris: to win the contest, she offered Helen as a bribe to Paris, thus inciting the Trojan War.

APOLLO: born on Delos; one of the twelve Olympian gods; symbol of light, youth, and beauty; synonymous with music, poetry, medicine, and prophecy; his temple of oracular prophecy at Delphi in central Greece was the most famous in the ancient world; twin brother of Artemis; archer renowned for his unfailing aim.

ARCADIA: mountainous province in the Peloponnesos.

AREOPAGOS: hill of Arês; a rocky hill northwest of the Athenian Akropolis; site of the court of justice that was situated there.

ARÊS: god of war unpopular among the Greeks; son of Zeus and Hera; lover of Aphroditê and probably father of Eros.

ARGADÊS: son of Ion.

ARGIVE: Homeric name for any Greek; a native of Argos; of or pertaining to ancient Argos.

ARGOS: ancient city in southeastern Greece in the northeastern Peloponnesos; also a region in which the city is contained.

ARTEMIS: daughter of Zeus and Hera; twin sister of Apollo; virgin huntress associated with wild places and animals; primitive birth goddess; known as an archer.

ASTYANAX: son of Andromachê and Hêktor; thrown from the walls of Troy by the Greeks.

ATHÊNA: daughter of Zeus, who sprang fully armed from his head; goddess of wisdom, skills, and warfare; chief defender of the Greeks at Troy; particular defender of Odysseus; in competition with Poseidon, who produced the horse, she won the favor of Athens by producing the olive tree, considered the more valuable, and for which she was made patron of Athens, her namesake.

ATHENS: independent city-state in southeastern Greece; center of Greek culture in the fifth-century BCE, when it was the capital of ancient Attika.

ATLAS: one of the race of Giants; as punishment for a revolt against Zeus, he was made to support the heavens with his head and hands.

ATTIKA: a peninsula of southeastern Greece; in ancient times a region dominated by Athens, its chief city.

ATREUS: king of Mykenê; father of Agamemnon and Menelaos; brother of Thyestes.

AULIS: port in Boiotia where the Greek fleet gathered to sail to Troy.

BAKKHOS: also known as Dionysos.

BELLEROPHON: hero; rode the winged horse Pegasos.

BRAURON: in Attika; site of a temple of Artemis.

CAPE MALEA: a perilous promontory off the southern coast of the Peloponnesos.

CASTALIA: scared spring near Delphi on Mount Parnassos.

CHALKIS: principal city of Euboia.

CHARYBDIS: whirlpool in a strait opposite Scylla.

CIRCÊ: goddess; sorceress; daughter of Hêlios.

CLASHING ROCKS: the Symplêgades; rocks guarding the entrance to the Bosporos; they clashed together to crush ships trying to sail through.

CYCLOPES: one-eyed giants who lived in caves on the slopes of Aitna in Sicily; in some versions the makers of Zeus's thunderbolts.

DANAANS: another name for Greeks or Hellenes.

DANAOS: king of Argos; gave his name to the Danaans; father of fifty daughters who fled from marriage to their Egyptian cousins.

DARDANOS: ancestor of Priam; founded Troy.

DELOS: island in the Aegean; birthplace of Apollo and Artemis.

DELPHI: Greek city on the southern slopes of Mount Parnassos in central Greece; site of the most famous oracle of Apollo; in the Greek world considered the world navel.

DÊMÊTER: Greek corn goddess; associated with fertility; a mother goddess; mother of Persephonê.

DIONYSOS: god of divine inspiration and the release of mass emotion; associated with wine, fruitfulness, and vegetation; son of Zeus and Semelê; leader of the Bakkhai; bestower of ecstasy; worshipped in a cult centered around orgiastic rites and veiled in great mystery; also known as Iakkhos and Bakkhos.

DIOSKOUROI: the heavenly twins Kastor and Polydeukês; sons of Zeus (or Tyndareos) by Lêda; deified by Zeus.

DIRKÊ: one of the two major rivers near Thebes.

DOROS: son of Xouthos and Kreousa.

EIDO: another name for Theonoê.

ÊLEKTRA: daughter of Agamemnon and Klytaimnêstra; brother of Orestês, Antigonê, and Ismênê.

ELEUSIS: town in Attika fourteen miles west of Athens; site in classical times of a mystical religious festival, the Eleusinian Mysteries, in which initiates celebrated Dêmêter, Persephonê, and Dionysos.

ENKELADOS: one of the Giants who battled the Olympians.

ERECHTHEUS: in classical times considered the first or an early king of Athens; born of the earth; raised by Athêna; worshipped with Athêna on the Athenian Akropolis; father of Kreousa.

ERICHTHONIOS: king of Athens; father of Erechtheus; grandfather of Kreousa.

EUBOIA: island in the west Aegean Sea; second largest island in the Greek archipelago; conquered by Athens with the help of Xouthos.

EURIPOS: channel between Boiotia and the island of Euboia; location of Aulis.

EUROTAS: river of Sparta.

EUXINE SEA: the Black Sea.

FURIES: the three terrible female spirits with snaky hair who punish the doers of unavenged crimes; spirits of vengeance.

GALENEIA: a sea nymph representing calm.

GANYMEDE: Trojan youth beloved of Zeus; swept up by Zeus's eagle to Olympos; served as cupbearer of the gods.

GELEON: son of Ion.

GIANTS: sons of Uranus and Earth; revolted against the Olympian gods.

GORGON: Medusa; one of three sisters killed by Perseus; to look at her was to be turned to stone.

GRACES: three goddesses associated with ideals of beauty and grace.

GREAT MOTHER: Dêmêter; goddess of fertility, grain, and agriculture; mother of Persephonê.

HADES: underworld abode of the souls of the dead; lord of the kingdom bearing his name; son of Kronos and Rhea; brother of Zeus, Dêmêter, and Poseidon; husband of Persephonê.

HÊKABÊ: queen and wife of Priam of Troy; mother of Kassandra, Hêktor, Paris, Polyxenê, and Polydoros.

HALAI: in Attika; site of a temple to Artemis.

HEKATE: a primitive goddess of the underworld later associated with Artemis; connected with sorcery and black magic.

HELEN: daughter of Zeus and Lêda; wife of Menelaos of Sparta; eloped with Paris to Troy and caused the Trojan War.

HELENOS: Trojan prophet and warrior.

HELLAS: originally a small territory and tribe in southern Thessaly; eventually applied to all of Greece.

HEPHAISTOS: lame son of Zeus and Hera; god of fire and the forge.

HERA: goddess; daughter of Kronos; sister and wife of Zeus.

HERAKLÊS: son of Zeus and Alkmênê; of outstanding strength, size, and courage; known for the performance of twelve immense labors imposed upon him by Eurystheus; fought with the Olympian gods against the Giants.

HERMÊS: Olympian god; son of Zeus and Maia; messenger and herald of the gods; associated with commerce, cunning, theft, travelers, and rascals.

HERMIONÊ: daughter of Menelaos and Helen; wife of Neoptolemos.

HIPPODAMIA: daughter of Oinomaös.

HOPLÊS: son of Ion.

HYACINTHOS: in a discus-throwing competition with Achilleus, he was killed when the North and the West Winds, jealous of Achilleus's love for him, blew the discus so that it killed him; wherever his blood fell hyacinths sprouted.

IDA: mountain and range southeast of Troy; favored seat of Zeus.

ILION: another name for Troy.

IO: daughter of Inachos; loved by Zeus; changed to a cow by a jealous Hera.

IOLAOS: son of Iphiklês; half-brother and companion to Heraklês.

ION: son of Apollo by Kreousa; servant in Apollo's temple at Delphi.

IONIA: ancient region in West Asia Minor, including a coastal strip and the islands of Samos and Kios colonized by Athens.

IPHIGENEIA: daughter of Agamemnon and Klytaimnêstra; sacrificed by Agamemnon at Aulis so that the Greek ships could embark for Troy.

ISTHMUS: the Isthmus of Korinth; connects the Peloponnesos and mainland Greece.

ITHAKA: island off the west coast of Greece; home of Odysseus.

KALKAS: Greek prophet of Agamemnon's army.

KALLISTO: Arcadian nymph; beloved of Zeus; Hera turns her into a bear; Zeus makes of her a constellation.

KALYPSO: detained Odysseus for seven years on her island during his voyage home from Troy.

KARYSTIAN ROCK: opposite Halai and Brouron.

KASSANDRA: daughter of Priam and Hêkabê; prophetess whose prophecies were never believed; taken as mistress by Agamemnon; killed by Klytaimnêstra.

KASTOR: twin brother of Polydeukês; sons of Zeus (or Tyndareos) by Leda; deified by Zeus; the Dioskouroi.

KEKROPS: first king of Athens; born of the earth; half-snake, half-man.

KLYTAIMNÊSTRA: wife of Agamemnon who killed him on his return from Troy; in turn killed by her son Orestês.

KREOUSA: daughter of Erechtheus and Praxithea; wife of Xouthos; mother of Ion by Apollo.

KRETE: island in the Aegean.

KYPRIS: goddess of love; also known as Aphroditê; named after the island of her birth.

LAËRTÊS: father of Odysseus.

LAOMEDON: king of Troy; father of Priam.

LÊDA: mother of Helen, Klytaimnêstra, and the Dioskouroi.

LÊTO: mother of Apollo and Artemis by Zeus.

LEUKADIA: island off the coast of Ithaka.

LEUKIPPOS: his daughters, Phoebe and Hilira, were carried off by the Dioskouroi and in one version were killed by the girls' cousins.

LIBYA: the Greek name for Africa.

MAIA: daughter of Atlas; mother of Hermês.

MARON: priest of Apollo at Ismaros; spared by Odysseus when he raided his city on the way home from Troy; gave Odysseus a case of wine in thanks.

MENELAOS: brother of Agamemnon; husband of Helen; king of Sparta.

MEROPS: king of Ethiopia.

MUSES: nine goddesses who preside over literature, the arts, and the sciences.

MYKENÊ: city in the Peloponnesos near Argos.

NAIADS: nymphs who lived in brooks and springs.

NAUPLIA: a coastal town in Argos.

NEOPTOLEMOS: son of Achilleus; married Hermionê; is killed by Orestês.

NÊRÊIDS: fifty nymphs of the sea; daughters of Nêreus.

NÊREUS: sea god; father of the fifty Nêrêids.

NILE: river in Egypt.

NYMPHS: female spirits of nature.

ODYSSEUS: son of Laërtes; king of Ithaka; known for his wily and cunning nature; hero of Homer's *Odyssey.*

OINOMAÖS: king of Pisa; father of Hippodamia, who he promised to anyone who beat him in a chariot race; Pelops won with trickery.

OLYMPOS: mountain in northeastern Thessaly; seat of the Olympian gods.

ORESTÊS: son of Agamemnon and Klytaimnêstra; smuggled to Phokis as a child for safekeeping during the Trojan War; kills his mother in revenge for her murder of Agamemnon.

ORION: gigantic hunter; turned by Zeus into a constellation.

PALLAS: alternate name for Athêna.

PAN: Arkadian god; son of Hermês and a nymph; a man with goat's legs, horns, and ears; god of fields, woods, shepherds, and flocks.

PARIS: son of Priam and Hêkabê; abducted Helen from Sparta.

PARNASSOS: mountain in Phokis in central Greece; on its southern slope is Delphi.

PELEUS: king of Thessaly; mortal married to the Nêrêid Thetis; father of Achilleus.

PELOPS: king of Argos; father of Atreus; grandfather of Agamemnon and Menelaos; gave his name to the Peloponnesos.

PERGAMON: a city near Troy.

PERSEPHONÊ: daughter of Zeus and Dêmêter; wife of Hades; queen of the underworld; also known as Korê.

PERSEUS: ancestor of Heraklês and Alkmênê; decapitates the Gorgon Medusa.

PHINEUS: king of Thynia, near the Bosporos; tormented by Harpies.

PHOIBOS: epithet of Apollo; means bright.

PHOKIS: region of Greece near Delphi; kingdom of Strophios and Pyladês.

PHRYGIA: general region in which Troy was situated.

PISA: country of Olympia; kingdom of Oinomaôs.

PLEIADES: seven-star constellation; daughters of Atlas placed in the heavens by Zeus.

POLYPHÊMOS: a Cyclops; son of Poseidon; lives on the slopes of Aitna in Sicily.

POLYXENÊ: daughter of Priam and Hêkabê; sacrificed on the tomb of Achilleus.

POSEIDON: son of Kronos and Rhea; god of the sea; brother to Zeus.

PRIAM: king of Troy; husband of Hêkabê; killed by Achilleus's son Neoptolemos at Troy.

PROMÊTHEUS: A Titan god who fought on the side of Zeus and the Olympians against his brother Titans.

PROTEUS: king of Egypt; father of Theoklymenos and Theonoê.

PSAMATHÊ: sea nymph.

PYLADÊS: son of Strophios; friend-lover of Orestês; husband of Êlektra.

PYTHIAN: relating to the temple of Apollo at Delphi.

RHION: city at the western mouth of the Gulf of Korinth.

SALAMIS: island in the bay of Eleusis; kingdom of Telamon; also capital city of Cyprus and kingdom of Teükros.

SATYRS: minor forest deities; human form but with goat's ears, horns, tail, and legs; associated with the revelry of Dionysos; sometimes the sons of Silênos.

SCYLLA: dangerous rock on the Italian side of the Straits of Messina, opposite the whirlpool Charybdis; in classical mythology personified as a female monster.

SICILY: large island at the foot of the boot of Italy; believed in ancient times the habitat of the Cyclopes.

SIDON: city in Syria on the Mediterranean coast.

SILÊNOS: drinking companion of Dionysos; in *Cyclops,* father of the satyrs.

SIMOÏS: river at Troy.

SIRENS: underworld goddess enchantresses who lured sailors to their island to eat them; also conduct the dead to Hades and mourn for them.

SKAMANDER: major river of Troy.

SPARTA: principal city in the southern Peloponnesos

STROPHIOS: king of Phokis; father of Pyladês; brother-in-law of Agamemnon.

SUNION: southernmost promontory of Attika.

TALTHYBIOS: Greek herald.

TANTALOS: king of Phrygia; son of Zeus; father of Pelops.

TAURIS: the Taurian peninsula to which Iphigeneia was transported from Aulis by Artemis.

TELAMON: king of Salamis; father of Aias and Teükros; exiled with Peleus from Aigina by Aiakos for killing Phokos.

TEÜKROS: banished by Telamon from Salamis for returning from Troy without his brother Aias; founded the city of Salamis on Cyprus with the aid of Apollo.

THEMIS: goddess of established law and custom.

THEOKLYMENOS: king of Egypt; son of Proteus; hater of Greeks.

THEONOÊ: daughter of Proteus; sister of Theoklymenos; virgin prophet.

THESTIOS: king of Aitolia.

THETIS: sea nymph; mother of Achilleus by Peleus.

THOAS: king of the Taurians.

THYESTES: brother of Atreus.

TITANS: race of gods that preceded the Olympians; vanquished by them.

TRITON: son of Poseidon and Amphitritê.

TROJAN: an inhabitant of Troy.

TROY: city in northeastern Asia Minor; site of the Trojan War.

TYNDAREOS: king of Sparta; husband of Lêda.

XOUTHOS: son of Aiolos; grandson of Zeus; husband of Kreousa; won the kingship of Athens by helping Athens in the conquest of Euboia.

ZEUS: chief god of the Olympians.

Aristotle. *The Poetics.* Translated by Gerald Else. Ann Arbor: University of Michigan Press, 1967.

Arnott, Peter. *Public and Performance in the Greek Theatre.* London: Routledge, 1989.

————. *Greek Scenic Conventions in the Fifth Century BC.* Oxford: Oxford University Press, 1962.

Barlow, S. A. *Euripides: Trojan Women.* Warminster, UK: Aris and Phillips, Ltd., 1986.

Bieber, Margarete. *The History of the Greek and Roman Theater.* 2nd ed. Princeton: Princeton University Press, 1961.

Blundell, Sue. *Women in Ancient Greece.* London: British Museum Press, 1995.

Burian, Peter. *New Directions in Euripidean Criticism.* Durham, NC: Duke University Press, 1985.

Burkert, Walter. *Greek Religion.* Cambridge, MA: Harvard University Press, 1985.

Burnett, Anne Pippin. *Catastrophe Survived: Euripides' Plays of Mixed Reversal.* Oxford: Clarendon Press, 1971.

Bury, J. B., and Russell Meiggs. *A History of Greece to the Death of Alexander the Great.* 4th ed. New York: St. Martin's Press, 1991.

Buxton, R. G. *Persuasion in Greek Tragedy.* Cambridge: Cambridge University Press, 1982.

Conacher, D. J. *Euripidean Drama: Myth, Theme and Structure.* Toronto: University of Toronto Press, 1967.

Cropp, M. *Euripides: Iphigenia in Tauris.* Warminster, UK: Aris and Phillips, Ltd., 2000.

Csapo, Eric, and William J. Slater. *The Context of Ancient Drama.* Ann Arbor: University of Michigan Press, 1995.

Dale, A. M. *Euripides: Alcestis.* Oxford: Oxford University Press, 1954.

Dunn, Francis M. *Tragedy's End: Closure and Innovation in Euripidean Drama.* New York and Oxford: Oxford University Press, 1996.

Easterling, P. E., ed. *The Cambridge Companion to Greek Tragedy.* Cambridge: Cambridge University Press, 1997.

Else, Gerald F. *The Origin and Early Form of Greek Tragedy.* Martin Classical Lectures, Vol. 20. Cambridge, MA: Harvard University Press, 1965.

Goldhill, Simon. *Reading Greek Tragedy.* Cambridge: Cambridge University Press, 1986.

Grube, G. M. A. *The Drama of Euripides.* London: Methuen, 1941.

Halleran, Michael. *Stagecraft in Euripides.* London and Sydney: Croom Helm, 1985.

Hornblower, Simon, and Antony Spawforth, eds. *The Oxford Classical Dictionary.* 3rd ed. Oxford: Oxford University Press, 1996.

Hornby, Richard. *Script into Performance.* Austin: University of Texas Press, 1977.

Jones, John. *On Aristotle and Greek Tragedy.* Stanford, CA: Stanford University Press, 1980.

Just, Roger. *Women in Athenian Law and Life.* London and New York: Routledge, 1991.

Kannicht, Richard. *Euripides: Helena.* Heidelberg: C. Winter, 1969.

Kitto, H. D. F. *Form and Meaning in Drama: A Study of Six Greek Plays and of Hamlet.* 2nd ed. London: Methuen, 1964; New York: Barnes and Noble, 1968.

―――. *Greek Tragedy: A Literary Study.* 2nd ed. New York: Doubleday, 1964; 3rd ed. London: Methuen, 1966.

―――. *Word and Action: Essays on the Ancient Theater.* Baltimore and London: Johns Hopkins University Press, 1979.

Knox, B. M. W. *Word and Action.* Baltimore: Johns Hopkins University Press, 1979.

Kott, Jan. *The Eating of the Gods: An Interpretation of Greek Tragedy.* New York: Random House, 1973.

Lattimore, Richmond. *The Poetry of Greek Tragedy.* Baltimore: Johns Hopkins University Press, 1958.

————. *The Story-Patterns in Greek Tragedy.* Ann Arbor: University of Michigan Press, 1964.

Lee, K. H. *Euripides: Ion.* Warminster, UK: Aris and Phillips, Ltd., 1997.

————. *Euripides: Trojan Women.* London: St. Martin's Press, 1976.

Lesky, Albin. *Greek Tragedy.* London: Ernest Benn, 1978.

Lloyd-Jones, Hugh. *The Justice of Zeus.* Sather Gate Lectures, Vol. 41. Berkeley and Los Angeles: University of California Press, 1971.

Mastronarde, D. *Contact and Disunity: Some Conventions of Speech and Action on the Greek Tragic Stage.* Berkeley and Los Angeles: University of California Press, 1979.

Michelini, Ann Norris. *Euripides and the Tragic Tradition.* Madison: University of Wisconsin Press, 1987.

Murray, Gilbert. *Euripides and His Age.* London: Oxford University Press, 1946.

Neils, Jenifer. *Goddess and Polis: The Panathenaic Festival in Ancient Athens.* Princeton: Princeton University Press, 1992.

Owen, A. S. *Euripides: Ion.* Oxford: Oxford University Press, 1939.

Pickard-Cambridge, A. W. *The Dramatic Festivals of Athens.* 2nd ed. Oxford: Clarendon Press, 1968.

————. *The Theatre of Dionysus in Athens.* Oxford: Clarendon Press, 1946.

Platnauer, M. *Iphigeneia in Tauris.* Oxford: Oxford University Press, 1938.

Powell, Anton, ed. *Euripides, Women, and Sexuality.* London and New York: Routledge, 1990.

Rehm, Rush. *The Greek Tragic Theatre.* London and New York: Routledge, 1992.

Seaford, Richard. *Euripides: Cyclops.* Oxford: Oxford University Press, 1984.

Segal, Charles. *Interpreting Greek Tragedy: Myth, Poetry, Text.* Ithaca, NY: Cornell University Press, 1986.

Segal, Erich. *Oxford Essays in Greek Tragedy.* Oxford: Oxford University Press, 1984.

————, ed. *Euripides: A Collection of Critical Essays*. Englewood Cliffs, NJ: Prentice-Hall, 1968.

Steiner, George. *The Death of Tragedy*. New York: Alfred A. Knopf; London: Faber and Faber, 1961.

Sutton, D. F. *The Greek Satyr Play*. Meisenheim am Glan, 1980.

Taplin, Oliver. *Greek Tragedy in Action*. Berkeley and Los Angeles: University of California Press; London: Methuen, 1978.

Thucydides. *The Peloponnesian Wars*. Translated by Rex Warner. Harmondsworth, UK: Penguin Classics, 1972.

Vernant, Jean-Pierre, and Pierre Vidal-Naquet, eds. *Myth and Tragedy in Ancient Greece*. New York: Zone Books, 1990.

Vickers, Brian. *Towards Greek Tragedy*. London: Longman, 1973.

Walcot, Peter. *Greek Drama in Its Theatrical and Social Context*. Cardiff, UK: University of Wales Press, 1976.

Walton, J. Michael. *The Greek Sense of Theatre: Tragedy Reviewed*. London and New York: Methuen, 1984.

————. *Greek Theatre Practice*. Westport and London: Greenwood Press, 1980.

Webster, T. B. L. *The Tragedies of Euripides*. London: Methuen, 1967.

Whitman, Cedric. *Euripides and the Full Circle of Myth*. Cambridge, MA: Harvard University Press, 1974.

Wiles, David. *Tragedy in Athens*. Cambridge and New York: Cambridge University Press, 1997.

Winkler, John, and Froma I. Zeitlin, eds. *Nothing to Do with Dionysus*. Princeton: Princeton University Press, 1990.

Zuntz, G. *The Political Plays of Euripides*. Manchester, UK: Manchester University Press, 1963.

CARL R. MUELLER has since 1967 been professor in the Department of Theater at the University of California, Los Angeles, where he has taught theater history, criticism, dramatic literature, and playwriting, as well as having directed. He was educated at Northwestern University, where he received a B.S. in English. After work in graduate English at the University of California, Berkeley, he received his M.A. in playwriting at UCLA, where he also completed his Ph.D. in theater history and criticism. In addition, he was a Fulbright Scholar in Berlin in 1960–1961. A translator for more than forty years, he has translated and published works by Büchner, Brecht, Wedekind, Hauptmann, Hofmannsthal, and Hebbel, to name a few. His published translation of von Horváth's *Tales from the Vienna Woods* was given its London West End premiere in July 1999. For Smith and Kraus, he has translated volumes of plays by Schnitzler, Strindberg, Pirandello, Kleist, and Wedekind, as well as Goethe's *Faust, Parts I and II*. In addition to translating the complete plays of Euripides and Aeschylus for Smith and Kraus, he has also cotranslated the plays of Sophokles. His translations have been performed in every English-speaking country and have appeared on BBC-TV.